THE PRODUCER AND THE PLAY

By the same author

THE OTHER THEATRE

NORMAN MARSHALL

The Producer
and the
Play

DAVIS-POYNTER · LONDON

This edition published in 1975 by
Davis-Poynter Limited
20 Garrick Street
London WC2E 9BJ
First edition 1957
Second edition 1962

Copyright © 1957, 1975 by Norman Marshall

ISBN 0 7067 0173 9

Printed in Great Britain by
Stellar Press Limited
Welham Green, Hatfield

CONTENTS

FOREWORD TO THIRD EDITION

This book was first published in 1957, when the director was still called the producer. Six years later it was re-published in a new edition to which I added a Postscript dealing with the trends and developments during those six years. I have left that Postscript unchanged but have added to it another, a PPS., as it were, which brings the book up to the end of 1974.

From time to time I have received letters from readers of the book regretting the lack of any account of the work of the directors in the American theatre. The omission is not due to any lack of appreciation of their contribution to the development of the art of direction; it is simply due to the fact that had I not confined myself to the European theatre the book would have become either too long or too cursory.

NORMAN MARSHALL

I

THE ADVENT OF THE PRODUCER

It is, I suspect, difficult to do any job passably well for long without believing it to be a little more important than it really is. For more than twenty-five years I have been producing plays. Consequently I may tend to over-rate the importance of the producer in the theatre. Nevertheless, I do not think it is any exaggeration to claim that during the past hundred years the producers have had so much influence on every aspect of the theatre that a study of their work is the simplest and most direct method of tracing the development during these years of that conglomeration of many different arts sometimes dignified by the title of The Art of the Theatre.

The producer is not nearly so late an arrival in the theatre as is generally supposed, although the name has only come into use comparatively recently. There has, of course, always been someone in charge of the rehearsals of a play ever since the theatre began. It is impossible even to get up a charade at a Christmas party without somebody taking charge and giving directions. But in the theatre, until about a hundred years ago, these directions needed to be only of the simplest kind, and did not require a specialist to issue them. Production was merely a part of the work of the leading actor or the stage-manager or the prompter. Acting was governed by tradition and convention much in the same way as operatic acting used to be until very recently. Movements and groupings were stereotyped; there was no attempt at teamwork. An actor on tour in the eighteenth century could play a leading part with a local stock company without any rehearsal at all, just as in the old days of the international seasons at Covent Garden a singer could arrive in London from Milan, or Berlin, or Paris on the day of performance and sing his rôle that evening without even having met the rest of the company beforehand.

When Kean first appeared in London, at Drury Lane in 1814, as Shylock, his only rehearsal-call was for twelve o'clock on the morning of the performance. That there was nothing unusual in this is proved by a letter written by Kean when he was at the height of his fame to the stage-manager of the Croydon theatre where he was about to act with the company for the first time in *The Merchant of Venice* and *The Iron Chest*.

"Sir,
I shall not require rehearsals for my plays; but be particular in your selection of Wilford. He is all-important to me. I will run through the library scene when I come down. He must be young, mind.

Yours obediently,
E. Kean."

Stirling, the actor who played Wilford, wrote an account of this rehearsal.

"When Kean arrived he sent for me to his dressing-room.
'You are rather tall, sir.'
'Yes, sir. What do you wish me to do?'
'Why, in the library scene, sink gradually on your right knee with your back to the audience. When I place my hand on your head to curse, mind you keep your eyes fixed on mine.'
'Is that all, sir?'
'Yes—do whatever you like after that, it will be all the same to me.'"

One gets some idea of what rehearsals were like in Macready's day from reading his diaries. The actors muttered through their lines, apparently considering that the only purpose of a rehearsal was to fix their entrances and their exits and their positions on the stage, which were given to them by the stage-manager. Macready's resolve "to rehearse with the same earnestness as I should act" astonished the rest of the cast, accustomed to leading actors who never troubled to read any of their speeches during rehearsal, contenting themselves with merely giving the cues. Because Macready's determination to rehearse at least his own part properly meant longer rehearsals it nearly caused a strike among the company.

So far as I have been able to discover, Drury Lane was the first London theatre to acknowledge that someone had been responsible for the staging of a production. In 1828 the play-bills for *The Queen Bee, or Harlequin and the Fairy Hive* informed the public that the pantomime was "Invented and Produced by Mr. Barrymore".

At that time, and for many years to come, the use of the word producer seems to have been confined to musical shows and pantomimes. But in 1863 the playbills for *Manfred* at the Lane announced: "The general action of the Tragedy arranged by Mr. Phelps." Gradually it became fairly usual to give credit on the playbills to the producers of straight plays as well as musicals, though in every case the producer was also the stage-manager, or the author of the play, or the manager of the theatre, or one of the actors in the company. It is not until 1890 that I have been able to find mentioned on a programme a producer who was engaged solely to direct the production. In that year, at the St. James's Theatre, then under the management of Lily Langtry, *As You Like It* was "Produced under the direction of the Hon. Lewis Wingfield".

Usually Lily Langtry herself directed the plays in which she appeared, but as she had acted Rosalind before, she saw no necessity for rehearsing with the company until shortly before the opening. Bored at the idea of having to attend rehearsals merely to direct the other actors, she engaged Wingfield to produce and went off on a holiday to Paris.

Wingfield was a colourful and versatile character who arrived at the profession of producer late in life by a somewhat devious route. In his early twenties he acted at the Haymarket. His next engagement was with a nigger-minstrel troupe. Then he took to travel, was one of the first Englishmen to journey into the interior of China, and wrote *Under the Palms in Algeria and Tunis*, which became a best-seller. He qualified as a surgeon in Paris during the siege, and at the same time was war correspondent for *The Times*, sending his despatches by balloon. On his return to England he took up painting, exhibited at the Royal Academy, and designed stage costumes for several leading actresses, including Mary Anderson and Lily Langtry. He contributed dramatic criticism to *The Globe* under the pseudonym of Whyte Tyghe, wrote fashion notes, published a novel, adapted Schiller's *Mary Stuart* for production at the Court Theatre, and lectured at the International Health Exhibition of 1884 on "Hygienic Underwear". Then he joined the army in the Sudan, but his health broke down and he was invalided out. It was on his return to England that Lily Langtry appointed him her producer. The cast of *As You Like It* appears to have resented being directed by an outsider, by someone who was not their manager, or the author, or the leading actor. They became increasingly restive when they discovered that Wingfield had new-fangled ideas about how Shakespeare should be acted, and would not allow them to use the traditional business. Eventually Lily Langtry had to be hurriedly recalled from Paris as the cast had gone on strike.

Wingfield's brief career as a producer was ended by his death a few months later, but on the strength of that one production at the St. James's he has his place in theatrical history as the first independent producer in the English theatre. The first producer to work regularly as a director of plays with which he was not concerned in any other capacity was Dion Boucicault (son of the Victorian playwright of the same name), who from 1902 to 1915 was permanent producer for Charles Frohman at the Duke of York's.

It seems that by the beginning of the century the critics and the more knowledgeable playgoers were becoming sufficiently aware of the existence of the producer for some of the actor-managers to consider it worth their while to mention on their programmes that they had themselves been responsible for the production of the play. For instance, in 1901 the programme at

His Majesty's Theatre announced for the first time that the play was "Produced under the direction of Mr. Tree". At the St. James's it was not until 1915 that George Alexander put himself down on the programme as producer. When in 1905 Gordon Craig in *The Art of the Theatre* argued the case for the new type of artist-director who had recently made his appearance in the theatres of Germany, France and Russia, the title of producer was seemingly still so rarely used in connection with straight plays that Craig calls him the stage-manager.

Although the word producer only came into general use during the present century, modern methods of production date back to the eighteen-thirties. They were introduced by Madame Vestris. When she went into management at the Olympic she refused to tolerate the slovenly free-for-all methods of those days and insisted upon long, detailed rehearsal. She took the rehearsals herself, and demanded from her players a far more natural style of acting than was then in vogue. One of her first reforms was to forbid the wearing of the traditional costumes in which every light comedy used to be performed. The "Comedy-juvenile", for instance, wore a claret-coloured coat, salmon-pink trousers with a broad black stripe, a sky-blue neckcloth fastened by a huge paste brooch, and an eyeglass with a pink ribbon. The audience accepted the convention of a young country squire rigged out in this fantastic costume much in the same way as a modern audience accepts the conventional costume of a pantomime principal boy. Vestris insisted on the characters in a contemporary comedy dressing like their counterparts in the audience. Clothed like ordinary human beings, the actors immediately became aware of the absurdity of the artificial mannerisms of speech and gesture which had been well enough suited to their ludicrous stage costumes. The playwrights, too, discovered that dialogue which had passed muster when spoken by a light comedian in pink trousers, sounded preposterously stagey when spoken by a young man who would not have seemed out of place dining at their house or their club.

The scenic innovations which Madame Vestris made at the Olympic were a further means of compelling the actor to behave more naturally. A box set with a ceiling was first seen in an English theatre on the stage of the Olympic Theatre in 1832. It was solidly built with practical doors which opened and shut with a realistic click, windows which appeared to be of glass, hung with curtains and with blinds which could be pulled up and down. There were real pictures on the walls, real books in the bookcases, clocks that chimed the hour, a carpet and rugs on the floor, plenty of comfortable furniture, flowers, ornaments and a solid-looking fireplace in which a log fire blazed realistically. All this at a time when the conventional "chamber set" consisted of a backcloth and wings, two or three chairs, and pictures, ornaments and fireplace painted on the canvas. The actor accustomed to stalking on to the stage from between two wings as he declaimed his opening lines could not help behaving much more like a normal human being when he had to begin his scene by performing the ordinary everyday business of opening and shutting a door and then found himself surrounded by the familiar objects of everyday life.

Madame Vestris's scenic innovations were not confined to chamber sets for light comedies. In a play called *Burlington Arcade* she created a street scene in which the passers-by, the shopkeepers and their customers peopled the stage with such realistic effect that *The Athenaeum* described it as "the first living mise en scène we have seen in our theatre". The paper's dramatic reporter described the scene in detail: "The extreme front of the stage is occupied by the pavement in front of the arcade, and the audiences have a complete view of the entrance, with the shops on each side, to an almost vanishing distance. These shops have not mere painted windows, but are transparent, and completely furnished with all which a genuine tradesman would employ to make an effective show. The hairdresser's shop, fitted up with a fine assortment of wigged busts and perfume bottles, is only outshone by the fascinating exhibition of artificial flowers at the window opposite. The windows on the first floors are open so as to display the interiors where people are seen moving about. A dozen or more lamps extending down the paved arcade are lit up at dusk with real gas by an actual lamplighter, producing an admirable effect."

When Vestris moved to the Lyceum the larger stage gave her scope for still more elaborately realistic settings. *The Illustrated London News* of 1852 dramatically describes the exuberant realism of her production of *The Chain of Events*: "Fires blaze, bells ring, firemen clatter over the stage with the engine; a fountain spouts water in the square of an illuminated street in Paris, horses draw carriages, a donkey pulls a water-barrel cart, and a ship smashes into a reef and sinks. The tossing and the rolling of the vessel amid the tumult and the darkness, made visible by the lightning flash, was managed with a reality that brought at once sea, sky, and storm-tossed bark not only before the imagination, but the vision. Then the sudden going down of the ship! It was terrible. The horrified shriek of the audience almost substituted that of the crew."

Even in these lurid Lyceum melodramas Madame Vestris insisted on her actors abandoning the stagey, traditional type of acting. What seems particularly to have impressed the critics was that none of the company ever declaimed their lines at the audience, but always gave the impression of talking to one another in an intimate, natural manner. But it was in light comedy that Vestris excelled both as a producer and as an actress. Her leading man was her husband, Charles Mathews, who, as a young man, started his career at the Olympic because, in his own words: "I had no respect for traditional acting. The lighter phase of comedy, representing the more natural and less laboured school of modern life, and holding the mirror up to nature without regard to the conventionalities of the theatre, was the aim I had in view. The Olympic was then the only house where this could be achieved, and to the Olympic I at once attached myself." Reading contemporary criticism of a Vestris production the word that occurs again and again is "natural". Typical of innumerable other notices is G. H. Lewes's review of *A Day of Reckoning* in *The Morning Leader*: "Vestris and Mathews were *natural*—nothing more, nothing less. They were a lady and gentleman such as we meet with in drawing-rooms, graceful, quiet, well-bred, perfectly dressed, perfectly oblivious of the footlights."

One of the plays produced by Vestris during her later years in management was by a new playwright, Dion Boucicault. Rehearsals were stormy because Vestris required much of the script to be re-written to suit her naturalistic style, and the stubborn young author was by no means easy to persuade; but Boucicault's subsequent work, both as an author and a producer, showed how much he had learned from Vestris.

It may seem curious to describe Boucicault as a naturalist, as most of his plays were romantic melodramas, but their popularity was largely due to the care he took to make his characters real people and to establish them in realistic everyday surroundings before involving them in exciting adventures. In his big scenes he made full use of the spectacular effects which Vestris had introduced at the Lyceum. The burning of the Mississippi steamer in his production of *The Octoroon* created an even greater sensation than the shipwreck in *The Chain of Events*. In *The Colleen Bawn* he had a cave scene in which the heroine was pushed into the water by the villain and saved just as she was going down for the third time by the hero making a spectacular dive from a high rock. In *Arrah-na-Pogue* the incarcerated hero climbed out of a window in an ivy-clad tower, which then sank gradually down through the stage as he clambered up the ivy and reached the platform at the top just in time to seize the villain by the ankle and send him hurtling to his death as he was about to force the heroine to yield to his advances.

Among the members of Boucicault's company was the young Squire Bancroft who later went into management and continued the naturalistic methods of production he had learned from Boucicault. It was Bancroft who produced the "cup-and-saucer dramas" of T. W. Robertson. Because of the naturalism of Robertson's dialogue and the detail with which he describes his domestic interiors and the clothes and behaviour of the caracters who people them, he is usually credited in histories of the drama with being the founder of the realistic school of acting and production; but it is doubtful if Robertson would have written his plays in the realistic idiom had he not known that there was already in existence a style of acting and production suited to it.

Another early realist, Strindberg, was less fortunate than Robertson. In 1888, twenty-three years after the Bancrofts had staged Robertson's first success, *Society*, we find Strindberg complaining bitterly in the preface to *Miss Julie* of the frustrations of writing naturalistic drama for a theatre as yet unprepared for it. "There has been no new form devised for the new contents and the new wine has burst the old bottles. . . . Nothing is harder than to get a room that looks something like a room although the painters can easily enough produce waterfalls and flaming volcanoes. No doubts the walls must be of canvas but we might be done with the painting of shelves and kitchen utensils on the canvas. We have so much else on the stage that is conventional and in which we are asked to believe, that we might at least be spared the too great effort of believing in painted pans and kettles."

In an attempt to escape from the scenery of his day, Strindberg in his stage directions stipulated that the ceiling and the side walls of the kitchen in which the play takes place should consist of draperies and that on the only wall shown there should be "two shelves full of utensils made of copper, brass, iron and tin, the shelves themselves trimmed with scalloped paper". Another of his stipulations was that the rear wall and the table should be set diagonally across the stage to get away from the visual effect of what he describes as "the fatiguing right angle", and to enable the actors to be seen both full face and in half profile when they sat opposite each other at the table. In the preface he pleads that "crucial scenes may not be played in the centre of the proscenium, like duets meant to bring forth applause; instead I should like to have them played in the place indicated by the situation". He sadly confesses that he hardly dare hope that "the ladies will listen to me and look more lifelike than beautiful" but begs that "they should at least use a minimum of make-up because in modern drama the subtlest movements of the soul are reflected on the face rather than by gestures and noise".

The first company on the continent to stage and act their plays in a naturalistic manner were the Saxe-Meiningen Players. Their director and producer was the royal amateur, George II, Duke of Saxe-Meiningen. In 1874 he reorganised the company at his court theatre with the deliberate intention of reforming the methods of acting and scene design on the German stage. An accomplished painter and draughtsman, he designed his own scenery and costumes. He did not merely make a picture of the settings; he also made innumerable sketches showing the grouping of the actors during the scenes. He went further than just considering how the actor would look in the setting. He considered how the setting would influence and control the movements of the actor. In these days interior scenes were almost invariably rectangular in shape, and the actors made nearly all their crosses parallel with the footlights. In the old prompt books the most frequent direction is: "Cross stage L. to R." The Duke deliberately designed his settings so that a great deal of the movement had to be diagonal or up and down stage. Whenever possible he achieved variety of movement by breaking up the monotonous surface of the stage floor by means of rostrums, staircases, sloping paths, rocks and banks.

At a time when the stage was flatly illuminated by a blaze of light, with the shadows painted on the scenery, the duke introduced more realistic methods of lighting, using varying intensity of light so that parts of the stage could be in shadow. Nowadays we are so accustomed to lighting which is both realistic and imaginative that it is interesting to read of the sensation created by the lighting of the scene in Schiller's *Mary Stuart* when Queen Elizabeth signed Mary's death warrant at a table apparently lit by only four candles, leaving the rest of the stage in darkness except for what appeared to be the reflected light of the candles glowing on Holbein's portrait of Henry VIII on the wall behind, so that the king seemed to be gloating malevolently over the proceedings.

In collaboration with his stage director, Chronegk, the Duke trained his actors to abandon all the old stagey conventions of gesture and speech. His productions of Ibsen's *Ghosts* and

Björnson's *The Bankrupt* are usually claimed to be the first productions in the modern naturalistic manner—a claim which ignores the work of Vestris and the Bancrofts. But their productions were never seen outside England, while the Duke spread his ideas throughout Europe as a result of the many tours undertaken by his company. (Between 1874 and 1890 they visited thirty-six cities, giving a total of 2,591 performances.) The Duke is also usually given the credit of being the first producer to insist on historical accuracy in the production of Shakespeare's plays, but he was forestalled by Kemble fifty years earlier and by Charles Kean during his Shakespearian seasons at the Princess's Theatre during the 'fifties.

Although the Duke was not the originator of naturalism and historical accuracy, he developed them further than his English predecessors. In this he was helped by his wealth, which enabled him to give more rehearsals to a play than any English manager could afford. In his costume productions the air of ease and authenticity with which his actors wore their clothes was largely due to the fact that instead of having to cope with costumes, properties, swords, wigs, beards, and furniture all for the first time at a single dress-rehearsal, the Meiningen players rehearsed in costume, with furniture and properties, almost from the beginning. If one compares photographs of the members of the Meiningen troupe in costume with similar photographs of English actors in those days, one sees at once a marked difference. The English players mostly look like Victorian ladies and gentlemen attending a fancy-dress ball; the Meiningen players look as if they might have stepped out of a painting of the period. This was not only due to the detail with which the Duke sketched for his perruquiers every wig and beard, but also to the fact that he taught his actors to acquire the proper stance and gestures appropriate to their costumes by studying the work of painters contemporary with the period of the play.

The Meiningen company appeared for a season at Drury Lane in 1881. At a time when the star system was at its height in the English theatre what particularly impressed the London critics was the ensemble playing of this company in which no actor was regarded as more important than any other. One night an actor would appear in a leading Shakespearian rôle and next evening, if there was nothing to suit him in the play, he would be one of the leaders of the crowd. There were no supers in the Meiningen productions. Every member of the crowd was a trained actor who toured with the company wherever they went. The mob in *Julius Caesar* was very different from the collection of obedient supers, dutifully reacting in unison, to which English audiences were accustomed. Each actor in the Meiningen crowd was first produced as an individual, and each individual performance was then fitted, with infinite care, into the general pattern of the scene.

In Lee Simonson's *The Stage Is Set* there is a description of the most celebrated of their mob scenes—the coronation procession of the Dauphin in Schiller's *Maid of Orleans*: "The crowd packed a shallow square under the portals of Rheims Cathedral. The stage was too small to hold them as they waited for the first sight of the cortège; they disappeared off-stage, strained against soldiers trying to keep a lane free, climbed on each other's backs, stood on tiptoe, hopped up and down, packed every spare ledge on a fountain, jammed the stairways of near-by houses, leaned over window-sills on each other's shoulders. The mounting excitement was carefully timed as the royal procession crossed the stage into the cathedral and increasing bursts of cheers greeted each notable when he was recognised. The crescendo of jubilation swelled at the sight of the Dauphin under his canopy. All the while trumpets repeated a single theme adopted from one of Brahms's chorales, with clarion insistence that mounted higher and higher until at the appearance of Joan it reached a climax of frenzy that usually incited an echoing ovation from the audience."

In England the Duke of Saxe-Meiningen's influence was reflected in the productions of Irving and Tree, who were much impressed by his handling of crowds and the historical detail of his productions. In Russia it was the visit of the Meiningen company in 1890 which inspired Stanislavsky, then a young amateur actor, to become a producer. In Germany the Duke's methods were handed on to Reinhardt by Otto Brahm, who copied and developed the naturalism of the Meiningen productions at the Deutsches Theater in Berlin, where Reinhardt was for some years a member of the company. The Meiningen troupe never visited France, yet it was the French theatre which was most strongly influenced by their productions through the work of Antoine, who saw them for the first time at Brussels in 1888.

There could hardly have been a greater contrast between the wealthy Grand Duke of Saxe-Meiningen and the clerk in a Paris gas-works who had just founded the Théâtre Libre with thirty-seven subscribers and a debt of several thousand francs. Antoine, the year before his visit to Brussels, had already put on the stage the first detailed realistic interior to be seen in a Paris theatre. A notice hanging beside the door of the room exhorting the last one out to turn off the gas was considered to be the perfection of realism. But it was not until Antoine saw the Meiningen players that he realised there was a style of acting which could match the realism of a naturalistic setting.

On his return to Paris the acting in the French theatres seemed ludicrously unreal compared with the naturalism of the Meiningen company. In his letters to Sarcey he describes performances at the Comédie Française in which actors declaimed long duologues facing the audience without once looking at one another. "Those footlights hypnotise them; everyone tries to act as near to the audience as possible. In the theatres where there are gas footlights most of the actors have singed trousers as a result of the practice of coming down to the edge of the stage to address the audience instead of speaking to the other characters in the play." A detail of the Meiningen performances which particularly impressed Antoine was that an actor would occasionally turn his back to the audience to speak to someone upstage. When he himself, acting in one of his own productions, introduced this touch of realism he was angrily booed because the Parisian audience considered it a gross breach of good manners for an actor to turn his back on them. In the English theatre the tradition that an actor should never speak with his back to the audience died so slowly that when the Lunts first appeared together in London in 1929 the fact that Alfred Lunt played a brief scene with his back to the audience was considered a startling and daring innovation.

Another of Antoine's letters describes the complete lack of production in the French theatre. "The comings and goings of the players are not regulated according to the text or in accordance with the sense of the scene, but according to the convenience and the caprice of the individual actor who plays each for himself with no regard for the others." He writes of the difficulties he had in getting his own actors to walk naturally across the stage instead of strutting, to sit down at a table without striking an attitude and staring into the audience, to speak rather than to shout, to abandon irrational, superfluous gestures and meaningless, mechanical movements.

By introducing into the French theatre a naturalistic style of acting and scene design Antoine made the stage habitable for the French realist writers—novelists like Zola, whose *Thérèse Raquin* had been hissed off the stage a few years earlier, and playwrights such as Henri Becque, author of *La Parisienne*, which had no success while the old declamatory style of acting was still in vogue. "The characters in *La Parisienne*," protested Antoine, "should not be living in vast rooms the size of cathedrals, but in interiors such as our own, by their firesides, beneath their lamps, around their tables, and not in front of the prompter's box; their voices are like our own, and they speak the language of our everyday life, with its abbreviations and colloquialisms, instead of the noble rhetoric of our classics."

Shortly after the founding of the Théâtre Libre Antoine published a pamphlet in which he describes his ideal theatre as one "in which the spectator will be able to enjoy in an intimate play the simple and appropriate gestures of a modern man living our everyday life. Actors will not constantly come out of the picture to pose before the audience, but will move among the furniture and accessories, and their acting will be amplified by a thousand and one details which have become indispensable in moulding a character logically. Feelings will be expressed by objects which are real and familiar; a pencil turned round in the fingers, a cup overturned, will be as significant and have an effect as intense on the mind of the spectator as the grandiloquent exaggerations of the romantic drama."

Antoine was not an innovator; he did not contribute anything to the art of production which had not already been practised by the Duke of Saxe-Meiningen, by Vestris and Bancroft; but he revolutionised the French theatre by bridging the gap between drama and literature, which had hitherto been separate professions in France. Most of the serious writers despised the stage because the public and the critics insisted upon the "well-made play" in which reality was sacrificed to the exigencies of an elaborately artificial plot. Antoine brought to the Paris stage the naturalistic plays of Ibsen, Tolstoy, Björnson, Strindberg, Turgenev and Heijermans; and by demonstrating that there was a style of acting and staging which could give an illusion of actuality, he enticed into the theatre many of the French realistic novelists, including the Goncourts, Lavedan, Paul Margueritte and Brieux.

It was Antoine's productions at the Théâtre Libre which aroused the first revolt against the realistic movement. The opposition was led by Paul Fort, a young poet still in his teens, who in 1890 opened the Théâtre d'Art. Fort was one of a group of writers and painters known as the Symbolistes. Believing that the theatre should be a place for fantasy and imagination, that settings should be evocative rather than descriptive, they accused Antoine of debasing the stage by filling it with "the trivial and accidental details of actuality". The Théâtre d'Art was the first to abolish the realistic perspective backcloth, substituting a formalised, decorative design symbolising the mood of the scene. The rest of the setting generally consisted simply of draped curtains. "The spoken word creates the décor as it does all else," declared the theatre's manifesto. "It is enough that the settings do not disturb the illusion, and for that they must be very simple." So it was the Théâtre d'Art which first put into practice the theory that the spectator can abandon himself far more completely to the play if his imagination is allowed to run free, unhampered by the "naturalistic lies" of the

scene painter, "because"—to quote again from the manifesto—
"the individual images of different people in the audience
will never be in harmony with a painting on the stage, and
representational décors are only a nuisance to the audience as
well as to the poet-playwright".

Fort's intentions went far beyond the replacement of scenery
by an abstract form of décor. He believed that the theatre
should completely renounce reality and become an abstract
art. But like so many other anti-realists he was defeated by the
inconvenient fact that nothing is more indubitably real than
the living actor. It was this same fact that so exasperated Gordon
Craig twenty years later that he angrily demanded the banishment of the actor "with his distracting tremors of the flesh"
and predicted the coming of the Uber-Marionette "to free the
stage from its enslavement to reality".

Some of the anti-realist producers who followed Fort sought
to fuse the abstract and the concrete by means of elaborately
stylised acting, and by obliterating the faces of the actors with
masks of abstract design. Fort himself took the first tentative
steps in this direction by producing his actors in a series of
statuesque poses, eliminating movement and gesture as far as
possible. But it is a denial of the nature of drama to deprive it
of action, so the inevitable result of Fort's experiments in acting
was sheer dullness. He abandoned the theatre after only two
years. Nevertheless, during his brief directorship of the Théâtre
d'Art he initiated the movement towards simpler and more
imaginative settings at a time when plays were constantly being
smothered to death beneath a mass of fussy, irrelevant detail.
His successor at the Théâtre d'Art was Lugné-Poë, who made
modified use of the ideas of the Symbolistes, gradually combining them with much that was best in the realistic productions
of Antoine and Brahm. By the time he founded his own theatre
—Le Théâtre de l'Oeuvre—he had evolved a naturalistic
method of production in which imaginative and selective use of
realistic detail, both in staging and acting, replaced the excessively factual realism of the early naturalistic producers.

Meanwhile the cause of anti-realists was helped by the publication of three books which set forth their doctrine. In 1899 Adolph Appia published his *Die Musik und die Inscenierung,* which was followed almost immediately by George Fuchs's *Die Schaubuhne der Zukunft;* six years later came Gordon Craig's *The Art of the Theatre.* All three writers argued that stage settings should not attempt to reproduce an exact image of the locale of the play, but must seek to give the illusion of imaginative truth, not actual truth. Appia's oft-quoted dictum that in *Siegfried* "it is not necessary to try to represent a forest; what one must give the spectator is man in the atmosphere of a forest" is echoed by Gordon Craig's "Let us not, in *Julius Caesar,* try to represent the Roman Forum (or our idea of it), but show for that scene simply a man speaking to a hundred thousand men".

Appia and Craig sought to rid the theatre of its scene-painters, replacing painted scenery by three-dimensional settings of a flat, uniform grey or cream so that lighting could be used to vary the colour of the set according to the changing mood of the scene. The determination of Appia and Craig to expel the painter from the theatre was not shared by Fuchs, who had been greatly impressed by the symbolistic settings at the Théâtre d'Art, designed by some of the best of the younger French painters, including Bonnard, Vuillard, Dérain and Utrillo. He argued that as it is impossible to achieve true perspective in the theatre, the third dimension should be abandoned altogether, and easel painters (instead of scene painters) be employed to design flat, decorative backgrounds against which the actor would stand out in sharp relief.

Although Fuchs's theories on staging were much the same as Fort's, he had no use for the so-called symbolistic acting at the Théâtre d'Art, which in his opinion amounted to no more than a series of static, impersonal recitations. He equally disliked "monkey-like imitations of every-day life". It seemed to him that under the influence of the realistic producer the actor was so busy smoking, spitting, drinking beer, belching, poking the fire, coughing, and blowing his nose that he had no time to think of anything but the outward characteristics of his part. What Fuchs sought from the actor was "inner realism". He envisaged a style of naturalistic acting in which realistic gesture, movement, and stage business would be used sparingly, imaginatively, and significantly.

Craig, on the other hand, was uncompromisingly against the slightest concession towards realism in acting. But his discussions on the art of acting are of little practical value, as most of them reach the conclusion that the actor must eventually be abolished. If one does away with a real tree, he argued, one must do away with reality in speech and gesture, and having got as far as this "you tend towards doing away with the actor". In the theatre of his dreams there would be no longer a living figure to confuse us into connecting actuality with art. "Who knows," he mused, "whether the puppet shall not once again become the medium for the beautiful thoughts of the artist." He thought it incorrect to speak of the actor as an artist. "For accident is an enemy of the artist. Art is the exact antithesis of pandemonium, and pandemonium is created by the tumbling together of many accidents. Art arrives only by design. Therefore in order to make any work of art it is clear we may only work in those materials with which we can calculate. Man is not one of these materials." Yet it is typical of Craig's contradictory genius that his book on Irving is one of the most understanding studies of an actor ever written, and he himself as a young man, when he was a member of Irving's company at the Lyceum, was by all accounts (including those by Granville-Barker and Shaw) an actor of exceptional promise.

Appia's ideas on acting were strongly influenced by Jacques Dalcroze. In *L'Oeuvre d'Art Vivant* he expounds at great length his theory that all art must be rhythmic, that nothing must be left to the chance inspiration of the actor, that the lines of the actor's body, his movements, his gestures, must be exactly related to the lines of the setting until the two are fused into a complete, rhythmic pattern. By means of fluctuating lighting the emphasis of the setting was to be constantly varied "so that the rhythms of its lines change in accord with the rhythmic movements of the actors". Although Appia in his writings constantly stresses the importance of the actor, he shows not the slightest interest in him as a human being, and denies him any freedom to think for himself. The actor is only important to Appia because he is the most flexible and easily movable element in the rhythmic patterns created by the designer-producer. The valuable part of Appia's theorising on acting is contained in his discussion of the Wagnerian operas. He insists that in opera the action must be suited not to the word but to the music, that all movement and gesture must be governed by the score, that it is as important to move to the music as it is to sing to the music—a fact which has only recently and somewhat reluctantly been admitted by English opera singers.

Whether Appia's theories on acting and production had much influence is doubtful. His books are appallingly difficult to read. The meaning has to be laboriously disinterred from beneath a soggy mass of Teutonic philosophy and metaphysics obscured by a cloud of romantic mysticism. On the other hand, the influence of his theories on scenery and lighting was considerable, not because he expressed himself on this subject any less obscurely, but because *Die Musik und die Inscenierung* contained eighteen designs which vividly revealed his ideas on stagecraft even to those who had not read a word of his text. Each of these drawings convincingly proves his contention that "the light which is most important in the theatre is the light that casts shadows". It is the contrast of brilliant light and deep shadow which gives Appia's imaginatively simple settings their appearance of tremendous, sculpturesque massiveness; it is his fluent use of light from many angles which dramatically accentuates different figures in the scene and varying aspects of the setting according to the development of the play.

On the strength of these illustrations Appia is usually given the credit of being the first to envisage new methods of stage lighting which today are standard practice. For instance, it has often been stated that it was due to Appia that producers began to use light to create shadows instead of flatly illuminating the stage and leaving it to the scene-painters to provide the shadows by painting them on the scenery; yet the Duke of Saxe-Meiningen and Henry Irving had both been using lighting in this way for more than twenty years before the publication of Appia's book. It is difficult to say which of them originated the method. Each seems to have evolved it independently about the same time. Although theatrical historians (who are curiously relucant to credit the English theatre with any initiative) generally attribute the "modernism" of Irving's lighting to the influence of the Meiningen company's visit to London in 1881, the fact is that Irving had given up depending on his painters for the highlights and shadows in his settings some years before this. One of his favourite devices was the dramatic use of figures moving from deep shadow into a blaze of light. Like Tyrone Guthrie today, he was sometimes accused of being more intent upon darkening the stage than lighting it. A typical example of his lighting was the opening of *Richard III* (produced four years before he saw the Meiningen company), a scene deeply shadowed by the arches of the narrow London street, so that a strange, eerie effect was created by the passing of the king's funeral as it emerged from the greyness into a patch of light and then became dim and ghost-like again as once more it moved on into the shadows.

Contemporary accounts of Irving's productions constantly refer to the softness and mellowness of the lighting, the rich glow it shed upon the costumes and scenery, the way it enhanced the mood of a scene, the skill with which it was used to give the effect of blazing sunshine, or the coolness of evening, or the dank cold of a winter's day. In achieving these effects Irving had one great advantage over the modern producer—he was using gas lighting. The light which comes from an electric lamp is a hard, cold, dead light. Gaslight is alive; it is never quite still. However steadily it seems to burn, there is always movement, a constant, almost imperceptible flicker which enlivens whatever it sheds its light upon. Compare the flash and sparkle of a crystal chandelier lit by candlelight or gaslight with the lifeless thing it becomes when it is lit by the motionless glare of electric bulbs. Whatever devices are used in the theatre to colour and soften electric light, it can never have the softness of gaslight. Ellen Terry has described how "the thick softness

of gaslight gave illusion to many a scene which is revealed in all
its naked trashiness by electricity". Electric lighting was installed at the Lyceum by Daly, the lessee of the theatre, while
Irving was on tour. When Ellen Terry saw the harsh effect of
the electric light on the scenery and the faces of the actors she
burst into tears and entreated Irving to restore the gas lighting.

The essential difference between the method of lighting
practised by Irving and the Duke of Saxe-Meiningen and the
theory expounded by Appia is that one was realistic, the other
deliberately unrealistic. In a production at the Lyceum or by
the Meiningen company the lighting only changed when there
was a logical reason for it—the rising of the sun, the approach
of dusk, the gathering of a storm, the dimming of a lamp, the
kindling of a fire, the drawing of a curtain across a window.
The continual and infinitely detailed changes of lighting which
Appia worked out deliberately ignored nature; they were
dictated by the changing moods of the play; or they were used
as a means of emphasis. During a scene parts of the stage would
be faded into darkness, for no natural reason, in order to concentrate attention on essentials—the theatrical equivalent to a
close-up in the cinema. Colours would change with an equal
disregard for reality so as to heighten the emotional tension.
This is, after all, simply a development of a method of lighting
which has always been used in Christmas pantomimes. When
the principal girl, dressed as a village maiden, sings her pretty,
sentimental song the producer seeks to make it seem still prettier
and more sentimental by bathing her in a pink light such as
never shone from heaven, and certainly not at high noon on the
village green. If a little later the Demon King should arrive,
black night will instantly descend, and he will stalk the stage
followed wherever he goes by an obliging pool of lurid green
light. After the Fairy Queen has appeared (in a beam of pure,
silvery light) and sent him packing, high noon returns as
suddenly as it departed. Nobody protests that all this happens
in defiance of the laws of nature, because pantomime is recognised to be a fantastic and illogical entertainment which makes
no pretence of reality.

Appia applied his theory of lighting mainly to opera, a still more deliberately unrealistic form of art belonging to a never-never land where people converse with one another in song instead of by the easier and more convenient method of every-day speech. The fundamental unreality of opera makes irrealism in acting, production, scenery, and lighting not only permissible but essential.

When Appia applied his theories to plays he chose the plays of Shakespeare, who wrote for a theatre in which realism in speech and stagecraft was as yet unknown. What Appia never attempted to do was to force his ideas willy-nilly upon a realistic play. In this he was more sensible than most of his disciples, including Gordon Craig, who sought to make irrealism an immutable principle to be applied to the production of every play, irrespective of the author's intentions.

When Craig designed the setting for Duse's production of *Rosmersholm* at the Pergola Theatre in Florence in 1906 he wrote in a programme note: "We are not in a house of the nineteenth or twentieth century built by Architect this or Master Builder that, and filled with furniture of Scandinavian design—that is not the state of mind Ibsen demands we shall be in. Let us leave period and accuracy of detail to the museums and to curiosity shops." Ibsen, in his stage directions, asks for "a room that is spacious, old-fashioned and comfortable". He describes the sofa and easy chairs grouped round the stove, the pots of flowers, the family portraits on the walls, "mostly clergymen, officers and government officials in uniform". Isadora Duncan in *My Life* describes Craig's setting. "He has been pleased to see the high interior of a great Egyptian temple with an enormously high ceiling extending upwards to the skies with walls receding into the distance. Only, unlike an Egyptian temple, at the far end there was a great square window . . . Craig had been pleased to see this in dimensions of ten metres by twelve. It looked out upon a flaming landscape of yellows, reds, and greens which might have been some scene in Morocco." (Ibsen describes a view of an avenue of fine old trees leading up to the house.) "Oh, how can I describe what appeared before our

32

astonished, enraptured eyes? Did I speak of an Egyptian temple?
No Egyptian temple has ever revealed such beauty. No Gothic
cathedral, no Athenian palace. Never have I seen such a vision
of loveliness. Through vast blue spaces, celestial harmonies,
mounting lines, colossal heights, one's soul was drawn towards
the light of this great window which showed beyond, no little
avenue, but the infinite universe. Within these blue spaces was all
the thought, the meditation, the earthly sorrow of man. Beyond
the window was all the ecstasy, the joy, the miracle of imagination." At this point in the panegyric Isadora Duncan is suddenly
assailed by a moment of doubt. "Was this," she asks herself,
"the living-room of Rosmersholm? I do not know what Ibsen
would have thought." She comes to the somewhat over-optimistic
conclusion that "probably he would have been—as we were—
speechless, carried away". But the incongruity between this
setting and the realism of Ibsen's play was irreconcilable. Even
Isadora Duncan had to admit that when Rosmersholm made
his entrance, with his hands in his pockets, he looked like a
stage-hand who had strayed on to the stage by mistake.

It is extremely difficult to write about Gordon Craig without
taking sides. The romantic charm of his personality and the
persuasive eloquence of his writing have won him a large and
devoted band of disciples who adopt so belligerent an attitude
towards anyone who dares to question the infallibility of the
master that the inevitable result has been the creation of a
vigorous resistance movement. The headquarters of the
resistance is inside the theatre. We who work in the theatre do
not deny our great debt to Craig as a vivid and inspiring theorist,
but most of us refuse to accept the claim made by Craig's
disciples (and by Craig himself) that he is a practical man of
the theatre, a great producer and designer who has been denied
the opportunity to practise his art because of the stupidity and
timidity of those in control of the theatre.

Craig worked for only two years as a producer, directing six
plays, not all of them full-length. When he was a young man in
his twenties he produced, in 1900, three performances of *Dido
and Aeneas* at the Hampstead Conservatoire. The following

year he revived it at the Coronet Theatre in Notting Hill Gate, together with *The Masque of Love* from Purcell's opera *Dioclesian*. In 1902 he produced *Acis and Galatea* for a fortnight's run at the Great Queen Street Hall, and, at Christmas, Laurence Housman's *Bethlehem* at the Imperial Institute. When in 1903 his mother, Ellen Terry, went into management at the Imperial Theatre, Westminster, he produced for her Ibsen's *The Vikings at Helgeland* and *Much Ado About Nothing*; but the venture only survived two months. In the same year he was assistant-producer for Fred Terry's production of *Sword and Song* at the Shaftesbury, and designed two of the scenes.

These productions were remarkable for their extreme simplicity at a time when more and more realistic detail was being crammed on to the stages of every country in Europe. Instead of painted backcloths Craig used richly coloured curtains and put nothing on the stage which was not absolutely essential to the action of the play. His costumes were austere in line and detail, but of brilliant and daring colours. He used lighting, grouping and movement to suggest a mood instead of imitating reality.

His production of *Acis and Galatea* was criticised on the grounds that he had produced a pastoral and put nothing pastoral into the scene. Arthur Symons, in his *Studies in Seven Arts,* says: "This criticism is partly just. Yet there are parts, especially the end of Act I, where he has perfectly achieved the rendering of pastoral feeling according to his own convention. The tent is there with its square walls, not a glimpse of meadow or sky comes into the severe design, and yet, as the nymphs in their straight dresses and straight ribbons lie back laughing on the ground, and the children, with their little modern brown straw hats, toss paper roses among them, and the coloured balloons (which you may buy in the street for a penny) are tossed into the air, carrying the eye upward, as if it saw the wind chasing the clouds, you feel the actual sensation of a pastoral scene, of country joy, of the spring and the open air, as no trickle of real water in a trough, no sheaves of real corn among painted trees, no imitation of a flushed sky on canvas, could trick you into feeling it. The imagination has been caught; a suggestion has been given which strikes straight to 'the nerves of delight'; and be sure those nerves, that imagination, will do the rest, better, more effectually, than the deliberate assent of the eyes to an imitation of natural appearances."

Since 1903 Craig has not been solely responsible for a single production. In *Who's Who in the Theatre* he is credited with having produced another four plays (in Germany, Italy, Russia and Denmark), but for these he was either responsible only for the designs or he gave some indication as to his ideas on the production and left the actual direction to an experienced producer.

The small total of Craig's practical work in the theatre has, of course, been used by his disciples to promulgate the legend of the misunderstood genius condemned to live most of his life in exile at his Florentine villa. But the truth is that Craig received many offers from all over the world, some of which he accepted—on conditions. These conditions were generally so fantastic that it was simply not possible for any theatre to grant them. For instance, when Jacques Rouché invited him to take over the artistic direction of the Théâtre des Arts, he accepted on condition that the theatre was closed to the public for at least ten years while he prepared his productions.

Cochran tells how he offered Craig a production "of any play, in any theatre or hall, with any actors. . . . Although it was in the days when I sought no financial assistance in my productions, and backed my losing ventures with the profits of my winners, for a production by Craig I was offered any sum I wanted. Money was no object—'the sky was the limit'. 'Perhaps these old hands have lost their cunning', was Craig's reply. He sent my wife a delicious woodcut, and went back to Rapallo".

Perhaps Craig was unhappily aware that he was a dreamer who did not know how to make his dreams come true, so he used his exorbitant demands as a means of avoiding having to make the attempt, while at the same time strengthening the legend of the misunderstood, persecuted genius. Bernard Shaw dealt summarily with this legend in an interview with George Bishop published in *The Observer*. "If there ever was a spoilt child in artistic Europe, that child was Teddy Craig. The doors of the theatre were wider open to him than anyone else. He had only to come in as the others did, and do his job, and know his place, and accept the theatre with all its desperate vicissitudes, and inadequacies, and impossibilities, as the rest of us did, and the way would have been clear for all the talent he possessed." But Miss Janet Leeper, who wrote the preface to the King Penguin edition of Craig's designs, argues that Craig, "seeing the theatre steadily and seeing it whole, could not be expected to descend into the arena and make ignoble bargains with actor-managers out for their own glory".

In 1922 *The English Review* said bluntly: "The theatre is waiting for Gordon Craig to return to active work. His theories are beginning to win through; it is for him to see that somewhere, somehow, he returns to practice. We grow tired of the reiteration of what Gordon Craig did in nineteen hundred and something; we grow sceptical of what Mr. Craig will do when a perfectly equipped theatre with efficient assistants and endowment complete is placed in his hands. Gods are sometimes born in stables, and if there is no room at the inn . . ." This provoked a thunderous reply from Craig in which he grandiloquently declared: "For the theatre I have tuned my ambition up to the right key—to the standard—with my eye on the British nation as it is. Tell others about the necessity for their being this, that, and the rest—tell all the young men who need that to encourage them. But do not tell it to me, because to do so is to laugh at the mighty Empire which when it likes, and without haste, can give me the means to do as is fitting."

Lee Simonson, the American scene designer, after a detailed study of Craig's work, come to the conclusion that "he has never shown the slightest capacity, either as a critic or as a designer, for the work involved in pushing to a solution a single problem he has posed. Long before the point was reached he struck another attitude and, in order to conceal his failure, strutted once again in the mantle of a prophet which he manipulates with the skill of an eighteenth-century tragedian playing in the grand manner. He can bare his breast to the 'slings and arrows of outrageous fortune' and present a perfect picture of a misunderstood genius who has never been given an opportunity to execute his dreams. He has not been prevented from doing so by a mean and jealous world, but by his own lack of authentic creative power. He has all the superficial attributes that we associate with a romantic and disordered type of genius but he has not the essential force of genius, the sullen determination to come to grips with the material difficulties of his instrument and so arrive at the creative pitch that turns dreams into their embodiment".

When Stanislavsky engaged Craig to produce *Hamlet* he found him of little practical assistance during the two years he spent struggling to translate Craig's noble vision of the play into terms of the theatre. When it was at last produced Stanislavsky had to admit that he had failed to find a way of realising Craig's intentions. One of the problems for which Craig could offer no solution was how to make the setting manageable. He had conceived an arrangement of mobile screens which would, before the eyes of the audience, glide about the stage, changing the shape of the scene according to the varying moods of the play. He saw it all vividly in his imagination. "At each appointed cue a single or double leaf of my screens moves— turns and advances—recedes—folds or unfolds." Unfortunately Craig had given little thought to the technical problem of how the screens were to be made to stand up safely and yet still be mobile. Although he claimed that they were "able to stand by themselves, dispensing with the braces, struts, pulleys, ropes and counterweights of the changeable sceneries", the technicians of the Art Theatre experimented for many months in an endeavour to solve the problem of what Stanislavsky describes as "those terrible and dangerous walls". An hour before the dress-rehearsal one of the screens swayed and fell, knocking over others in its fall, and in a few seconds the entire set had collapsed like a house of cards. Craig denies this ever happened, but it is recorded in *My Life in Art*. "In order to avoid a catastrophe," wrote Stanislavsky, "we were forced to deny ourselves the joy of moving the screens in full view of the audience and to accept the use of the traditional theatrical curtain, which coarsely but loyally hid the work of the stage-hands."

Nevertheless, these screens—which Craig called The Thousand Scenes in One—are his most practical contribution to the art of the theatre, in spite of the fact that nobody has yet discovered a way of making them move in the way he dreamed they would. I can speak of them from experience. The Cambridge Festival Theatre, where I worked as a producer, was equipped with a complete set of Craig's screens. We found they could be arranged in innumerable combinations and permutations to provide an infinite number of finely effective settings, provided we made imaginative use of the theatre's exceptionally elaborate and flexible lighting equipment. But to re-arrange them, even during the intervals, was a considerable task. When Craig visited the theatre we tried in vain to discover how he had envisaged them being moved in view of the audience. I remember him standing on the stage peering in puzzled silence through his pince-nez at these screens, as if he were surprised and pained by their obstinacy in remaining so immobile.

As Craig's ventures into the theatre have been so few, his fame as a designer is based almost entirely on his drawings. The producer and the designer look at these drawings rather differently from the layman, who is entranced by their beauty and imaginativeness, and filled with indignation against the theatre for not allowing these magnificent conceptions to be realised upon the stage. The producer looks at them through an imaginary proscenium and sees that the soaring lines of those great pillars and arches rise thirty, forty, fifty feet beyond the highest proscenium opening ever built. Lee Simonson has made measurements and models of some of Craig's designs. Using as the basis of measurement either the treads of a stairway or the human figure sketched in the designs, he finds that one of Craig's settings for *Macbeth* would require a proscenium opening a hundred feet wide and ninety feet high. In another of these designs for *Macbeth* a stairway winds around a column which is twenty-seven feet in diameter, therefore more than eighty-four feet in circumference. The setting for Act I, Scene 5, is fifty-three feet high and fifty-three feet deep, yet the scene plays for less than five minutes, and Craig gives no indication of how the set is to be changed or adapted for the scene which follows. "A Scene for a Play by Shakespeare" rises to a height of seventy feet, is eighty-eight feet wide (exactly twice the width of the proscenium opening at Covent Garden) and extends to a depth of a hundred and forty-four feet, which is double the size of the Covent Garden stage from the setting line to the back wall.

Measurements such as these do nothing to shake the faith of the idolaters in Craig as a practical man of the theatre. They are convinced that, given the opportunity, he would have been able to translate these undisciplined fantasies into practical stage settings, in spite of the fact that their impressiveness depends largely on the splendour of their dimensions, on scale and space. Miss Enid Rose, in her book, *Gordon Craig and the Theatre*, ridicules Joseph Harker for having used a foot-rule to convince Tree that the roof would have to be taken off His Majesty's Theatre to accommodate the designs for *Macbeth* which he had commissioned from Craig. According to Miss Rose, "Craig's way of obtaining impressions of the high and mighty was a way which did not enter into Harker's calculations at all; it was based on the principle of relativity." But surely it is his disregard for the principle of relativity which is the basic weakness of so many of Craig's designs for the theatre. Scene designing is governed by the relation between the unchangeable size of the human figure and the height of the scene, which is dictated by the size of the proscenium opening. A Craig drawing of a six-foot figure standing beneath an archway sixty feet high is immensely impressive because of the relation of the figure to the soaring lines of the arch; but when the height of the arch is reduced to twenty feet (which is about as high as it could be in a theatre) the figure of the actor still remains six feet high, with the result that the size of the arch in relation to the figure standing beneath it is no longer particularly impressive. Miss Rose counters such arguments by telling us "Craig knew that practice with his device of 'The Scene with a Mobile Face' would give him power over line and space, over light and shadow, which would make possible the seemingly impossible". If so, I can see no reason why he should not have demonstrated his intentions by the normal method of drawing his designs to scale.

Craig's disciples do him a disservice by persisting in their claim that he is a practical man of the theatre, a great producer and designer debarred from the stage by the stupidity of those within the theatre. From time to time the theatre is driven to defend itself against this charge, and the ensuing arguments are apt to obscure Craig's real reputation, which does not depend upon what he might or might not have achieved as a producer and a designer, but upon his influence on other producers and designers. It now matters little whether his designs could or could not have been translated into stageworthy sets; what does matter is that the spirit of these dreams and visions has inspired innumerable designers with something of the splendour of Craig's imagination, stimulating them to seek to depict moods rather than facts, to suggest rather than to imitate.

It is perhaps not too fantastic to see in those romantic visions of a strange, twilit world where lonely figures wander like lost souls among the shadows or crouch at the foot of vague, towering shapes, shrouded in a silver mist, something symbolic of Craig's own state of mind. In his later years he seems to have been groping in the darkness towards not just a new conception of the theatre but towards an entirely new form of art as yet undreamed of by man. "To save the theatre we must destroy it," he cries. But what then? "We shall build," he declaims, "the Theatre of the Future . . . While we are about it, let us measure for an art which will exceed in stature all other arts, an art which says less yet shows more than all . . . I prophesy that a new religion will be found contained in it. That religion will preach no more, but it will reveal. It will not show us the definite images which the painter and sculptor show us. It will unveil thoughts to our eyes, silently—by movement—in visions."

The vagueness of these oracular pronouncements does not seem to trouble Craig's disciples. Challenge them to elucidate passages such as these and they smile scornfully. The secrets of the master, they imply, are not to be revealed to everyone. But

Craig himself, in his old age, sadly admitted that the mists still obscured the shape of the new form of art of which he was the prophet. "I once said that there are just two kinds of theatre, the old theatre of my master, Irving, and its successor, which I once called the theatre of tomorrow. I have changed my ideas. The old theatre has been effectively destroyed. In its place we have a new kind of theatre which is infinitely better, but is, in fact, no more than a re-edit of the old model, brought up to date, streamlined, and improved. The *real* theatre, the theatre which is an art in its own right like music and architecture, is yet to be discovered and may not come for several generations."

Craig's most valuable book is his first, *The Art of the Theatre*, written before he assumed the mantle of a prophet. *The Art of the Theatre* is a clear and persuasive statement of the theories of the symbolists and other little groups who for the past fifteen years had been forming pockets of resistance against the onrush of realism. Few of the ideas in the book are altogether original. Many of them are derived from Appia—a fact more freely and generously acknowledged by Craig himself than by his disciples. But if Craig is indebted to Appia, he in turn is equally indebted to Craig for popularising his ideas, making them not only understandable but also provocative and exciting.

The most famous and frequently quoted passages from *The Art of the Theatre* are those in which Craig envisages a new theatre with a producer in absolute control co-ordinating all those elements which, when fused together, comprise the art of the theatre. Craig is often credited with having virtually invented the modern producer. But in 1905, when *The Art of the Theatre* was published, the idea was by no means new. It had been expounded by Appia and Fuchs, and put into practice before these books appeared by the Duke of Saxe-Meiningen, Stanislavsky, Antoine, Fort, Brahm, and Lugné Poë. The importance of *The Art of the Theatre* was not in the originality of its ideas but in its readability. Because it was written vividly, entertainingly and excitingly it reached a public which had never even heard of the dry and unpersuasive works of the other theatrical theorists.

We producers ought to be particularly grateful to Craig for publicising our arrival in the theatre and for so brilliantly arguing our case. But soon he began to make exorbitant claims for the producer. He was to be no longer the servant of the playwright but his master, not an interpreter but a creator, using the play as the raw material for his own work of art, giving it a "symbolical development" suggested by "the broad sweeps of thought" which the play evokes in the producer's mind. Craig's conception of the producer's rôle is best illustrated by his opinion that *Hamlet* does not belong to the theatre because it is so complete in itself that the producer can add nothing to it.

The Art of the Theatre became the handbook of a revolution— the revolt against the drab, factual theatre of dialectics. Although Craig was not the instigator of the revolt, he became its acknowledged leader. He protested that the theatre had become overburdened with words; its origin was in dance and mime; once again it should subordinate speech to movement. He defined the good dramatist as one who knows that the eye is more swiftly and powerfully appealed to than any other sense, that an audience is more eager to see what the actor will do than to hear what he will say. On the first page of *Towards a New Theatre* he quotes the dictionary's definition of THEATRE as "derived from the Greek Θέατρον, a place for seeing shows, derived from the Greek Θεᾶσθαι, to see". To this Craig adds the note: "Not a word about its being a place for hearing 30,000 words babbled out in two hours." In one of his letters he describes how, on a visit to Germany, he went through the stage-door of a theatre and saw a notice which said: *Sprechen Verboten.* "The first moment I thought I was in heaven. I thought, 'At last they have discovered the Art of the Theatre.'"

Of all the productions I have seen the one which would probably have pleased Craig most was Jean-Louis Barrault's production of Kafka's *The Trial* adapted by André Gide. *The Art of the Theatre* is one of Barrault's five gospels. (The others are *The Poetics* of Aristotle; *Les Trios Discours* of Corneille; *La Préface de Cromwell* by Hugo; and *Le Théâtre et son Double* by Artaud.) Like Craig, Barrault has been described as an enemy of speech. Paul Arnold, the editor of *La Revue Théâtrale,* in his notice of *The Trial* estimated that the entire dialogue could be spoken in fifteen minutes. The production was symbolistic, both in décor and acting, a combination of pantomime, rhythmic movement, and shadowgraphs, with speech used merely as an accessory to visual means of expression. But the production of *The Trial* did not go far enough to accord with Craig's later and more extreme theories in the years when he was demanding the banishment from the theatre of the actor as well as the playwright. In the 'twenties an Italian, Enrico Prampolini, followed Craig far further than Barrault. Prampolini considered the actor "a useless element in theatrical action and moreover one that is dangerous to the future of the theatre . . . We are tired of seeing this grotesque rag of humanity agitating itself futilely under the vast dome of the stage in an effort to stimulate its own emotions. The appearance of the human element on the stage destroys the mystery of the beyond, which must rule in the theatre, a temple of spiritual abstraction". So Prampolini invented an abstract "theatre of mechanics", a theatre without actors, a super-human performing machine, which he called "The Polyexpressive and Magnetic Theatre".

The magnetic puppet is already in use. The recent film of *Hansel and Gretel* was performed by a company of these stringless puppets which, according to the publicity, "are capable of thousands of expressions". In these inventions are perhaps the beginnings of the fulfilment of Craig's later daydreams.

But it is to Craig's earlier and less extreme writings that one returns again and again whenever one's faith in the theatre weakens. When he wrote about the theatre of the future he may not have been exactly explicit, but he wrote about it with such passionate fervour that at least he convinced one that the theatre *has* a future, and that it can be a future full of splendour and dignity and beauty and excitement—"a place in which the entire beauty of life could be unfolded, and not only the external beauty of the world, but the inner meaning of life".

2

THE REVOLT AGAINST REALISM

By the beginning of the twentieth century the realists had so firmly entrenched themselves in the theatre that their opponents were making little progress. In Germany the realistic producers were aided by new inventions which simplified the changing of elaborately realistic settings. Stages were now being built which could revolve; there was another kind which slid off into the wings while its companion stage, complete with scenery, slid on from the other side; most elaborate of all were the stages which sank on hydraulic lifts into vast cellars where another stage, fully set, waited to rise up and take its place. Before the invention of these revolving, sliding, and sinking stages, photographically realistic interiors with their unwieldy mass of furniture and properties were only feasible in plays which needed no change of scenery during an act. Now solidly built realistic sets complete in every detail could follow one another with no more than a few seconds' pause.

Another invention which aided the realists was the plaster cyclorama. This "sky dome", as it was first called, curving round the back and over the top of the stage, replaced the back-cloth and did away with the necessity for the unconvincing hanging borders of painted foliage which had hitherto been necessary for masking "up above". When properly lit, the cyclorama gave a convincing illusion of sky and space such as had never been achieved with the old-fashioned painted sky cloth.

The realists considered their case was now complete. Hitherto they had been criticised on the grounds that it was impossible to imitate nature convincingly on the stage. But now, with the aid of the cyclorama, they could give an illusion of the open air; they could put a forest of real trees upon the stage without the effect of reality being destroyed by painted tree-borders hanging above the three-dimensional trees. Now that tons of solid scenery could be moved by machinery they could build real houses of wood and plaster instead of flimsy constructions of canvas which had to be light enough to be pushed about by stage-hands. On the new mechanical stages it was possible to build a complete, life-size village, and to show different aspects of it during the course of the play—the main street, the church-yard, the inn, the bridge over the canal, and so on. Surely there could no longer be any logical objection to realism. But their opponents were not impressed. They pointed out that they considered the theatre was an art, and that it was pointless for art to reproduce reality.

The most triumphant demonstration of the new mechanised stagecraft was Reinhardt's production of *A Midsummer Night's Dream* in 1905. He saw the play as dominated by the woodland; therefore "the wood must live and breathe and seem infinite and inexhaustible". Fuerst and Hume in *Twentieth Century Stage Decoration* describe how "veritable trees, not painted but plaster ones, were placed on the stage, and the space below was covered not with a painted ground-cloth but with what seemed to be palpable grass in which the feet sank among the flowers; while here and there were seen bushes and little beeches grow-ing between the trees, and in the midst of all a little lake mirrored between two hills. And now (constructed on the revolving stage) all this forest began slowly and gently to move and to turn, discovering new perspectives, always changing its aspect, presenting ever new images inexhaustible as Nature. And while the stage turned and changed, the elves and fairies ran through the forest, disappearing behind the trees, to emerge behind the little hillocks. These beings with their green veils and leafy crowns seemed to form a part of the forest itself. Puck, who up to that time had been usually dressed in the costume of the fantastic ballet or opera, was covered only with grass and became at last the true elf, who rolled with laughter like a child in the green of the forest".

This production is usually described as the apotheosis of realism. Actually it was the beginning of Reinhardt's break-away from the bleak realism of Otto Brahm who was at this time the most powerful influence in the German theatre. Rein-hardt had begun his career as an actor in Brahm's company, and his first notable success as a producer was a meticulously realistic production of *The Lower Depths*. But Reinhardt was a Jew who had lived his early life in Vienna, and the charac-teristics of his race and the atmosphere of the city in which he had spent his youth had combined to give him a love of colour and gaiety, richness and display. It seemed to him that realism was draining all colour from the theatre, depriving it of its sen-suousness, leaving it grey and factual. In his production of *The Dream* he sought to use realism imaginatively.

To the confirmed anti-realist, imagination and realism are incompatible. Reinhardt proved that it is not necessarily so. Having built himself a real forest he transformed it into a mysterious, magical woodland by peopling it with half-seen beings flitting among the trees, filling it with strange sounds, and lighting it so that it was a place of ever-changing moods. "Another part of the Wood" was no longer just a stage direc-tion. On the revolving stage it was possible to show so many different aspects of the wood that it was easy to believe in Lysander losing himself in its "dark, uneven way". Nowadays we may wince at the idea of this much realism in a Shakespeare play, priding ourselves that we can conjure up the forest in our imagination with no more help than Shakespeare's lines and one or two stylised trees against a neutral background; but by the standards of 1905 this production seemed far less realistic in intention than the canvas-encumbered productions of the play to which audiences of those days were accustomed. The critics praised it for its sense of poetry, for its romanticism, and, above all, for its "unearthly" quality.

By now there were signs that the tide of realism was on the turn. Stanislavsky, having perfected his naturalistic style in the

last of his Chekhov productions in 1904, was restlessly beginning
to consider other methods. He encouraged Meierhold, a member of his company, to experiment with stylised productions
in the Art Theatre Studio, and he himself, in 1907, attempted
his first "irrealistic" production when he produced Andreyev's
The Life of Man on a stage hung with black curtains against
which skeleton doors and windows were outlined in rope. The
acting was highly stylised, purged of all naturalistic movement and gesture. Reinhardt made his first experiment in
stylisation in 1906 when he engaged Edward Munch, the im-
pressionist painter, to design a production of *Ghosts* in which
the clash of lines and colours in the setting symbolised the clash
of ideas in Ibsen's play.

Reinhardt's influence changed the entire character of the
German stage. He began to produce at a time when showmanship (in the good sense of the word) was completely lacking in
the German theatre, which was regarded not as a place of
entertainment but as an educational institution. Producers of
the classics had to be scrupulously faithful to long-established
and carefully cherished traditions and conventions. The slightest
deviation aroused the wrath of the critics, most of them university professors, who considered it their duty to guard the
academic interpretation of the classics against any producer or
actor with ideas of his own.

Ernst Stern in his autobiography, *My Life, My Stage,* describes
how at performances of Goethe, Schiller, and Shakespeare "the
audience was expected to sit there humbly and listen to the
words as though to a sermon in church addressed to the good of
their souls. Leading theatres, like the Deutsches Theater, were
in the hands of literary men who carefully avoided all experiments and did their utmost to see that everything was done in
exactly the same way as it was always done before. The result
was that when the classics were performed the audience saw
what might be compared with a blackened masterpiece in which
all colour and life had been deadened by layer after layer of
ancient varnish. And now imagine that overnight the dirt was
cleaned away and the colours all shone in their pristine glory,

47

and that a thing which had been dull and uninteresting was now a delight to the eye. That was what happened when Reinhardt presented his productions of Kleist's *Katchen von Heilbronn* and Shakespeare's *The Merchant of Venice* and *The Winter's Tale*. When he gave the audience something to see as well as something to hear (which, one would have thought, was exactly what the theatre was there for) the critics howled 'Sacrilege!' 'Reinhardt detracts from the essential!' 'Meretricious superficialities!' 'A debasement of the classical spirit!' And so on. They seemed to regard his productions as a personal insult, as an attack on their supreme right to determine what should and what should not be done in the theatre, and they did their best to put him out of business".

It was not only the traditionalists who attacked Reinhardt. He was equally fiercely criticised by the new school of German realists. What they particularly disliked about his work was its unashamed theatricality, a quality which they scrupulously avoided in their own low-toned productions. One of Reinhardt's greatest services to the German theatre was that he restored to it its theatricality—but a theatricality purged of staginess. In doing so he revolutionised German acting. In his productions of modern plays he taught his actors a style which was realistic in feeling but which avoided the drab, painstaking exactness of the realist school; it was warm, vivid, and colourful, always a little larger than life. In his productions of the classics he demanded lively, supple speaking in place of the slow, ponderous delivery of the traditionalists. He made his actors think afresh about the characters instead of dutifully assuming the ready-made characterisations approved by the professors. Above all, he insisted that the classics belonged not to literature but to the theatre and that the actors should be encouraged to re-discover their forgotten theatricality.

Reinhardt was constantly accused of having no style of his own, of annexing other people's ideas. (One of his critics described the Reinhardt organisation as the cleverest and most sensitive receiving station in the world of art.) But as most of the producers whose ideas Reinhardt used were dogmatically proclaiming that their method was the one and only way in which plays ought to be produced, it was hardly reasonable of them to become indignant when another producer adopted those methods. Reinhardt was in fact a great missionary for the new ideas in the theatre because he popularised styles of production which but for him might never have reached more than a coterie audience. Perhaps the reason why the originators of these ideas were so abusive about Reinhardt was because he would not give his allegiance to any one school of production. For instance, when he created wordless dramas, such as *Sumurun* and *The Miracle*, he was enthusiastically hailed by the followers of Craig as one of themselves, a powerful ally in their struggle to free the theatre from the domination of the spoken word. But soon he was producing the plays of Bernard Shaw, using his skill and prestige to popularise the drama of dialectics, and the disappointed disciples of Craig were angrily accusing Reinhardt of being a turncoat, a plagiarist, a copy-cat.

Edward Dent has described him as "typically German, not in his creative power, but in his power to appreciate". There was no known form of theatrical production which he did not practise at one time or another. It is true that he had no style of his own, no formula to which he worked. He simply sought for each play the style of production best suited for it. His most remarkable quality as a producer was that he so seldom repeated himself.

Outside Germany the importance of Reinhardt's work has been underrated, chiefly through insufficient knowledge of it. In England we saw little of it apart from some of his largest and most spectacular productions, such as *Oedipus Rex*, *Sumumun*, *Venetian Night*, *The Miracle*, and *Helen*. English theatregoers travelling abroad saw his *Everyman* at Salzburg, and if they went to Germany they probably chose to go to the most lavish of the several Reinhardt productions running in Berlin—perhaps his *Tales of Hoffman* or *Danton's Death*. So it is understandable enough that in England his success was attributed to showmanship, vastness and quantity. He was described as "The Sultan of the Grand Spectacle", accused of being vulgar and tasteless, achieving splendour without grandeur, size without style. That may have been true of some of Reinhardt's gigantic spectacles, but others, particularly those in mime, had an imaginativeness and an excitement surpassed only by the early spectacular ballets of Diaghilev, such as *Tamar* and *Scheherezade*.

The mime play *Venetian Night* was magnificently described by Bridges Adams in a broadcast talk about Reinhardt. "He chose not the Venice of the Magnificos or of Casanova, but the Venice of the Victorian Grand Tour, with a good deal of help from Mendelssohn. Imagine, then, a small piazza, backed by a hotel and encircled on your left by a shadowy canal with a bridge across it. On the bridge there appears a flaxen-haired German student, complete with his rucksack and his Goethe, taking in the Venice of his dreams and dutifully reading what the revered Goethe has to say about it. Under the bridge shoots a gondola, bearing an English milord and his lady with an incredible amount of baggage. The milord is old and dry; the lady is young, beautiful, and unhappy. The spectacle is too much for an Austrian lieutenant of cavalry on the opposite bank of the canal; he catches her eye. She throws him a rose, but it drops short, on the open page of the student's Goethe; he is transfigured—but he has noted the lieutenant. The stage now revolves until we are inside the hotel, with its staircase, galleries, and corridors. The ill-matched couple are shown obsequiously to their rooms, the student, less obsequiously, to his attic under the tiles. In his white nightgown, he says his prayers and goes to sleep, with his Goethe and the rose upon his pillow.

"I forget how it came to pass—in his dream—that the student made his way to the lady's room, the stage turning to help him. But in the room he found the lieutenant, up to no good. He slew him; and I remember the ashen horror on Maria Carmi's face (I think it was Maria Carmi) as she swept the bed-curtains round the body. But it was impossible to leave it there, so the poor student manfully took the thing on his back, and there ensued a hideous tiptoeing through the dim corridors—the stage still moving—and down the stairs and out onto the bridge, where he flung it into the water. Instantly the bells in the hotel began jangling, and the porter ran out, and plunged his arms into the canal, and fished out not one dead lieutenant but six of him in quick succession. He tossed them high in the air and they landed on their toes, bouncing and quite dead. Still bouncing, they chased the student through the labyrinth of the hotel and out again onto the bridge, where, with a wild gesture, he threw himself over. But at that moment his bed came floating down the canal, and he dropped into it, fast asleep. End of Part I. In a time when you were beginning to hear it said that scenery was a menace to true illusion, it was refreshing to find a man who could pile a few tons of it on the stage and set it twirling, merely to spin a thread of gossamer."

Reinhardt's spectacular productions were only a small part of his work. During his lifetime he staged over five hundred productions, including twenty-two of Shakespeare's plays, Greek drama, expressionist drama, plays by authors as different as Molière and Shaw, Ibsen and Goldoni, Goethe and Maugham. The productions I remember with most pleasure were not his vast spectacles but his subtle and intimate work at the little Kammerspiele Theatre.

Although Reinhardt had, as a producer, no taint of dogmatism or sectarianism, he was at heart a realist—but an imaginative realist. His best productions united a modified form of stylisation with a realism which was never merely literal. In his settings he sought to reduce detail to one or two significant features, such as the corner of a street, or part of a bridge, or the masts and sails of ships showing above a dyke. A churchyard was suggested by two cypresses and a single great tombstone; the cathedral in *Faust* by two immense columns soaring upwards to lose themselves in shadows. The barbarous age of Lear was evoked by draped curtains painted in fierce, clanging colours, the garden of Aglavaine by green gauze draperies.

In the later years of his life his work began to suffer from his dependence on other men's ideas. As he grew older he seemed to lose the power to absorb yet more new ideas of production and make them his own. He had little in common with the spirit of post-war Germany, little sympathy with the experiments being made in its theatre. He slipped back to the style of his early realistic productions, often cluttering and encumbering his stage with irrelevant and distracting detail. In New York I saw his last production, when he had become an exile from his own country. It was the work of a weary man fumbling among the memories of his past successes in the hope of finding something to fire his old enthusiasm.

During all the years of Reinhardt's life in the theatre the battle between the realists and the anti-realists continued to rage, but no sound of the turmoil of this battle penetrated the peaceful English theatre. Here there was no reaction against realism because in England it was still far from reaching its full development. It was in our theatre, as we have seen, that realism was born, but it is one of our characteristics that we originate ideas, invent new machines, make discoveries in science, and then leave it to other countries to develop them. It is typical of us that we invented and taught the world to play most of the games at which we are nowadays defeated. And so in the theatre, having originated realistic methods of production, we had by the beginning of the twentieth century lagged far behind the Continent in the development of realism. Vestris and Bancroft had evolved the realistic setting mainly as a means of imposing a more natural style of acting, but the producers who followed them confined their realism mainly to the visual aspect of production and allowed the acting to lapse back into theatricality. The blame for this was due to the playwrights rather than the producers. The naturalism of Robertson's plays had not exerted anything like the influence with which they are credited in histories of the drama. Playwrights were still sacrificing human nature to theatrical effect, so producers were compelled, as Desmond McCarthy complained, to train their actors to avoid natural acting for fear of challenging in the spectator a standard of comparison, "so that the art of acting became the art not of reproducing emotions but of behaving in such a way that the audience was astonished into not noticing whether the acting was good or bad, or whether the emotions expressed were true or false".

In 1905 a young producer who fiercely resented the way in

which actors were being tyrannised by the writers of "the well-made play" decided to go into management with the avowed intention of getting back to actuality. This producer was Granville-Barker, who, in partnership with J. E. Vedrenne, took over the Court Theatre. Under Granville-Barker's direction the Court in many ways resembled Antoine's Théâtre Libre. Both theatres appealed only to a limited public, so runs were brief and money was short, which meant that a constant flow of new productions had to be provided as quickly and as economically as possible. (At the Court thirty-two plays were produced in thirty-three months.) Both producers were accused of teaching their actors "not to act" because they trained them to avoid over-exaggeration, to behave as normal human beings. Both were enemies of the star-dominated productions of those days and sought to achieve a balanced ensemble, taking particular pains over the small parts.

Granville-Barker was far less intent than Antoine upon the visual aspects of realism. His settings were not nearly so detailed, and in his direction of the actor he was far less interested than Antoine in the exact imitation of outward characteristics and idiosyncrasies. He taught his actors to create a part by identifying themselves so completely with the character that gesture, movement, and facial expression were not just reproduced from observation of every-day life but were the natural expression of the character's thoughts and feelings. At a time when actors considered a sense of the theatre to be more important than anything else and had no hesitation in sacrificing character for the sake of a flamboyant theatrical effect, Granville-Barker laboured with endless patience to achieve his aim of making the characters in a play "seem to live and move by the laws of their own being". He was more interested in plays which gave scope for exact and detailed characterisation than in those where the characters were painted in broad, sweeping strokes—which is one of the reasons why he was not at his happiest as a Shavian producer. Shaw himself has described Granville-Barker as "a man whose fastidiously delicate taste made him the worst possible producer for my plays. Granville-Barker's productions of his own plays and Galsworthy's were exquisite; their styles were perfectly sympathetic, whereas his style and taste were as different from mine as Debussy's from Verdi's. His fault was to suppress his actors when they pulled out all their stops and declaimed. They either under-acted, or were afraid to act at all lest they should be accused of ranting or being ham."

Granville-Barker applied his standard of naturalism not only to the acting but to the play. He demanded from the playwright the same degree of naturalism that he expected from the actor. Desmond McCarthy, in his book on the Court Theatre, has described how "the whole play had to be tugged at and tested in rehearsal until the coherence of its idea and the soundness of its sentiment were perfectly established". What Granville-Barker taught his playwrights and his players was that "a play's business is to interpret life, not to imitate other plays; an actor's business is to interpret life, not just to imitate other actors".

At a time when the realists were providing settings which competed with the actors for the attention of the audience, and the anti-realists were maintaining that the audience could conjure up the scene in their imagination with no more help from the designer than one or two hints and suggestions, Granville-Barker's attitude was refreshingly sensible. His theories on staging were based on the simple fact that the audience's powers of attention are limited, and must be husbanded by the producer so that they are expended as profitably as possible. He argued that if the audience has to imagine the background of the play or fill in details which can be provided by the producer and the designer, time and attention is stolen from the actors, so that too little detail becomes just as distracting as too much detail.

What was so exasperating about the wranglings of the realists and the anti-realists was that both were fanatically determined to impose their own theory of staging upon every play, without regard for its particular requirements. Granville-Barker agreed that realistic settings are unnecessary and irrelevant in Shakespeare's plays because "it seldom matters where exactly the characters are (when it does he takes care to tell us), and at times we might wonder if we stopped to think about it (though he does not let us) if he knows himself". But in most modern plays, Granville-Barker maintained, background made actual becomes part of the play and the producer can make dramatic use of it. "Hedda Gabler's surroundings—she herself such a contrast to them—are very much part of the play; so is the gallery, up and down which we hear—with his wife's ears —and later with our own eyes see John Gabriel Borkman pacing. And as for the studio and that queer garret in *The Wild Duck,* there is as much dramatic life in it, one could protest, as in any character in the play."

In his book, *On Dramatic Method,* Granville-Barker warns those who are opposed on principle to realistic settings that "one may rest too much upon the conviction to be carried by the actor's mere embodying of a character". He points out that there is a strong disposition on the part of the audience to refuse to believe that the individual they see on the stage (and whose real name they have just read in the programme) is Hedda Gabler or Hjalmar Ekdal, and that the producer can do much to counteract this by establishing the characters in convincing surroundings. He goes on to discuss why realistic detail in acting and staging is so essential in a play by Ibsen and so unessential in a play by Aeschylus. The reason, he finds, is that in an Ibsen play the focusing on action and character is far sharper. "If a Greek play could be said to have some of the attributes of sculpture, there is added now to dramatic art something of the quality of a picture, the least touches of light and shade can be made to tell."

Many theatrical theorists of today have nothing but derision and contempt for what they call "the picture stage"; but it was the stage for which Ibsen wrote his plays, and in his stage directions he gives his producers exact instructions on how to use actors, setting, furniture and properties to compose the pictures as he imagined them. Few dramatists have taken more care to express character and thoughts by means of minute touches of visual detail. Granville-Barker takes as an example the opening of *Rosmersholm.* "Rebecca sits crocheting 'a large white woollen

shawl which is nearly finished'. Even in this (and even in the
fact that it is a 'large' shawl and 'nearly finished') there is a
touch of dramatic significance; for it is the occupation of a
woman—of such a woman as we see before us, at least—who
sits and waits and watches and thinks, and has been so sitting
(since it is a 'large' shawl 'nearly finished') through long hours.
She is waiting now and watching, her eyes turning every few
seconds or so to the window. It is open, so that we may hear if
not see the pastor coming; she is listening intently, too. She
must not stand openly watching; when Madame Helseth tells
her he is coming we find that she only 'peeps out between the
curtains'. This is our first sight of Rebecca, in repose but for
the competent fingers busy at the crochet, yet with every sense
alert. And the actress, without a word to say on the subject,
will tell us plainly (if she is fit to play the part at all) that this
man she is waiting for means much to her."

Now turn back to the first chapter of this book, re-read
Isadora Duncan's description of Craig's setting for *Rosmersholm*
and imagine this scene played in what appeared to be "the
high interior of a great Egyptian temple" with Rebecca peeping
out between non-existent curtains through "a great square
window, ten metres by twelve", looking out upon "a flaming
landscape of yellows, reds, and greens which might have been
some scene in Morocco". In Germany during the 'twenties I
saw a production of *Rosmersholm* by an anti-realist producer
who had deprived Rebecca of her crochet, which he evidently
considered an irrelevant and distracting detail, leaving it to the
actress to mime the business of crocheting a shawl. No shawl in
the world could possibly have distracted the attention of the
audience from the play more effectively than the spectacle
of an actress crocheting (or was she knitting?) an imaginary
something-or-other with imaginary needles. The shawl in *Rosmersholm* is not an irrelevant detail. Ibsen was too good a
dramatist for that. To quote again from Granville-Barker's
notes on the play, "When the curtain rises on the fourth act,
and there is Miss Rebecca West standing in that same room,
with her cloak, hat, and that same white crocheted shawl,

finished now, hanging over the back of the sofa, we may, if we are superior people, smile a little at the shawl, but Rebecca West will be, by now, very much more real to us—and our smiling will be one sign of it."

It would be foolish to judge the anti-realistic producers by their excesses. Their protest against photographic realism was fully justified, but all protests must inevitably be exaggerated and over-emphatic. The more moderate arguments come later when the excitement has subsided. They are put forward not by those who made the first, heated protest, but by others who have had time for cool consideration.

The most moderate and reasoned protest against realism was made by Jaques Copeau when he founded the Vieux Columbier in 1913. Like so many other pioneer producers, Copeau came from outside the theatre. When he founded the Vieux Columbier at the age of thirty-five he was a literary critic and editor of *La Nouvelle Revue Française*. His only experience of the stage had been when the Théâtre des Arts produced his adaptation of *The Brothers Karamazov*. His motive for becoming a producer and gathering together his own company of actors was a profound dissatisfaction with the ways plays were being acted in the Paris theatres. As a literary man his primary interest was the play. Reading a play by a contemporary dramatist after seeing it on the stage, he invariably found that in performance it had been under-developed owing to the shallowness of the acting and production. As for the classics, in France they were so tightly swathed in the trappings of tradition that they were unable to breathe.

Copeau studied the writings of Appia, Fuchs, Craig and the other anti-realists without finding much with which he was in agreement. He had no sympathy with Craig's campaign for the curtailment of the power of the spoken word. He thought that Appia and Fuchs, in their concentration on the visual aspects of production, gave too little thought to the actor and the play. What interested Copeau above all else was what the actor had to say and how he said it. The only producer whose ideas approximated to his own was Granville-Barker. These two men stand apart from the other producers of their time insofar as they were men of letters besides being men of the theatre. At a time when the theorists were exalting the theatre at the expense of the drama, both were opposed to what was called the "theatrically creative" treatment of plays. Their task, as they saw it, was to interpret the author's script honestly and modestly.

It was typical of Copeau that when he founded the Vieux Columbier he made no pronouncement about his theories of production. He had none. That was something which he hoped he and his actors would evolve in the course of their daily work. In a manifesto very unlike the opinionated statements issued by most new theatre groups he said: "Whatever our avowed preferences as critics, our personal direction as men of letters, we do not represent a school . . . We bring with us no formula in the belief that from it there must inevitably spring the theatre of tomorrow. Herein lies a distinction between us and the undertakings that have gone before. These—and it can be said without umbrage to the best known among them, the Théâtre Libre, and without depreciation of the high merit of its chief, André Antoine, to whom we owe so much—these fell into the imprudent and unconscious error of limiting their field of action with a programme of revolution . . . We do not know what is to be the theatre of tomorrow. But in founding the Théâtre du Vieux Columbier we are preparing a place and haven of work for tomorrow's inspiration."

Copeau began with a company of eleven actors. One of these was Charles Dullin, who played Smerdiakov in Copeau's version of *The Brothers Karamazov*. Another was Louis Jouvet, a young man studying to become a pharmacist, who had formed a company of his own called Le Théâtre de Château d'Eau, which speedily lost most of its tiny capital of five thousand francs.

Before opening the Vieux Columbier Copeau took his little company away from Paris to his home at Le Limon in the department of Seine-et-Marne. Here they read plays aloud, improvised scenes, and practised exercises designed to make their bodies and voices flexible instruments. In their improvisations they learned much from Dullin, who had been a reciter in the cafés of Montmartre and an exponent of the traditional "comédie improvisée", which was still popular in the cabarets of Paris and the fairs of provincial France. From Copeau they learned to beware of originality. "The one originality of interpretation which is not anathema," he told them, "is that which grows organically from a sound knowledge of the text."

These warnings against originality may sound strange coming from a producer who has the reputation of having worked in a highly mannered style of his own, but this reputation is largely due to the fact that the few sketchy descriptions of Copeau's work published in England have made too much of the unusual design of his theatre and the balletic movement in some of his revivals of the classics. My own recollections of the productions I saw at the Vieux Columbier during the early 'twenties are that they were simple, sincere, and very well acted. Admittedly the theatre itself was somewhat startling on first acquaintance because it was so unlike any other theatre one had ever seen. It was simply a long, narrow hall at the end of which shallow, curving steps led to a platform with a door on either side and, at the back, a couple of pillars, and a stairway leading to a balcony. The stage was left unframed. There was no suggestion of a proscenium, no wings (the actors simply made their exits through the doors into the adjoining rooms) and no definite line of demarcation between stage and auditorium. Décor was used rarely and sparingly, seldom consisting of more than one or two painted screens, or a balustrade, or a draped curtain. Only the barest minimum of furniture and properties was used, and nothing was put on the stage merely as an aid to realistic illusion. The atmosphere for each play was created almost entirely by the lighting.

In the productions that I saw, Copeau seemed to have taken pains to avoid drawing attention to the unusual features of his stage and the absence of scenery. But one gathers from a letter to Copeau from Granville-Barker that in the early days he made more ostentatious use of his new stage. "I fancy," wrote Granville-Barker, "that you were at first a little too intrigued by all those clever devices of staging and decoration that were then in their heyday. This was natural. Some of them were very good and others quite amusing. But the game of dressing up your stage in odd shapes is such an easy one to play and it contributes just as much to the art of the theatre as the costume of the actor does to the playing of Hamlet or Tartuffe—just as much and no more. The art of the theatre is the art of acting, first, last, and all the time. You very soon found that out. It was interesting to see how quickly you absorbed all that was fruitful in the new staging, and I believe what chiefly attracted you to it was that it is essentially the old staging restored. For you are, like all good Frenchmen, like all good artists possibly, a traditionalist (by which I do not mean a conservative) at heart."

The acting at the Vieux Columbier was, in a modern play, at first sight completely realistic, although the detailed business of the ordinary realistic production was reduced to a minimum. But watching more closely one realised that gesture was being used sparingly and selectively, so that each gesture was given unusual significance. In Copeau's productions of the classic comedies the acting had the balletic quality which so many producers attempt to achieve though the result is generally no more than a series of self-conscious posturings and caperings. At the Vieux Columbier the actors, as a result of their training, seemed to adopt this style of acting naturally and spontaneously. What I chiefly remember about these productions was their lightness, their grace, and their gaiety. Pictorially they were exquisite because of the skill with which Copeau composed his grouping and movement on the various levels of his stage, sometimes varied by the addition of one or two rostrums or a few steps. But one was never conscious of a producer composing effective groupings for their own sake; they seemed the natural result of the action of the play, just as the movement about the stage had an ease and fluidity which gave the impression that it had been spontaneously created by the actors themselves instead of being the work of the producer.

In 1924 Copeau closed the Vieux Columbier and retired with some of his company to Pernand-Vergelesses in Burgundy because he felt they must renew their strength by "kissing the soìl". Granville-Barker, by now a close friend of Copeau's, did his best to dissuade him from leaving Paris. "I beg you," wrote Granville-Barker, "to spend no more time kissing the earth or laying foundations, but to go ahead with your building; that is to say, with the interpreting of one good play after another, letting the art of one beget the better art of the next. For—to keep the apter metaphor—once the strain is sound, that is how good art does naturally increase, and after painful years of gestation it will suddenly come to amazing fertility and flower in a hundred unexpected ways. Moreover, all the virtue goes out of a simplicity that is guarded too faithfully and too long, and it becomes an affectation of the barrenest sort."

In Burgundy the company studied acting and worked in the fields and in the carpenter's shop. They took part in the local wine festivals, performing what they described as "diversions" The peasants called the group "Les Copiaux", and it was under this name that they first appeared before a town audience at Bale in 1926. The most characteristic of their productions was *La Danse de la Ville et des Champs*, described as a "Spectacle Burguignan, joué, dansé, chanté, mimé, par Les Copiaux". It was written and produced by Michel Saint-Denis, who had begun his theatrical career as secretary to Copeau and then became in turn stage-manager, stage-director, and eventually assistant-producer at the Vieux Columbier. In 1931 Copeau handed over the direction of Les Copiaux to Saint-Denis. The company was renamed Le Quinze and returned to Paris for a three-month season at the Vieux Columbier which since 1925 had been used as a cinema. The plays were *Noé* and *Le Viol de Lucrèce*, both by André Obey, who two years previously had joined the company as their permanent playwright. A programme note described these two plays as "the first fruits of a close collaboration between a dramatist and a company of players. The collaboration was smooth and happy, but at first it required such an effort of adjustment that it would have been impossible for us to adapt ourselves to more than one author at a time". Further fruits of the collaboration were *La Bataille de la Marne, Loire, Don Juan,* and *Venus et Adonis.*

Obey, when he joined the company, was already a playwright of some experience, with one of his plays in the repertoire of the Comédie Française. If he had never seen the work of Copeau's troupe he would presumably have continued to write plays, but they would certainly have been very different from the plays he wrote for the Compagnie des Quinze. It would have been pointless to write a play such as *Le Viol de Lucrèce* for the ordinary theatre, because it demands actors equally highly trained in speech and mime—which the Compagnie des Quinze alone was able to provide. And yet, as Copeau so often pointed out, there was nothing novel in their technique. It was based on the two great traditions of the French theatre—fine speaking and expressive miming. The art of mime, which in the English theatre died centuries ago, has always been kept alive in the French theatre and forms a considerable part of the actor's training, but Copeau taught his troupe to mime with a subtlety and conviction such as probably had not been seen upon the stage since the days of Molière.

The miming of the Compagnie des Quinze made so strong an impression on English audiences that it was insufficiently realised that the speaking of the company equalled the perfection of their miming. Obey made full use of their training in the delivery of the traditional "tirade", confidently giving them rhetorical speeches such as Noah's outburst invoking God's vengeance on the scoffers, the narrations of the Messenger in *La Bataille de la Marne*, the elderly taxi-driver's account of the famous drive of the Paris taxis rushing the Sixty-second Division to the front, the Daughters of Loire lamenting the ravages of the floods in Touraine, Le Récitante in *Le Viol de Lucrèce* describing Tarquin furiously galloping through the night along the Roman road.

Among my most vivid recollections of the miming of the company are the stylised movements of the masked actors robed in brown representing the winter waters of the Loire, and a scene in *La Bataille de la Marne* in which a whole army in retreat was symbolised by a little group of exhausted soldiers dragging themselves across the stage, so conquered by fatigue

that victory or defeat had become equally meaningless to them.
James Agate's description of the opening of this play gives an
impression of how the company and their producer could evoke
in the imagination of the audience what could not be shown
upon the stage. "On the stage nothing save a few dun hangings
veiling the bare theatre walls, and the floor artificially raked
to enable the actors to move on different planes. Off the stage
an immense distance away a military band is playing, and in
the wings the armies of France go by. We see them through the
eyes of five or six peasant women clothed in black and grouped
as you may see them in the fields of France or the canvases of
Millet." Agate described the acting as the kind "which begins
where realism ends . . . The whole cast played with a perfection
of understanding and a mastery of ensemble beyond praise.
This is great, perhaps the greatest acting, since on a bare stage
the actors recreated not the passion of one or two, but the agony
of a nation".

The best illustration of the company's method of combining
speech and mime is the scene in *Le Viol de Lucrèce* depicting
Tarquin's stealthy approach to the bedchamber. At the back
of the stage, on a rostrum, was the curtained bed, the rest of the
stage empty except for the hangings which formed the background; on either side of the proscenium the masked figures of
Le Réciteur and La Récitante. The woman, who speaks for
Lucrèce, describes her quiet, untroubled slumber; the man,
harsh and ominous, tells of Tarquin's approach. As he speaks
we see Tarquin miming his journey through the dark corridors
of the sleeping palace, feeling his way with outstretched hands
through the blackness, losing himself among the winding
passages, hesitating, retracing his way, stumbling over unseen
steps, fumbling with unfamiliar locks, until at last he forces the
door of the bedchamber with his knee. On the little stage of the
Arts Theatre, where I saw the play, the actor (it was Pierre
Fresnay who played Tarquin) was never more than a few feet
away from the bed as he mimed his journey through the palace,
yet so completely had we been induced to forget the conventions of the realistic theatre that the bed, instead of being an

incongruous distraction, became the symbol of Tarquin's desire; we saw it not as a tangible object but as the image burning in Tarquin's brain, drawing him irresistibly towards his crime. The tremendous climax of the scene was orchestrated rather than acted. First Le Réciteur crying four times: "Tarquin-roi! Roi des Romans! Roi! Roi!" in a despairing effort to restrain him by the reminder of his kingship; then Tarquin's savage cry of triumph as he forced Lucrèce's submission, followed by her cry of despair, echoed by two short, sharp cries of horror from the masked figures crouched at the sides of the stage. Each cry on a different note, each with a different meaning, the effect was more piercingly dramatic than anything I have ever experienced in the theatre.

The staging of the Compagnie des Quinze, like its method of acting, dated back to Molière—not the Molière settled in Paris and performing for the court of Louis XIV, but the Molière who toured the towns and villages of France, playing in a tent or in the open air, on a bare trestle platform. It was this "tréteau nu", as Copeau called it, which was the basis of the setting used by the Compagnie des Quinze—a light, collapsible rostrum which could be divided into four so as to form separate platforms, or piled upon one another to represent, for instance, with the aid of a ladder, the prow of Noah's Ark. The background was formed by a kind of tent, or rather three sides of a tent suspended from the flies on a ring. The panels forming the sides could be rolled up or draped to form entrances. This tent-like surround to the stage did away with the need for wings or sky borders, served equally well to suggest an exterior or an interior, could be used in a theatre or a hall or a barn, and could be packed into a single large hamper. Sometimes one or two pieces of scenery of deliberate naïveté were added to the setting. In *La Bataille de la Marne,* for instance, a village was suggested by some roofs and a church steeple modelled in miniature and set upon a little platform in the corner of the stage supported on four poles. In *Don Juan* the setting consisted of the five "mansions" of the mediaeval mystery plays, represented by simple Gothic arches of wood placed in a semi-circle round the stage. Descriptions of settings as simple as these are apt to give an impression of drabness and austerity—which is all that most of the imitators of the Compagnie des Quinze have ever achieved. But these productions by Saint-Denis were enchanting to the eye because of the beautifully composed groupings, the loveliness of the costumes, and the colourfulness of the lighting. After many years there are still scenes which linger in the memory—for instance, Lucrèce at her spinning wheel surrounded by her chattering maidens, a picture so exquisitely composed that it might have been grouped by one of the early Italian masters.

In 1934 the company, feeling they had become stale and repetitive, decided, as Copeau had done ten years before, to withdraw to the country. They rented the estate of Beaumanoir, near to Aix-en-Provence, and here they planned to spend four months of each year studying, rehearsing, and training ten pupils, while the rest of the year was to be divided between four months touring in France and abroad and four months of open-air productions in Provence. But it is always dangerous for a company of actors to work together and live together in isolation from the rest of the world. The ideal life which they had envisaged was marred by human frailties. The company disbanded and Michel Saint-Denis left France to settle in England where for many years, both as a producer and a teacher of acting, he did much to enrich the English theatre. But without a company of his own he achieved nothing which equalled his productions with that company created by Copeau.

Copeau's reaction against realism seems no more than the mildest of protests compared with the ruthlessness with which every vestige of realism was banished from the stages of the post-war revolutionary theatres of Germany and Russia. The producers seemingly regarded the old bourgeois theatre as a kind of gigantic hoax. They inveighed against "the trickeries, the shams, and the deceits" by which the producers had sought to beguile their audience into believing that they were seeing real life upon the stage. The audience was no longer to be hoodwinked into forgetting that what they were watching was anything but a theatrical performance. Meierhold declared that the task of the producers was to destroy the illusion of actuality. "The actual world exists and is our subject; but this play and this stage are not it." Scenery was abolished. The stage became a bare platform upon which were set one or two rostrums and a few steps. The back wall of the stage was nakedly revealed because in their worship of functionalism the revolutionary producers were "proud to grant the naked bricks a dignity which the realistic theatre had constantly denied them." The spotlights, the floods, and all the rest of the lighting equipment were deliberately exposed to view. If a rostrum or a piece of furniture had to be moved between scenes, the curtain was kept up so that the stage-hands could be seen at work.

I have never been able to discover any good, logical reason for this extreme anti-illusionist method of production, although I have had plenty of experience of it, as my early years as a producer were spent in the one theatre in England which consistently practised it. This was the Cambridge Festival Theatre, which was founded in the mid-'twenties to make war on what its director, Terence Gray, described as "the old game of illusions and glamour, hocus-pocus and bamboozle". At one time, in his determination to make certain that the audience were under no illusion that they were "spying on reality", he removed the side walls of the proscenium so that throughout the performance the audience could see the actors waiting to make their entrances, the stage-hands standing about, the electricians at their switchboard, the prompter with the book in his lap, the furniture and props for the next scene stacked in a corner. Such drastic methods of convincing the audience that they are not "spying on reality" seem to me completely unnecessary because I find it hard to believe that any audience ever becomes entirely unconscious of the fact that they are in a theatre watching an impersonation of reality. For instance, the burst of applause which sometimes follows the exit of an actor after a well-played scene is proof that an audience, however completely they may be held by that scene, remain aware that what they are seeing is not real life but a clever impersonation of it.

The Revolt Against Realism

The attempt to destroy the representational theatre in Russia required the actors to abandon their old technique. The detailed and subtle portrayal of emotions was described as "worthless soul junk". The actor was ordered to "forget his little, rickety ego" and become "an instrument for social manifestos". The producers, in their hatred of an individualistic society, exercised every kind of ingenuity to deprive the actors of their individuality. "The principles of the propagandist theatre," declared Meierhold, "are in entire conformity with those of Marxism because they seek to emphasise the elements which make prominent what is common to all men, the *unindividual*." He demanded from his actors "the vigorous elimination of all humane feeling and the creation of an order based upon mechanical laws". He invented what he called bio-mechanics —"the geometrisation of movement based on deep study of the human body and the laws of movement and space". Meanwhile in Germany Piscator was enforcing "unindividualistic acting" by dressing his actors in harsh, angular costumes which were deliberately at variance with the lines of the human body, so that the players seemed more like robots than human beings. Tairov made his actors wear fantastically exaggerated make-ups to ensure that they would not resemble anyone in real life and thus become individuals in the eyes of the audience. It was Tairov who invented the constructivist setting, a gaunt scaffolding supporting a few bare platforms on different levels, with every strut and bolt ostentatiously exposed to view. The aggressive functionalism of this kind of setting was regarded as having considerable propaganda value at a time when the Russians were being taught to revere the machine as part of their training to become one of the great industrial nations of the world. The lack of colour and any form of decoration in these bleak constructions was considered to be part of their virtue because (to quote from an article by John Mason Brown written after a visit to Russia about this time) "The ornamental was despised for its past, and hated as the flowering of a decadent and acquisitive idleness".

I saw Meierhold's constructivist production of Ostrovsky's

The Forest when his company was appearing in Berlin. Imagine a play performed on a builder's scaffolding by the Crazy Gang and a troupe of acrobats and you may get some idea of what this performance was like. The actors, grotesquely dressed and made up as drolls and buffoons, somersaulted, swung on trapezes, and depicted excitement by means of handsprings and flip-flaps. Naturalistic speech was forbidden; they shouted, chanted, intoned, and chorused. The stage was bleakly lit in a glare of harsh, white light from floodlights hanging immediately above the setting in full view of the audience. As slapstick entertainment it was immensely exhilarating, though in the end one became wearied by its crudity and noisiness. I heard someone sitting behind me say, "I wish we had brought the children. They would have loved it." Meierhold might have considered this a compliment to his production, for at this time the Russian producers were catering for a huge new audience which had never been inside a theatre before the revolution, an audience which was mainly illiterate and still almost childishly unsophisticated. For this audience every point had to be heavily underlined, humour had to be reduced to its simplest elements, characterisation had to be converted into caricature, everything had to be enlarged and exaggerated so that it was obvious and unmistakable even to the simplest member of the audience. Few plays had yet been written to fit the new style of production or the revolutionary mood of the moment, so the plays of the Czarist regime were still performed—but in productions that savagely satirised the bourgeois characters and mocked everything that was sentimental and idealistic.

In Germany the shortage of material for building scenery inspired producers to evolve another style of anti-realistic production in which actors on a bare, darkened stage were picked out by shafts of light against a black background. If there was any scenery at all, it was limited to one or two small pieces, symbolic rather than realistic. Stylisation in staging inevitably led to a stylised method of acting which in turn demanded stylised writing, and it was thus that the short-lived German school of expressionist drama was created. People in the plays became symbols instead of characters. They were deprived even of their names. They became Mr. One, Mr. Two, Mr. Three, or Mrs. X, Mrs. Y, Mrs. Z, or Mr. Anybody, Mrs. Everybody, Mr. Somebody, Mrs. Nobody; or just plain Mr. Zero. The lines these figures spoke were stripped of all but the key words and phrases, so that the dialogue resembled the staccato wording on a telegraph form. The actors' speech was drained of naturalistic inflections until it approximated more to the clatter of typewriters than the sound of the human voice.

Later in the 'twenties, when steel, timber, and other materials became more plentiful in Germany, Piscator created a brief sensation in Berlin with a series of expressionist productions in which he made ingenious use of elaborate and expensive machinery. The front of his stage was constructed on the principle of the conveyor belt, so that it was possible to give the impression of crowds of workers and soldiers on the march while the stage moving in the opposite direction kept them stationary. (It was a device which had been used at Drury Lane in 1910 for a scene in *The Whip* when three racehorses galloped against the movement of the conveyor belt.) In the centre of Piscator's stage a cantilever bridge moved up and down; sections of the stage rose, sank, revolved, slid; lantern slides and cinema films were projected on to the back wall; above the proscenium Communist slogans blazed in lights; the gigantic shadows of pulsating machines were thrown on to gauzes behind which the actors went on with their performance; searchlights swept to and fro across the acting area; motor cycles roared up and down steep ramps, and to add to the din there were the blaring of loudspeakers, the beating of drums, the throbbing of machinery, the rat-tat-tat of machine-guns, the tramping and shouting of the crowds.

For a while the novelty and strident vitality of the productions at the Piscatorbühne drew Berlin, but a theatre devoted to virtuoso displays of production can never gain the allegiance of the ordinary playgoer who will always be more interested in the play and the players than in the producer. Amidst the rumble and turmoil of Piscator's productions the play was lost and the actor reduced to a nonentity. Audiences dwindled, the theatre closed, and Piscator left Germany for America where he became director of the Dramatic Workshop of the New School for Social Research.

Another German producer who, like Piscator, made exuberant use of the end of restrictions on the use of building materials in theatres was Leopold Jessner, whose favourite form of setting was a vast flight of steps extending the entire width of the stage, rising steeply to a high platform at the back. In his production of *Richard III* the steps were blood red to symbolise Richard's bloodstained path to the throne which stood at the top of the steps. When he appeared as King, seated on the throne wearing a red cloak and a huge, bloated crown, his followers, also dressed in red, prostrated themselves below him so that they suggested a great pool of blood. At the end of the play he staggered along the platform at the top of the steps naked to the waist, and as he cried "A horse! A horse! My kingdom for a horse!" he straddled his sword as if it had been a hobby-horse and wearily lolloped down the steps to fall exhausted to the ground. Then a white curtain descended and Richmond spoke his final speech in front of it clad in white armour, in contrast to the opening of the play when a black-clad Richard spoke the opening soliloquy against a black curtain. Another example of Jessner's use of what were nicknamed "the Jessnersteppen" was at the end of Crabbe's *Napoleon*, when the Emperor, who throughout the play had appeared only on the topmost step, was seen crouched dejectedly on the lowest step of all, with a setting sun on the backcloth. In this production, too, the stage was dominated by a throne at the top of the steps, the throne of Louis XVIII, with richly-patterned curtains behind it suggesting a throne-room. When Napoleon entered he tore down one of these curtains so that it fell across the throne, shrouding it from sight, symbolising the extinction of the Bourbon dynasty; meanwhile files of soldiers marched on to the stage to indicate Napoleon's return to power.

Jessner was greatly influenced by the work of the Russian producers. No doubt his elementary symbolism would have been an aid to the new Russian audience in the years immediately after the Revolution, but it was scarcely flattering to the intelligence of the Berliners and did great disservice to authors by over-simplifying characters and their motives. In *Continental Stagecraft* MacGowan and Jones describe Jessner as "directing in words of one syllable . . . It is symbolism in baby-talk, presentational production in kindergarten terms".

A frenzied neuroticism characterised Jessner's productions of plays by contemporary German authors. Figures darted about the steps like hunted, furtive criminals, then froze into immobility, transfixed by sharp, stabbing beams of harsh white light. The plays were driven along at frantic speed. Jessner conceived Wedekind's characters as people possessed, wildly, blindly pursuing their aims. I did not see his famous production of *Der Marquis von Keith*, which I know only from a description of it by Julius Bab, for many years director of the Berlin Volksbuhne. "The background was a white screen in front of which, on a high rostrum, the characters could rage at will. On a lower level was a realistic room for the middle-class, harmless people. Above, the possessed ran in and out, not really passing through doors but through partitions in the white wall which sprang apart and then shot together again on springs. In place of bells sounded a fast tattoo of drums; the champagne glass was a pointed piece of wood. Nothing was allowed to distract, nothing cause a delay, when the figures on this upper platform flared up in their wild frenzy."

The parrot-cry of the new producers was that the theatre was now a popular art, no longer an entertainment for the rich bourgeois. It was believed that the popular theatre must be a huge theatre. Russia began to build theatres of fabulous size like "The Theatre of the Masses" at Kharkov. Max Reinhardt opened the Grosses Schauspielhaus in Berlin as "The Theatre of the Five Thousand". The vast cycle-racing pavilion in Leipzig, seating fifty thousand, became a theatre for dramas of the mass revolt. Plays were performed in circuses, in skating rinks, in city squares, in sports stadiums, on parade grounds. The fact that no kind of subtlety was possible in these vast auditoriums was considered to be all to the good. The drama was to express "the mass soul of the victorious workers and sing the joys of collective man". The individual gave place to huge crowds marshalled by the producers into diagrammatic patterns symptomatic of a period which envisaged society organised into highly disciplined groups.

The more enterprising English and American papers sent their dramatic critics to visit the German and Russian theatres, and some of them returned enthusiastically declaring, *"The new drama has arrived."* But Ivor Brown was more cautious and farseeing. "Although not a man but mankind is the tragic hero now, the 'alone-standing man' may be on his legs again more quickly than the Teutonic dramatists and their foreign admirers imagine. For the mass, however majestic, or however cunningly symbolised, has its artistic limitatons. You can enjoy the march of a crowd for half an hour, but to know one member of it may be the delight of half a lifetime."

Today all these experiments in Russia and Germany may seem crude, violent, and ingenuous, but they were not just producers' stunts. They were the expression of the detestation of everything which the bourgeois theatre stood for and an attempt to create a new means of theatrical expression which would give birth to a new race of playwrights who would write about the aspirations of collective man instead of about the petty, personal, private feelings of the individual, "the clandestine adulteries of gilded loafers". The movement failed because the theatre is essentially a human place and because when an actor is reduced to the level of a puppet he can only express a few emotions, and those only in their simplest form. The work of the producers in the post-revolutionary theatres contributed little that was lasting to the theatre, though still, from time to time, an attempt is made to revive some of the conventions of the extremist practitioners of "irrealism".

3

THE EXPERIMENTALIST PRODUCERS

During those years of hectic experiment in Russia and Germany the French theatre went on its way much as before. It had taken many years for Antoine's example to have much effect, but now, as a result of his influence, the acting was being curbed of its excessive theatricality and there was a marked improvement in the settings which in the Paris theatres had been notoriously slipshod and often ludicrously unsuited to the play. The Comédie Française had tightened up its discipline and recognised the authority of the producers, who were now insisting upon a properly balanced ensemble. As yet Copeau's work had made little impression on the Paris theatre, but his influence was soon to be spread much more widely by Jouvet and Dullin, who left him in 1922 to form companies of their own. Dullin opened what he called a "workshop theatre" at L'Atelier in Montparnasse. Jouvet during his first three years of management shared the Théâtre des Champs Elysées with Pitoëff, a Russian exile who before arriving in Paris had founded a theatre in Petrograd and another in Geneva, both with companies which were mainly amateur.

During those early years in management Pitoëff had always been desperately short of money, so he had learned to stage his productions with the minimum of scenery and the maximum of invention. For instance, he would suggest a tent under a night sky by looping up two pieces of silver ribbon against a background of black curtains. Producing a historical play which called for a crowd of soldiers, he could not afford to pay supers to stand about holding spears, so he simply stuck the spears into the stage and lit only their tips, so that the light glinting on the spearheads gave the impression of a great throng of men-at-arms. In his production of *Androcles and the Lion* he got over the expense of the elaborate setting needed for the arena by playing the whole scene in shadowgraph.

If Pitoëff had been able to spend more money on his productions his method of staging would, I think, still have been very much the same. He believed that the primary aim of the producer should be to focus attention on the central idea of the play, to eliminate all external detail of décor and acting which might lead to obscure it from view. Yet in his direction of the actors there was no hint of stylisation. He merely used stage business and movement more sparingly than most producers, instinctively separating the essential from the inessential. I doubt if the ordinary spectator noticed anything unusual about the acting, though he probably felt that the essentials of the play were revealed with exceptional clarity. Pitoëff's only obvious idiosyncrasy as a producer was sometimes momentarily to arrest the action to emphasise some particularly significant piece of grouping. It was as if a photographer had suddenly shouted "Hold it!" in order to take a picture of the scene. The device may sound a little crude and obvious, but it achieved something of the same effect as a sustained chord in the orchestra.

Pitoëff's use of this device was one of his many ways of emphasising the author's intention by pictorial means. When he produced Pirandello's *Henry IV* he stressed the fact that the chief character is living in a world of make-believe by making the setting look as if it were built of cardboard, so that at the climax of the play, when the pretender is nearly driven to admit his pretences, he rushed about the stage frantically propping up the flimsy, tottering walls which threatened to fall around him. There is nothing in the author's script to suggest any such scene, but Pirandello approved it as a vivid pictorial illustration of the play's theme.

Sometimes Pitoëff's method resulted in an over-simplification of the author's intentions. For instance, his production of Shaw's *St. Joan* stressed the mystic quality of Joan's saintliness as the dominant theme of the play. The permanent setting, in the form of a triptych, was suggestive of a mediaeval mystery, and deliberately stressed the religious background of the play. Throughout the production everything was subordinated to the idea that this was the story of a divinely inspired miracle. With Ludmilla Pitoëff as St. Joan the performance was often profoundly moving, but the final impression was the opposite of what Shaw intended. It was a beautiful, conventional, stained-glass-window picture of sainthood. Admirers of the production argued that it had a unity of atmosphere entirely lacking when the play was produced in London by Lewis Casson, but to me it demonstrated the dangers of a tidy-minded producer seeking to find a single, unifying theme to bind together a great, sprawling, argumentative masterpiece.

During the years Pitoëff and Jouvet shared the same theatre nobody could have predicted that Jouvet was to become one of the greatest producers of the French theatre. At a time when the producer was being encouraged to consider himself the creator of a new form of theatrical art, Jouvet held the view that in the theatre it is the playwright who alone creates. He took infinite care to discover the author's intentions and to interpret them with absolute fidelity, but at first Jouvet's fidelity to his authors took the form of a dogged faithfulness which resulted in productions which were flat and dull. In his painstaking determination to give full value to each line of the script he made every line sound equally important until the meaning of the play was smothered in its own words. In those days he had nothing of Pitoëff's gift for highlighting the essentials of a play; there was no sense of perspective in his productions. Although his later work was full of invention, at first he shrank from introducing any ideas of his own into a production. For a time it seemed that the unwavering allegiance to the text which he had learned from Copeau was becoming an obsession which would stultify his development as a producer. Copeau himself realised this and wrote to Jouvet urging him to use his personality and his ideas "to fertilise with new capital the traditions you have inherited from us".

Pierre Brisson in an article in the *Revue de la Société d' Histoire du Théâtre* has described Jouvet's development as a producer as "a continual compromise between boldness and timidity . . . With a literary judgment sharpened by constant reading he refused to step out of what he considered to be his domain. This was due not to modesty but to loyalty. Yet he knew that after each success his doubts would return. This fear deterred him from too ambitious endeavours, led him back with ceaseless questioning to seek the exact, the perfection of fidelity. Full of ideas as he read through a script, but full of distrust in the tumult of his imagination, he passed all projects through a crucible, tested them, followed them to their source, scanned them again and again. So he came at the height of his career, to that equilibrium between audacity and respect of which *Ecole des Femmes* is surely the perfect example".

Jouvet's productions of Molière were his most important contribution to the French theatre. He freed the plays from the weight of tradition which was stifling them on the stage. It was not, as was generally supposed, a genuine theatrical tradition handed down from the days of Molière. It had been imposed upon the actors by the scholars when they made Molière a "subject" and claimed that he belonged to literature rather than to the theatre. Jouvet has described how before his first Molière production he "conducted a long and careful enquiry. From commentaries by actors who had played or dreamed of playing in this piece, from commentaries by critics and spectators, from explanations by authors who had rewritten the play many times, I gathered all that could be known about the subject. The play seemed to me to be choked with opinions, oppressed by explanations, shrouded in theories, asphyxiated by controversy, but still green in the sap of the text". His own approach to the play was, as usual, cautious, thoughtful, hesitant; but at least he had no hesitation in rejecting the traditional conception of Molière as a moralist. Here for once he felt on firm ground. He was dealing with the work of another man of the theatre who was not only a playwright but, like himself, an actor, a producer, and a manager. To Jouvet it was unthinkable that such a man "would attempt an adventure as perilous, as consuming as the theatre merely in order to give others a lesson. For the man who knows what it is to entertain people and to count his costs at the end of the day, for the man who knows what it is to perform a comedy or direct a theatre, there is only the choice, when he thinks of such a conception of dramatic art, between a Christian indulgence and a mild hilarity".

Jouvet taught his actors that Molière is not a moralist but a humanist, that the right approach to his characters is not through their brains but their hearts, that his humour is not farcical but graceful, that the greatness of his plays is in "their incomparable blend of tenderness, charm and reason". What Jouvet stressed above all else in his productions of the plays is that they are not realistic or naturalistic, but poetry first and foremost. "Molière, who has been labelled the man of reason, is the man who has best felt and best understood the irrational, and his plays, which appear to be the triumph of reason in the eyes of his commentators, are actually the kingdom of that marvellous unreasonableness that we call poetry."

All that Jouvet recognised in Molière was completely and exquisitely expressed in his famous production of *Ecole des Femmes*. It was hailed by the French critics as "le retour à l'art classique"—"le retour au véritable esprit de Molière et son siècle". Yet it was a production which was in no way a pedantic reproduction of the conventions of the theatre in Molière's time. Christian Bérard's settings exactly expressed the tone of the production in décor which re-created the style of the period without copying it. When the curtain rose it was, for a moment, somewhat disconcerting to see four chandeliers hanging above a setting representing the front of a house, especially as the elegance of these chandeliers seemed oddly at variance with the simplicity of the plain, white screens and narrow arches used to suggest the house and the colonnade surrounding it. "Where are we?" asked one of the French critics. He answered the question himself. "Rein ne rappelle exactement une époque et pourtant le plus inculte des spectateurs ne saurait s'y me prendre c'est le 17ᵉ siècle français, c'est Paris, c'est la place Royale, Le Marais, c'est lumaire du vieux théâtre, c'est le décor éternel de la Commedia dell' Arte." When the scene changed to the garden the screens forming the little enclosed forecourt of the house unfolded themselves and glided to the side of the stage to form the walls of the garden while four little flower-beds, each with a small tree in the centre, trundled themselves into position —all this without human aid or any discernible mechanical means. But it is typical of Jouvet that this ingenious transformation was not just an entertaining invention of his own for rapidly changing the scenery without lowering the curtain; it was based on the classic method of scene-changing in the old French theatre, and was achieved by using the same kind of machinery.

Jouvet was one of the most intensely serious men I have ever met. He made no attempt to hide his seriousness behind that façade of bonhomie and high spirits which most theatre people rapidly acquire. He came of peasant stock. His grandmother kept an inn in the Ardennes; his father was a builder. He himself had the large, capable hands of a good workman and it was as a builder of scenery that he started in the theatre. As a young man he was three times rejected by the Conservatoire: thirty years later he became one of its professors. It would be unfair to gibe at the Conservatoire for rejecting him at their auditions, for his development as an actor was slow. In fact everything in Jouvet's development came slowly and with difficulty. Although widely read, particularly in the history of the theatre, he considered himself to be poorly educated, so he mistrusted his own judgment and was cautious to accept ideas until he had pondered them a long time. "Problems lived with him all day," says Brisson. "He chewed them over, masticated them, pulverised them. He hammered at a question like a battering-ram at a beam; with a stubborn strength returned to it again and again till at last he overcame the obstacle."

When I first met Jouvet I asked him one or two questions of the sort for which one would have expected him to have ready-made replies, but before answering he ruminated on these questions then replied with great care and at considerable length. That was, I think, because he had no fixed ideas, no dogmas. If he were asked a question about something which he considered important he would consider it afresh, testing his opinion once again in his mind before replying. There was a profound humility in his approach towards his work and he inspired his company with something of his own spirit. Although his manner was brusque, even rather gauche, there was a warmth and tenderness in his nature which was reflected in his productions. Oddly enough, in spite of the seriousness of his character, his greatest successes as an actor were in comic rôles, such as Dr. Knock, which he played with tremendous speed and gusto.

While Jouvet subjugated himself to his author, Charles Dullin's productions were always strongly flavoured by his own personality. Meeting him for the first time one got the impression of a depressed, saturnine little man with a long nose, a pronounced stoop, and a thin rather whining voice. It was only when one noticed that he was watching everyone in the room with an amused twinkle in his sharp, shrewd little eyes that one got any hint of the character he revealed in his productions—an odd mixture of gaiety and cynicism. His productions of Ben Jonson's *Volpone*, his greatest success with the public, was a good example of how Dullin's own attitude to life coloured his interpretation of a play. There was little trace in this production of Jonson's ferocious moral fervour. The monsters of greed whom Jonson castigated were changed into gulls and buffoons, mocked by the producer with mischievous enjoyment. Jonson's savage humour was translated into gay satire, matched by the sharp bright colours of the décor. Much more in accord with Dullin's amused, uncensorious attitude to life were the amoral comedies of the Restoration, and of all his productions the one which perhaps most faithfully interpreted the author was *The Beaux Stratagem*.

Copeau's influence on Dullin was apparent in his elaborate use of expressive gesture and mime. In the school attached to

L'Atelier a great deal of time was devoted to training the actors in ballet and improvisation. One of his pupils was Jean-Louis Barrault. At rehearsals Dullin kept a very light hand on the reins, encouraging his actors to improvise—not only in movement and gesture, but even in words, for he had little of Jouvet's reverence for an author's text. He hated what he called "l'horrible naturel". "The world of the theatre," he used to say, is a fairyland where we can escape from our everyday existence." He loved brightness—bright colours, bright music, bright movements. He had never been converted to Copeau's asceticism in matters of décor, and employed as his designers some of the leading French painters, including Barsacq, Jean Hugo, Picasso and Marie-Hélèn Dasté. Among the composers who worked at L'Atelier were Milhaud, Auric, and Honneger. Whenever possible Dullin liked to introduce music into his productions, not only to heighten the atmosphere, but to comment on the action of the play and its characters, and to accompany the songs and dances and mimes which he interpolated, often with only the flimsiest excuse. The critics accused him of turning Balzac's *Mercadet ou le Fraiseur* into something very like a comic opera, and attacked some of his productions of comedies for being so full of exaggerated antics and noisy music that they belonged to the circus rather than the theatre. The writer of Dullin's obituary in *The Times* considered that his most successful productons were *Le Marriage de Figaro* (produced for the Comédie Française) and Evreinov's *La Comédie de Bonheur,* because in both plays there is that mingling of the elements of carnival and social satire Dullin sought to find in nearly every play he produced. I did not see either of these productions, but I remember how perfectly these two elements were mingled in his production of *The Birds* of Aristophanes.

Descriptions of Dullin's productions are apt to give the impression that he was a producer who deliberately twisted a play to suit his own tastes. It was not so. Although his view of life was too personal, too individual to make him a good interpreter of the work of those who saw life from a different viewpoint, he produced plays as he saw them, with complete sincerity, and was often genuinely puzzled when other people saw them differently.

Pitöeff, Jouvet, and Dullin, together with Gaston Baty, formed what they called the Cartel. It was a purely business arrangement designed to reduce expenses by advertising all four theatres on one poster, exchanging actors, maintaining a pool of properties, furniture and stage equipment, and forming a united front if one of their members was involved in a dispute with the Press or the ticket agencies. For instance, when a newspaper refused to send its critic to the theatre of a member, all four threatened to withdraw their advertisements. The Cartel enabled these small managements to enjoy some of the advantages of a big, monopolistic management while leaving each member completely free to pursue his own artistic policy.

Gaston Baty was the only one of "Les Quatres" who was not an actor as well as a producer. He served his apprenticeship under Reinhardt. On returning to France he did some productions for Gémier and then got together a little company called "La Chimère" which played in halls and out-of-the-way unfashionable little playhouses. His first theatre was an old army hut in the Boulevard St. Germain. Then he took over the little studio at the top of the huge building in the Champs-Élysées which houses two other theatres. Here he achieved his first popular success with Simon Gantillon's *Maya*. Later he moved to the Théâtre de l'Oeuvre, and finally settled in 1931 at a theatre in Montparnasse which had formerly been a music-hall.

Baty was the sole representative in the French theatre of the dictator-producer. In the French theatre the power and prestige of the playwright has always been much greater than in other countries, and Baty was accused by the critics of challenging the autocracy of the playwrights, of seeking to subjugate the author to the producer. Playwrights protested that he was only interested in plays which offered scope for production effects. Actors complained that he regarded them merely as one of the instruments to be used in creating his productions, no more important than his other instruments such as the scenery, the lighting, the music and the noises-off.

There is some truth in these allegations. But Baty could not have maintained his position as one of the leading French producers for nearly thirty years if he had merely been a brilliant and ruthless exhibitionist. His theory of production was based on his belief that in the theatre the expressive power of words is limited, and that the task of the producer is to aid the author by adding all that the words are unable to say. "To produce a play," said Baty, "is to illustrate it—to penetrate the mind and heart of the playwright in order to extend his thoughts and emotions beyond words." Early in his career Baty produced a play which exactly fitted his theory of "extending thoughts beyond words". The play was Jean-Jacques Bernard's *Martine*. Bernard has defined drama as "the art of the unexpressed". He shrinks from using dialogue to express thoughts and feelings which in real life would remain unspoken. He relies on inference rather than statement. He develops a scene with infinite skill and subtlety until the culmination is not a speech but a silence in which the audience is left to perceive the significance of all that has already been said. At this moment the author hands over to the producer. All depends on the exact positions of the characters in relation to one another, a movement, a look, a gesture, a turn of the head. Baty's production of *Martine* was exquisitely in accord with the author's intentions, but when producing plays more explicit he was apt to use tricks of production merely to elaborate and underline what had already been plainly said. Yet Bernard was by no means the only author who acknowledged his indebtedness to Baty. Herman Gregoire, for instance, said of him: "He knows how to add to the words everything that the words have not been able to say. He divines, understands all that has nourished the emotions of the playwright, and of which his writing leaves only a residue." Simon Gantillon was another of Baty's authors who defended him. "He sustains, develops, and vivifies the ideas endorsed in the writing. Let us destroy a stupid legend: even if he is not a slave to the text at least Baty submits himself to it scrupulously, seeking always to find the theatrical means of expression which conforms with the spoken word."

It was as a producer of the classics that Baty was most sternly criticised. He was one of those producers, familiar enough in England today, who feel they must "do something" with a classic. Whether what they do is in accord with the author's intentions matters little provided it is something nobody else has done with the play before. For instance, because *Le Malade Imaginaire* was Molière's last play, Baty conceived it as the work of a man obsessed with the fear of death and produced it as an hysterical mixture of wild farce and brooding horror, culminating in a grotesque, nightmarish ballet of doctors and domestics. In his production of de Musset's *Les Caprices de Marianne* Baty transformed the play from the sixteenth century to the end of the eighteenth century for the possibly justifiable reason that to modern audiences the costumes of the eighteenth century more effectively suggest the poetic atmosphere of the play; but it was much more difficult to justify the masked figures which he brought on between the scenes to recite and mime verses which de Musset wrote to his brother on his return to Italy. One felt that the only reason for these interpolations was to provide the producer with more opportunities to display his inventiveness than he could find in the play itself.

When Baty moved to the large theatre in Montparnasse his exhibitionism became more pronounced. From Reinhardt he had learned to handle crowds brilliantly and to use elaborate stage mechanism and lighting equipment with skill and showmanship. The size of the stage at Montparnasse enabled him to exercise these talents, and if the play did not—well, that had to be remedied. His finest productions at the Montparnasse theatre were his own adaptations of *Crime and Punishment* and *Madame Bovary*, tailor-made scripts which suited him perfectly. His pictorial sense was superb, his groupings and movements beautifully composed, but one remembered them for themselves rather than as part of the play. "If one has any unforgettable memories of Baty's productions," remarks Robert Brassilach in *Les Animateurs de Théâtre*, "they are of him and of him alone, not of his author or his actors." Myself, I find that although I have forgotten nearly everything about most of the plays I saw him produce I can still vividly recall the effects he created by means of his scenery, his lighting, and his elaborately orchestrated "noises-off"—the dazzling tropical sunshine beating down on the white walls of the steep, winding street of the African town in *Prosper*, and the contrast of the cool, shady room where one still heard as a distant murmur the innumerable sounds of the life in the street outside; the Atlantic liner towering above the quayside in *Departs;* the grotesque shadows thrown on the wall of a room by a flickering candle in a play even the name of which I have forgotten; the customers thronging the chemist's shop in *Madame Bovary*, and the box at the theatre with its glimpse in perspective of the auditorium beyond and the curtain rising and falling on the stage modelled in perspective.

In the Russian theatre, by the time the 'thirties had been reached, the more extreme forms of stylisation and anti-illusionism had been abandoned. The change had been brought about by the audiences, who plainly preferred those theatres where the acting was warm, human, and lifelike to those where the individuality of the actor was suppressed and the part he was playing reduced to an abstraction. They preferred, too, that their plays should be staged with at least some approach to realism instead of the aggressively anti-realistic manner of the revolutionary producers. Meierhold alone refused to yield to the tastes of the public and continued to create productions which André van Gyseghem in his book on the Soviet Theatre describes as "tapestries of fantastic devices woven by living puppets: theatrical tapestries composed not of colours and emotions and beauty but of geometrical designs, which fascinated the brain but never touched the emotions". In 1934 the government woke up to the fact that it was only to the intelligentsia that Meierhold's work made any appeal. Plans which were being made to build him a new theatre were cancelled. He was denounced as "the father of formalism", accused of anti-national tendencies, of desecrating the classics, and of having dedicated one of his productions to Trotsky. The Committee on Arts ordered all companies throughout the

Soviet Union to condemn him and endorse the government's action. Stanislavsky's response to this order was typical of his courage and generosity: he offered Meierhold a post at the Art Theatre. Meierhold declined it and little was heard of him until 1939. Seemingly the government had by then decided to reinstate him in public favour, for he was invited to be one of the speakers at the First National Convention of Theatrical Directors. He was, of course, expected to denounce his work in the past and declare his readiness to reform. The speech he made is recorded in Jelagin's *The Taming of the Arts*. "I, for one," said Meierhold in the course of that speech, "find the work in our theatres pitiful and terrifying. I don't know whether it is anti-formalism, or realism, or naturalism, or some other 'ism'. But I do know that it is uninspired and bad. This pitiful and sterile something which aspires to the title of socialistic realism has nothing in common with art. Go to the Moscow theatres and look at the colourless and boring productions which are all alike and which only differ in their degree of worthlessness. No longer can we identify the creative signatures of the Maly Theatre, of the Vakhtangov Theatre, of the Kamerny Theatre, of the Moscow Art Theatre. In the very places where only recently creative art was seething, where men of art searched, made mistakes, experimented, and found new ways to create productions some of which were bad and others magnificent, now there is nothing but a depressing, well-meaning, shockingly mediocre and devastating lack of talent. Was this your aim? If so you have committed a horrible deed. You have washed the child down the drain with the dirty water. In your effort to eradicate formalism you have destroyed art."

Next morning Meierhold was arrested. He was never heard of again.

Nowadays the productions in the Russian theatre are, by all accounts, conventional and, on the whole, undistinguished. When John Fernald visited the U.S.S.R. in 1953 he found the settings unexciting, often crudely lit, and he was surprised by an air of casualness in the work of the producers—"an apparent lack of feelings for nuance of tempo, for evocative grouping, for taking charge of a scene and sweeping it up to a climax". The only production which aroused his enthusiasm was *The Three Sisters* at the Moscow Art Theatre, a production made in 1938 by Danchenko, who was Stanislavsky's partner in the founding of the Art Theatre. In all the theatres he visited he found acting of an extraordinary high standard, untainted by the tendency to over-play which was for so long the weakness of Russian acting, and which was deliberately fostered by the revolutionary producers to please the new, unsophisticated, illiterate audience which was thronging into the theatres. But during these years Stanislavsky refused to make the slightest compromise for the sake of the new public. Because the revolutionary producers were destroying the actors' art by forcing them to concentrate on externals, he saw that the mission of the Art Theatre was to preserve a style of acting which the other theatres might emulate when the excesses of the revolution had abated. What he hoped for has come about. Today it is the standards and traditions of the Art Theatre which dominate the theatre everywhere in Russia.

Besides Stanislavsky's "inner realism" there is another kind of realism which is a feature of the present-day Russian theatre. It is the scenic realism of the old Drury Lane melodramas. In Moussorgsky's *Khovanschina,* for instance, the church bursts into flames so realistically that it is said that at most performances terrified members of the audience make for the exits believing that the stage is really on fire. In *Russlan and Ludmilla* a whole palace floats in the air, and in another scene the cast fly through the sky on a magic carpet while meteors stream through the firmament. In *The Bronze Horse* there is a tremendous gale which uproots bushes and hurtles them across the stage, sends newspapers sailing through the air, and rips the tiles from the roofs; then the river rises above its banks, flooding over the stage, and in the raging waters the refuse of the town swirls past—an upturned boat with people clinging to it as they struggle in the torrent, a sentry box, uprooted trees, and finally a horse still harnessed to its cart. The audience love it—and so would we: but it is all very different from the anti-illusionist theatre of the 'twenties.

86

The Experimentalist Producers

Although in Russia the producers no longer consider it their mission to destroy the illusion of actuality and constantly to remind the audience that they are not spying on reality, this "anti-illusionism" still persists in the work of the German producer Bert Brecht, who directs his own company in the Russian sector of Berlin. What Brecht calls "the markets of evening entertainment" have become in his opinion a branch of the drug traffic, places where the audience are transformed into "an intimidated, credulous, bewitched crowd". He asks us to go into one of these theatres and observe the spectators. "Looking around, one sees immobile faces. These theatregoers sit together like men who are asleep but are having unquiet dreams, because, as people say of those who have nightmares, they are lying on their backs. True, they have their eyes open. But they don't watch, they stare. They don't hear, they are transfixed. They look at the stage as if bewitched, a type of response which has its origin in the Middle Ages, the time of witches and clerics. Watching and hearing are *activities,* sometimes enjoyable ones, but these people seem to be released from all activity. They seem to be *people to whom something is being done.*"

The anti-illusionists are fond of drawing these lurid pictures of drugged, comatose, passive spectators, but although I have often watched the audience from a box in one of those "markets of evening entertainment" I have never seen an audience remotely resembling Brecht's description, though perhaps they are to be seen on the first night of an excessively boring play. However, as Brecht believes that his mission is to free the audience from the spell cast upon them by the witchcraft of the realistic producers who make a dream world of reality, let us examine his remedy. It all depends on what he calls the alienation effect. "An alienating image is one which makes a circumstance recognisable and at the same time makes it strange. . . . The theatre must astonish its audience, and it does so by means of a technique which alienates what is accepted. And this technique permits the theatre to use the method of the new science of society—dialectical materialism." Now what on earth

87

is this "new science of dialectical materialism"? Brecht explains it as "a method which, in order to show how society is susceptible of change, treats social conditions as though they were on trial and follows them up in all their contradictoriness . . . We say that man contains much and therefore much can be made of him. He need not remain as he is. He is to be regarded not only as he is but as he might be. We must use him not as a starting point but as our goal. This means that it is not enough for me simply to put myself in his place; as the representative of all of us I must put myself at some distance from him. This is why the theatre must *alienate* what it shows".

Now let us try to discover how, in terms of production, the theatre can alienate what it shows. "To produce alienation effects the actor has to forget everything he has learned about enabling an audience to feel its way into his creations. Since his intention is not to put his audience into a trance he should not put himself into a trance. At no point must he allow himself to be transformed into the character. If someone said: 'He didn't play Lear, he *was* Lear,' that would be a damning judgment. He has only to *show* the character. Or, to put it better, he has to do more than merely *experience*. This does not mean he must be cold when he portrays passionate people. It is only that his own feelings should not be entirely those of his character, lest the feelings of the audience become entirely those of the character. The audience must have complete freedom."

What this amounts to is a reversal of Stanislavsky's doctrine that the actor must identify himself completely with the part he is playing. Brecht demands an objective style of acting—what he rather oddly calls epic acting. "It is not enough that the actor give up attempting to deceive his audience into thinking that not he but the fictitious character is on the stage; he must make certain that he is not deceiving them into thinking that what happens on the stage has not been rehearsed but is happening for the first and only time. It should be apparent in all his acting that at the beginning and in the middle he already knows the end. And he should thus maintain a calm freedom throughout."

In Berlin in 1949 I was able to study Brecht's production of his own play, *Mother Courage*. Many features of the production were simply the old, familiar anti-illusionist devices which the revolutionary theatre of the 'twenties used to enforce Meierhold's dictum that "the actual world exists and is our subject; but this play and this stage are not it". For instance, as a means of destroying the illusion of actuality the stage was flooded in a glare of harsh white light throughout the performance, whether the action took place at daybreak or sunset, at midnight or at noon. In between the scenes captions, slogans and comments were projected onto a gauze curtain. Points were emphasised by songs which did not emerge out of the action of the play but were what Brecht calls "musical addresses to the audience" in which the actor stepped out of the story and commented on the play. Orchestral music was used in a similar manner. Normally incidental music is, of course, used to heighten the mood of a scene, but this is absorbed by Brecht as "helping the audience to give itself over to the occurrences on the stage". In *Mother Courage,* for example, a quiet, peaceful scene was accompanied by harsh, threatening music which was an ironical commentary on what we were being shown by the actors.

The stage (it was a large, finely proportioned stage of what used to be Reinhardt's Deutsches Theatre) was almost completely bare. The background was the cyclorama, not lit as a sky but bleakly exposed as a huge, bare, white cloth. The changes of scene were indicated by small, solidly built semi-realistic pieces of scenery isolated in the centre of the stage. This "space staging", as it used to be called, was common in the German theatre of the 'twenties. Mother Courage's cart, which is so important in the play, was a solidly realistic affair and at the end of the play, when the old woman harnesses herself to it and sets off once more on her journeyings, the revolving stage was brought into action so that, as she trudged along, the revolve moving in the opposite direction kept her stationary, like someone on a treadmill.

Although I had studied Brecht's ponderous and involved pronouncements on epic acting I had no clear idea of what sort of acting I expected to see. Much to my surprise, it was very like the best kind of naturalistic acting in the English theatre. It was controlled, exact, economic in the use of gesture, devoid of any suggestion of over-playing, but vividly effective. Perhaps I was foolish to be so surprised. After all, the essence of Brecht's theory of acting is that the actor's approach to his part should be objective, which is the way nearly every English actor approaches a part. The conditions under which he works make it almost impossible for him to abandon himself completely to a part and become the character he is playing. During his early years on the stage he is hustled from play to play in weekly repertory, and although when he reaches the West End he has three or four weeks of rehearsal, that still gives him no time to *become* the character in the Stanislavsky manner. Most of the time has to be devoted to the technical problems of the part, so in performance he remains to some extent aloof from the character he is playing, critically watching his performance and consciously controlling it by means of his technique. The English actor is really a superb puppet-master. In fact he does exactly what Brecht demands when he declares that "the actor, instead of *being* the part, must *show* the part to the audience".

Brecht has had more influence on German acting than any producer since Reinhardt. When Reinhardt and many of the leading players and producers were driven into exile the acting on the German stage tended to become undisciplined and over-emphatic. Much of it lapsed into exhibitionism and splurgy emotionalism. Ihering sums up Brecht's service to the German theatre when he says that "he took away the actor's obtrusive gemutlichkeit. He insisted on simple gestures. He had to have cool, clear speech. No emotional chicanery was permitted. The result was the objective, epic style".

During the years of experiment in the theatres of Europe the English theatre was constantly accused of isolationism. American writers on the theatre who came to Europe to write books with titles such as *The Theatre of Tomorrow, The Theatre in Revolt, The Theatre Unchanged, The New Stagecraft,* usually did not think it worth while to study the English theatre which they accused of "failing to respond to the radical impulses that have moved the theatres of the Continent". But the English producers were by no means oblivious to what was happening abroad. They watched these experiments cautiously and critically, occasionally giving them a trial. The Stage Society during the 'twenties staged productions of plays by several of the German expressionists; the Birmingham Repertory Theatre produced Kaiser's *Gas* in the expressionistic manner for which it was written; the Gate Theatre founded by Peter Godfrey in 1925 and the Cambridge Festival Theatre opened by Terence Gray the following year were uncompromisingly anti-realistic in their methods of production.

Admittedly it was only in the experimental theatres that the new forms of production could be seen, but these theatres gave plenty of opportunities for authors to study them and to write their plays so as to make use of them if they wished to do so. The only English playwright of any importance who did so was J. B. Priestley, who wrote *Johnson Over Jordan* to be produced in the expressionistic style.

While the German and Russian theatres retarded their normal development because of the fanaticism with which they accepted new forms which rapidly grew sterile, the English theatre went on its way much as before, occasionally discovering for itself a new style of production. Nigel Playfair, for instance, revolutionised the production of the English classics by finding an entirely new approach to them at the Lyric Theatre, Hammersmith; and there were ceaseless experiments in new ways of producing Shakespeare—which are the subject of a later chapter in this book. Otherwise the English theatre remained obstinately faithful to its realistic traditions.

The producers who had the greatest influence on the English theatre after the 1914–18 war were Gerald du Maurier and Basil Dean, who continued and developed the subtle and exact kind of realistic production, purged of all theatrical clichés, which Granville-Barker had introduced into the English theatre. Basil Dean was the first English producer whose name meant anything to the ordinary theatregoer—but that was due less to the excellence of his work than to some of his more exuberant experiments in creating startling weather effects at the St. Martin's on the first cyclorama installed in a London theatre. The public will always be interested in a producer mainly because of his pictorial effects, which are the most obvious part of his work but by no means the largest or most important part.

Dean had been brought up in the realistic school, first as an actor in Miss Horniman's company at Manchester and then as a stage-manager for Tree at His Majesty's. His productions were more photographic and less subtly imaginative than Granville-Barker's. He trained the young company he gathered together at the St. Martin's to give an exact imitation of the external characteristics of their parts instead of encouraging them to use their imaginations as Granville-Barker did, but the result was acting which had extraordinary clarity, sharpness and precision. Dean has had an enormous influence in developing the infinitely detailed realistic acting which is today the outstanding characteristic of the English theatre. He has a genius for filling the stage with a great deal of complicated movement which always seems perfectly natural, never fussy and distracting. One of his most remarkable feats of production was the party scene in *The Constant Nymph* in which the many characters seemed to drift chattering about the stage with the vagueness and aimlessness of people at a cocktail party, yet the movement and grouping were always so exactly composed that at every moment of the scene the attention of the audience was focused exactly where Basil Dean intended; and the timing of the lines and the modulation of the voices had been rehearsed with such skill that one got the impression of hearing the important lines almost by accident above the babble of conversation. His productions had a glittering efficiency, an extraordinary wealth of detail which nevertheless never obscured the outline of the scene which was always kept firm and clear. But when he abandoned realism for fantasies such as *Hassan* and *A Midsummer Night's Dream* his direction lacked imagination and a sense of poetry.

Apart from du Maurier and Dean the only other producer who had any particular influence on the English realistic production during the 'twenties was Alfred Lunt. When he and Lynn Fontanne made their first appearance together in London at the St. James's Theatre in 1929 in *Caprice* the lightness and vivacity of their playing, the speed at which lines were bandied to and fro, the crispness with which they made their points was something altogether new and exhilarating to English audiences. The result of the Lunts' visit was an immediate quickening of the lethargic tempo of English production and a much lighter touch in the playing.

The following year Coward's direction of *Private Lives* brought a new kind of understatement to English production. The abrupt, staccato playing of seemingly flippant scenes gave them a nervous tension which subtly conveyed the undercurrents of emotion.

Since then there has been no discernible development in English production apart from the direction of Shakespeare and the other classics. An occasional production of a French play such as *Ring Round the Moon* or *Time Remembered* gives an opportunity to our producers to prove that they are capable of productions which are fantastic and imaginative, but it is rarely that an English author asks for anything but realism from his producers. When Tyrone Guthrie wrote and produced *Top of the Ladder* one had a feeling he had done so because he was longing to do an irrealist production of a modern play and despaired of finding one to produce unless he wrote it himself. The most original and genuinely English productions in our theatre today are the Crazy Gang shows. If they could be persuaded to appear in a play they would give a vigorous shake-up to our methods of producing contemporary farce, at present the dullest and most conventional form of production in the English Theatre.

4

STANISLAVSKY AND THE MOSCOW ART THEATRE

From time to time I find among my post a leaflet announcing the aims of some newly formed group of young actors with fine intentions. There are the usual promises of "plays of high artistic merit"—"opportunities for new, experimental playwrights"—"the creation of a genuinely contemporary theatre, a People's Theatre in the fullest sense of the word"—and so on. But what interests me most about these manifestos is that they usually include an announcement that "Rehearsals will be conducted according to the Stanislavsky method", or some such phrase. Now just what exactly does this mean? Precisely which of Stanislavsky's methods is to be followed?

Stanislavsky began producing at the age of nineteen and was at work until a few days before his death fifty-six years later. These fifty-six years were a period of continual change and development in the European theatre, particularly in Russia where the Revolution swept out of the theatres most of the old audience, replacing them with an audience of an entirely different sort. Yet to the end of his life, in 1938, Stanislavsky retained his position as the world's greatest producer. He could not have done so if during all these years he had simply continued to practise the method of production which he brought to perfection comparatively early in his career. The theatre for whose advancement he had done so much would eventually have outpaced him, while his work degenerated into the merest mechanical repetition of a formula. There is no such thing as

"The Stanislavsky Method". Instead there are the various methods of production which he initiated, many of which he afterwards rejected, but only after he had worked on them for months, even years. It was during the later and more experimental stages of his career that he would wrestle with a production for a hundred rehearsals or more in his struggle to perfect his latest theories. In 1920 Byron's *Cain* was given one hundred and sixty rehearsals, but survived only eight performances. When Gogol's *Dead Souls* was produced in 1932 it had been rehearsed for a year and a half. In contrast, *The Seagull,* the first success of the Moscow Art Theatre, was produced in twenty-six rehearsals.

The danger to a producer or a group of actors attempting to base their work on the example of Stanislavsky is that they are apt to use methods which he himself eventually repudiated, although he may have practised them for a time, and, during that time, have written about them with complete conviction. A year or two ago I asked the producer of a company which claimed to be working "according to the basic principles of Stanislavsky" for some information as to how rehearsals were conducted. He wrote back saying that although they were fully aware that with only a limited time for rehearsals they could not hope to follow Stanislavsky's method completely, they did at least try to practise "three of the fundamental principles of his system". He went on to explain: "We try to live our parts not only during rehearsal but even when we are away from the theatre going about our ordinary life; we give as much time as we can to absorbing the atmosphere of a play by studying books, paintings, and photographs which tell us about the period and the country in which the play takes place; and we spend at least the first days of rehearsal sitting round a table and examining and discussing the play and its characters in very great detail."

What this producer describes is not so much a way of rehearsal as three ways of preparing for rehearsal. They have little to do with "the basic principles of Stanislavsky". It is true that at one time (it was when he was working with an amateur group) Stanislavsky believed that actors rehearsing a play should try to live "in character" even outside the theatre, but he eventually realised that acting in a perpetual off-stage charade results in a conflict in the actor's mind between his own improvisations and the author's intentions, so that it becomes difficult for the actor to speak the author's lines with the necessary technique and conviction when he has been enjoying the undisciplined freedom of inventing his own thoughts, words and deeds for the character he is portraying. It is also true that Stanislavsky used to believe in the actor preparing for rehearsals by studying the background of the play in books, pictures, and museums. Before starting rehearsals of Tolstoy's *The Power of Darkness* he took the whole company for a fortnight into the country to study peasant life, bringing back to Moscow for further and more intensive study a mass of material which included not only photographs, sketches, clothes, furniture, and domestic utensils but also an old peasant and his wife. Years later, in a lecture to his students, he confessed that he "used to stuff the heads of the actors with all sorts of lectures about the epoch, the history, and the life of the characters in the play, as a result of which they used to go on the stage with a head full to bursting and were not able to act anything". In his later years he used to discourage the actor from preliminary study of the play's historical background, merely giving him during rehearsal such facts as the actor found he really needed as he worked on his part. The "round-the-table" discussion of the play was also eventually discarded because "such an analytic method led the actor into the sphere of abstract reasoning, whereas it is the task of the producer to develop the active nature of the actor's creative work. Reasoning has nothing to do with art. The best analysis of a play is to act it in the given circumstances. For in the process of action the actor gradually obtains the mastery over the inner incentives of the actions of the character he is representing, evoking in himself the emotions and thoughts which resulted in these actions".

It is unfortunate that these three aids to rehearsal—living the part outside the theatre, studying the background of the play, discussion round the table—which were once practised by

Stanislavsky and then discarded, have been so much written about and talked about that it is generally believed that they were the basis of Stanislavsky's "system". This misconception has resulted in producers and actors with an insufficient understanding of his teachings wasting an appalling amount of rehearsal time in woolly, confusing discussions, and using up their energies outside the theatre in irrelevant games of make-believe.

In fairness to the more befuddled disciples of Stanislavsky it must be admitted that until recently it was not easy in this country to gather much information about his methods of producing during the later years of his life. His autobiography, *My Life in Art,* written in 1923, deals with the first half of his life in the theatre and gives a clear account of his methods during those years; but *An Actor Prepares,* published in 1936, and *Building a Character,* published after his death, deal mainly with the training of an actor, and tell us little about his later methods of production, except in the dramatic schoolroom. Fortunately we have recently become better informed about the later years since the publication of David Magarshack's biography, which enables us to trace the gradual change and development in Stanislavsky's methods of production throughout his life in the theatre.

He began as an autocratic dictator-producer. He did not collaborate with his actors; he simply imposed his own ideas upon them. His account of his preparations for rehearsals of *The Seagull* describes his method. "I used to shut myself up in my study and write a detailed mise-en-scène as I felt it and as I saw and heard it with my inner eye and ear. At those moments I did not care for the feelings of the actor! I sincerely believed it was possible to tell people to live and feel as I liked them to; I wrote down directions for everybody and those directions had to be carried out. I put down everything in my production notes: in what way a part had to be interpreted and the playwright's stage directions carried out, what kind of inflexions the actor had to use, how he had to move about and act, and where and how he had to cross the stage. I added all sorts of sketches for every mise-en-scène—exits, entries, crossings from one place on the stage to another, and so on and so forth. I described the scenery, costumes, make-up, deportment, gaits, the habits of the characters, etc." In the second half of his career his method became the complete antithesis of this. Magarshack's book records a conversation, twenty-five years after the production of *The Seagull*, in which Stanislavsky describes himself arriving at the first rehearsal of a play "no more prepared than the actor". By this time he had come to believe that "the producer must approach the play with a mind as fresh and clear as the actor's and then grow together with him. The whole development of the production of a play must evolve during the process of the work on the play and with the maximum regard to the individuality and the creative abilities of each member of the cast".

Although Stanislavsky wrote and talked with scorn about his early methods, nevertheless it was during this period that he created so many of his most famous productions, including *The Seagull, Uncle Vanya, The Three Sisters, The Cherry Orchard, Ivanov, Czar Fyodor, An Enemy of the People, The Lower Depths,* and *The Blue Bird.* Yet if one is to believe Stanislavsky's picture of himself during these years he was a tyrannical, exhibitionist producer, interested in the play mainly as a means of displaying his own skill and inventiveness, using the actors as the pawns with which he composed his effects. But it is unwise to accept the autobiography of any artist as an accurate record of his life in art. I think it was Holbrook Jackson who said that the inevitable desire to exaggerate or to subtilise ultimately turns all autobiographers into liars. In *My Life in Art* Stanislavsky looks back on his old methods with such abhorrence that he exaggerates them and denounces them with the fervour of a convert at a Salvation Army meeting reviling the life he lived before he was saved. Nevertheless, even allowing for the element of exaggeration, there is no doubt that for many years Stanislavsky achieved magnificent results by methods which today are generally condemned. Are we then perhaps wrong after all in condemning the autocrat producer who dictates to his cast his own ideas, moves, gestures, and inflexions, demanding mere obedience from his actors instead of seeking their collaboration? I do not think so. But I think we would be wrong to join in Stanislavsky's condemnation of himself for practising these methods fifty years ago, at a time when the Russian theatre had become the most backward and the most undisciplined in Europe.

When Stanislavsky began his work the producer was an almost unknown figure in Russia. Rehearsals were "supervised" by the stage-manager who sat somnolently in a huge armchair in front of the prompter's box, attempting to do little more than keep the peace between the actors. The theatre-going public was so small that a play could only be given for a few performances, and a new production had to be put on nearly every week. There was no time for proper rehearsal and no desire for it among the actors. They relied for their lines upon the continuous mutter from the prompter's box rather than upon their own memories. The plays, mostly French comedies and farces, or Russian imitations of them, were so stereotyped that the same performances, together with the same scenery, furniture, and costumes, could, with a few slight variations, be used week after week. Acting consisted mainly in selecting from a stock of theatrical clichés whatever seemed most appropriate to the moment. The groupings were so standardised that the actors automatically took up their positions without thinking, except when they were engaged in manoeuvring with one another for the best position on the stage.

Stanislavsky spent the first twelve years of his life in the theatre producing with amateurs and it was some of these amateurs, turned professional, who formed the nucleus of the Moscow Art Theatre Company, founded by Stanislavsky and Nemirovich-Danchenko in 1898. The amateur inevitably begins by copying what he sees upon the professional stage. If Stanislavsky had attempted in his early days to produce either with amateurs or professionals according to the method he evolved in later years, the result would have been disastrous. It would have been like prematurely thrusting democracy upon a people too politically immature to make it work. Besides, Stanislavsky would not have been capable, at the outset of his career, of producing according to the method he afterwards adopted. He was himself no exception to the rule that the amateur begins as a copyist. Both as an actor and a producer he developed slowly. He was not one of those actors who, even when they are young and inexperienced, instinctively do much that is right and effective. He was handicapped by being exceptionally tall, which made him self-conscious and clumsy. Yet he dreamed of playing elegant romantic lovers. He copied the gestures and deportment of the singers who played the romantic rôles in the operettas. He had his voice trained in the hope that some day he would be able to play these rôles. His ambition was "to be handsome, to sing tender love arias, to be successful with the ladies". All his early productions were light operas. He was at this time more interested in acting than producing, but being the producer was the simplest method of getting his own way about putting on the operettas in which he wanted to play. *The Mikado* was one of the operettas he produced and played in. Although as producer he took immense pains to create a realistic Japanese atmosphere, as an actor he could not bear to depart from his vision of himself as a handsome Italian opera singer, so he made no attempt to play the part as a Japanese, but "tried to look like the most banal, theatrically operatic, postcard beauty".

It was a visit of the Duke of Saxe-Meiningen's company to Moscow in 1890 which excited Stanislavsky's interest in production and determined his career. For some time he had been growing increasingly depressed over his slow progress as an actor and was considering giving up acting. But as he watched the performances of the Meiningen company he saw himself in a new rôle—the rôle of the producer exciting amazement and admiration by the beauty and dramatic effect of his groupings, the inventiveness of the stage business, the brilliant handling of the crowd scenes, the meticulous detail of the scenery and properties, the cleverness of the lighting, and the effectiveness of the "noises-off". All this was done with superb efficiency by

Chronegk, the producer of the Meiningen company, but in such a way that the audience were left in no doubt that it was he who was the star of the company and that the actors were simply carrying out his commands. This does not seem to have troubled Stanislavsky. Because he still longed to excite admiration he was eager to emulate this style of production in which the guiding hand of the producer could be seen in everything that happened on the stage. He justified Chronegk's despotism because it seemed to him to be grounded in necessity. The Meiningen actors were so ineffective that "it was necessary to take much from the actor's balance cup and put it into the director's. The necessity to create for everybody created the despotism of the stage-director". He saw himself, a producer of amateurs, in the same predicament as Chronegk. He too had to work without the help of talented actors: henceforth these actors must hand over to him the task of creation and he would conceal their deficiencies by the novelty and inventiveness of his production.

The meticulous correctness of the scenery and properties in Chronegk's productions particularly impressed Stanislavsky, because he himself already had a weakness for this kind of irrelevant pedantry. When he produced *The Mikado*, a troupe of Japanese acrobats appearing at the circus in Moscow were engaged to teach the cast "all the Japanese customs, the manner of walking, deportment, bowing, dancing, the handling of a fan. The women walked all day with their legs tied together as far as the knee, the fan became a necessary object of everyday life. We already felt the necessity to explain ourselves during conversation with the help of the fan, a Japanese habit. Returning from office or the factory, we donned our Japanese costumes and wore them all evening, and during holidays as well. . . . In the performance there was something never shown on the stage before—real Japanese life". In his enthusiasm for showing real Japanese life on the stage Stanislavsky overlooked the fact that he was not producing a real Japanese play but an Englishman's burlesque of how he imagined life was lived in Japan.

It does not seem to have occurred to Stanislavsky to consider *why* the standard of acting in the Meiningen company was so poor. The reason for the lack of first-rate actors could hardly have been shortage of money as the Duke spent huge sums on the scenery, costumes, and properties, and toured an army of supers. It may have been that Chronegk was a poor judge of an actor; or he may have deliberately chosen actors of mediocre talent so that he himself would remain the unchallenged star of the show; or he may have suspected that actors of intelligence and personality would not always be subservient to his will; or it may have been that he began with a company which had the potentiality of becoming a group of first-rate actors, but who lost heart when they discovered that the producer thought their performances less important than the clothes on their backs and the properties in their hands, and asked no more from them than absolute obedience to his commands. It was only years afterwards that Stanislavsky saw that as a result of Chronegk's methods "the director was obliged to create without the help of the actor, and the actor without the help of the director".

Soon after the Meiningen company's visit to Moscow Stanislavsky directed his first straight play. It was Tolstoy's *The Fruits of Knowledge,* put on by the Society of Arts and Literature, the group of amateurs with which Stanislavsky had been acting for the past three years. At the first rehearsal Stanislavsky immediately started to emulate Chronegk's disciplinary methods. He announced a system of fines. Lateness at rehearsal, talking during rehearsals, a badly learned part, absence from the rehearsal-room without permission, were to be punished with "special severity". Everybody must be soberly dressed. The huge hats which were then the fashion among women were condemned as frivolous and were not to be allowed at rehearsal. Flirting, he solemnly announced, was forbidden. He went on to lecture his cast on the subject of love. That was to be allowed because "serious love uplifts you. Shoot yourself for the sake of women, die, but do not indulge in flirtation which drags you downward". To us the solemnity of the young Stanislavsky may seem a little ridiculous, but it was one of his greatest gifts as a producer that he never had any difficulty in persuading his company to accept his own enthusiasms and beliefs. A producer must convince himself before he can convince his cast. There was no doubt in Stanislavsky's mind that Chronegk's despotism and ruthless discipline were the first essentials of a good production. His belief was justified by the results. The production was highly praised, especially for a quality which was to become an outstanding feature of all Stanislavsky's productions—the excellence of the ensemble.

It is interesting to note that Stanislavsky, like most inexperienced producers, had great difficulty in composing the groupings and movements. "I found," he wrote, "that I lacked the experience to make each of the quickly changing groupings interesting and typical." In his handling of the individual actor there was no attempt at collaboration. "I showed what my imagination saw to the actors and they imitated me. Where I was able to feel things rightly the play came to life. Where there was only outward ingenuity the play remained a dead thing. The only good quality of my work at that time was the fact that I tried to be sincere. I saw the truth, and falsehood, especially theatrical falsehood, became for me intolerable."

In this Stanislavsky was already showing himself more than a mere imitator of Chronegk. The acting of the Meiningen players was stagey and conventional. Stanislavsky was beginning to seek for a method of acting which would supplant the theatrical artificialities of the stage of that day. It would be a long time yet before he developed his theory of "inner feeling". His aim at the moment was "to chase the theatre from the theatre", but his conception of realism was more a matter of outward resemblance than of inner feeling.

Gutzkow's historical play *Uriel Acosta*, which Stanislavsky produced in 1895, provided him with his first opportunity to handle big crowd scenes. Afterwards he admitted that under the influence of Chronegk he had over-elaborated the crowd scenes and over-estimated the importance of historical exactitude. But in his handling of the individual actors he took a step forward, as he gave some rein to the more talented members of the cast, though he describes himself as "ordering the other actors about as if they were mannequins". In *My Life in Art* he justifies this by declaring that "all but the most talented amateurs require despotic treatment. Talentless people must be subjected to simple training, dressed to the taste of the director and made to act according to his will. If one is forced to give talentless actors big parts, one is also forced, for the sake of the performance, to hide their faults. For this there are many excellent ways which I learned to perfection at that time. These cover the lapses of the bad actors like screens".

What Stanislavsky did when he was dissatisfied with the playing of a scene was to invent some elaborate byplay to catch the interest of the audience. In the second act of *Uriel Acosta* he brought on to the stage a beautiful young woman and her handsome admirer, both of them exquisitely dressed, put them in the most prominent place on the stage, and invented for them a gay, flirtatious love-scene in dumb show. No doubt this most effectively distracted the attention of the audience from the shortcomings of the actors struggling to play the scene which the author had written. Stanislavsky somewhat ingenuously tells us that where it was necessary for the audience to listen to the dialogue in order to be able to follow the plot of the play, he "stopped the action of the extras temporarily to give the spectators an opportunity to hear the important words". Unfortunately Stanislavsky got so much satisfaction from exercising his inventiveness on these interpolated scenes that they were still a feature of his productions long after the shortcomings of his actors had ceased to be an excuse—if it ever really was an excuse.

Stanislavsky was at first a poor judge of a play apart from its more obvious theatrical qualities. Afterwards he attributed this to his lack of any real education. He did not go to school or to a university. The son of a wealthy mill-owner, he was tutored at home. The lessons which his parents considered most important were dancing, deportment, fencing, and gymnastics. The rest of his education does not seem to have continued beyond the elementary stages. He had little chance of developing any literary tastes, and for many years he avoided the company of writers and men of letters because he felt ill-equipped to take part in their conversation. His highly developed sense of the theatre, unrestrained by an educated sense of taste and judgement, led him to confuse what was genuinely theatrical with what was merely stagey. It led him to produce as melodrama plays which required to be handled much more delicately; it led him still further—to mutilating the texts of plays to suit them to his own melodramatic taste. For instance, in his production of Ostrovsky's *The Dowerless Bride* in 1890, he so altered this gentle, lyrical play about an impoverished but highly respectable aristocratic family that it became a lurid melodrama with the heroine "a half-gipsy brought up in Bohemia" and her mother a retired courtesan.

Each production of Stanislavsky's during the years immediately before the founding of the Moscow Art Theatre marked some new development in his work. It was in Hauptmann's macabre fantasy *Hannele,* which he produced in 1896, that he first experimented in combining the dramatic use of pauses with "the orchestration of voices", which afterwards became such a feature of his Chekhov productions. "I taught the actors to speak and move like the figures in our sick-dreams, when someone seems to whisper mysteriously in your ear—then a pause on a broken word, a long pause, then again a slow, broken, often-accented speech in a rising and falling chromatic scale. Again a pause, a silence—an unexpected whisper—the slow, monotonous movements of the crowd of ghostlike beggars casting their shadows across the walls and ceiling. Then suddenly the grating sound of an opening door, the harsh creaking of a hinge, the shrill, whining voice of the beggar woman who has just entered, the sharp, unpleasant voice one hears when one is in a fever."

It was in his production of another of Hauptmann's plays, *The Sunken Bell,* "a philosophic fairy-tale", that Stanislavsky began to experiment with three-dimensional scenery. He had come to the conclusion that the painted backcloth was of no real use to the actor. The actor, he argued, cannot see the backcloth hanging behind him: because he cannot see it, his acting cannot be inspired by it; nor can he make any use of it in his acting; in fact, he must keep well away from it, as otherwise he will seem far taller than the trees and houses painted upon it. When Simov, who was designing *The Sunken Bell,* produced his first model of the mountainous scene in which most of the play takes place, Stanislavsky said to him: "Why don't you give me, instead of all this painted canvas, which we actors never see, a great stone on which I may sit down to dream, lie in despair, or stand high in order to be near the sky?" From this Stanislavsky and Simov evolved the idea of breaking away from the convention that the floor of the stage must be flat. It was usual enough, of course, to have steps and a rostrum at the back of the stage, but at that time it was considered essential for the actor that the greater part of the stage should be as bare as possible in order to give him complete freedom of movement. Furniture was reduced to a minimum. In an interior scene at the Maly Theatre—the State Theatre of Moscow—it was still usual for the furniture to consist merely of a few gilt chairs ranged round the walls of the set. If in the course of a scene an actor wished to sit in a chair, he would place it in a convenient position, afterwards replacing it against the wall. To Stanislavsky it seemed that a bare, flat stage was like a concert platform on which the actor and the producer were confined to the monotonous repetition of a very limited number of movements and groupings. In *The Sunken Bell* he had the idea of building up the floor of the stage in a series of different levels representing boulders, winding paths, and the slopes of the hill. In his enthusiasm for this new idea he left no room anywhere on the stage where the actors could walk. "Let them creep," he said, "or sit on stones; let them jump from rock to rock, or clamber among the trees. This will force them to get used to a new mise-en-scène and to play in a way that is new to the stage instead of just standing near to the footlights." Indeed, there was nowhere for them to stand near the footlights because most of the front of the stage was filled with the great trunk of a fallen tree. Simov overcame Stanislavsky's objection to the backcloth by filling the back of the stage with a network of branches through which one saw a glimpse of a distant prospect of wild, mountainous country.

This production had a great influence on Stanislavsky's future work. For some time he had been seeking ways of compelling his actors to abandon the old, stereotyped movements and gestures. Now, as they clambered about the set for *The Sunken Bell*, they were so busy negotiating its hazards that subconsciously their movements became perfectly natural. Perched on the top of a boulder or sitting astride the branch of a tree, they were more concerned with keeping their balance than with taking up some stagey pose or making an unnecessary, conventional gesture.

Stanislavsky saw that this method of using the mise-en-scène to force actors to behave naturally instead of stagily could be adapted to a realistic modern play. Instead of boulders and tree trunks and rocks there would be sofas and chairs and tables —not just the bare necessities with which the stage was usually furnished, but all the clutter of the over-furnished rooms of that period; the innumerable spindly occasional tables, palms in pots perched on elaborately carved stands, whatnots, brass standard lamps, Japanese screens, gilt easels, marble busts on pedestals, footstools everywhere, and rugs from which the snarling heads of tigers and polar bears rose to make yet another obstacle to be negotiated. The actor threading his way among this labyrinth had no more chance of assuming stagey, conventional postures than when he was perilously surmounting the rocky inclines of *The Sunken Bell*. For Stanislavsky the mise-en-scène had become not just a background for the actor but something he could use and make a part of his performance. The knick-knacks which littered the occasional tables and the crowded mantelpiece, the photographs, books, family albums, ornaments and gewgaws of every sort were not there simply to dress the set. Stanislavsky believed that if the actor was constantly picking up and handling trivial, everyday things, the casualness and seeming unimportance of these little bits of business would not only subconsciously influence his movements and gestures but would also make him instinctively aware of the falseness of a stagey inflexion or intonation. And so, oddly enough, it was as a result of producing a fairy-tale, peopled with wood-sprites, witches, hobgoblins and toadlike monsters, that Stanislavsky brought to his productions of Chekhov's plays that minutely detailed visual realism which is so often described as "characteristic" of his work, although it was but one aspect of it, for the number of his realistic productions was comparatively small.

The Sunken Bell was Stanislavsky's last production for the Society of Arts and Literature. Six months earlier there had been the famous meeting with Nemirovich-Danchenko when, after talking for eighteen hours, they decided to found the Moscow Art Theatre. Nemirovich-Danchenko was a successful playwright and a distinguished literary critic who for some time had been teaching acting at the Moscow Philharmonic School, where he had been working on much the same lines as Stanislavsky, battling against the stale, trite traditionalism of the Russian theatre, endeavouring to make his pupils act simply and naturally. He had given a great deal of thought to the problems of theatrical administration and had submitted to the Government a detailed plan for the reform of the Imperial Theatre. Here was the ideal partner for Stanislavsky. Although Nemirovich-Danchenko had a knowledge of the theatre, he was essentially a man of letters rather than a man of the theatre. His highly cultivated literary taste was just what was needed to counteract Stanislavsky's bias towards melodrama. Nemirovich-Danchenko's ability as an administrator was equally necessary to Stanislavsky who was now chairman of the family business, and had to devote part of his time to the factory and the office. He continued to do so until the establishment of the Soviet regime, when the Government relieved him of these responsibilities.

Nemirovich-Danchenko shrewdly assessed the strength and the weakness of Stanislavsky as a producer. He said to him bluntly, "You are an exceptional regisseur, but so far only for melodrama and farce, and productions full of dazzling stage pictures, in which neither the psychology nor the words are of any great importance. You trample upon what other people create. Sometimes you have the good fortune to fuse with it; then the result is excellent. But more often, after a while, the author, if he happens to be a great poet or a great playwright, begins to call you to account for your insensitiveness to the play's inner meaning."

Stanislavsky was at this time primarily interested in the external, showy aspect of the theatre, in the highly coloured historical plays and macabre fairy-tales which gave him the opportunity to astonish the audience by the novelty of his ideas. "My problem," wrote Nemirovich-Danchenko, "was to awaken his interest in the depth of things, in the lyric qualities of the workaday world. It was necessary to divert his thoughts from fantasy and history, and to plunge him into the most ordinary, everyday realities, filled with our most ordinary everyday emotions." What Nemirovich-Danchenko admired in Stanislavsky's work was the extraordinary variety and dramatic effectiveness of the movements and groupings which he composed, the brilliance with which he handled crowd scenes, the vividness and originality of his theatrical imagination, the care he devoted to his décor, costumes, and properties, his mastery of lighting and all the technicalities of the stage, his rejection of the theatrical cliché in any form, the constantly varying tempi of his productions, his use of pause, his creation of atmosphere by means of lighting and subtle use of sound effects. But what seemed to Nemirovich-Danchenko more important than any of these qualities was Stanislavsky's gift of inspiring his cast with his own intense enthusiasm so that, setting aside all petty vanities, they worked together with a selfless devotion to the play and complete faith in their producer. The ensemble which Stanislavsky achieved from his actors was by now very different from the mere obedience which Chronegk demanded from his company. Chronegk's actors dutifully carried out his commands; Stanislavsky's actors obeyed him with an eager enthusiasm because he possessed the gift of effortlessly convincing them that what he asked of them was ineluctably right.

Nemirovich-Danchenko did not find Stanislavsky an easy character to understand. He seemed to him to have "a passionate and complex nature", still in some ways curiously undeveloped. (He was at times so ingenuous that his friends used to refer to him affectionately as "that great infant".) All through their association Nemirovich-Danchenko was perpetually bewildered by what seemed to him the contradictions in Stanislavsky's character and in his ideas. They were not really contradictions; it was just that Nemirovich-Danchenko could never get used to the suddenness with which Stanislavsky would decide that a long-cherished theory was wrong and would discard it without a moment's hesitation. There were traits in Stanislavsky's character which were maddening to Nemirovich-Danchenko's well-ordered mind. For instance, although he admired Stanislavsky's tremendous perseverance—he described it as perhaps the most dominant trait in his character—it was combined with a complete absence of any sense of time. The dress rehearsal of *The Merchant of Venice,* one of the early shows at the Art Theatre, had to be abandoned in the early hours of the morning, long before the end of the third act, because Stanislavsky had used up hours during the two intervals endlessly rehearsing one actor in the exact method of making a bow and another in how to handle a sword. That evening must have been all the more exasperating to Nemirovich-Danchenko because he thought the play hardly worth producing. He described it as a "trivial" play because the characters and events were so far removed from everyday life. He was only really interested in plays about contemporary life in which the characters were subtly and exactly delineated. He disliked exaggeration in any form and was incapable of appreciating or even understanding the magnificent theatricality of Stanislavsky's productions of costume plays. It bothered him, for instance, that, if an unusually high hat was a feature of a costume of a particular period, Stanislavsky would make it still higher; if a door in a castle wall was small, he would make it so small that the actors had to stoop to pass through it. Stanislavsky had read somewhere that the boyars in the presence of the Czar bowed thrice to the ground. "Well, in our rehearsals," complained Nemirovich-Danchenko, "the boyars got down on their knees, touched the floor with their foreheads, rose and went down again—at least twenty times!"

The playwright whom Nemirovich-Danchenko admired above all others was Chekhov. Here was the subtly exact portrayal of contemporary character, the half-tones, the delicate tints and shadings, which appealed to him so strongly. But there were no half-tones in Stanislavsky's productions. Nemirovich-Danchenko was very doubtful whether he was the right producer for Chekhov, and in all the advice and criticism which he gave to Stanislavsky at the beginning of their association one senses this uneasiness. Nemirovich-Danchenko was determined that the Art Theatre should do a production of *The Seagull* which would reveal the true quality of the play. A courageous ambition, because *The Seagull* had failed miserably when it was originally produced. After the first night Chekhov wrote to his family: "The play has fallen down with a crash. In the theatre there was a heavy atmosphere of depression, perplexity and humiliation. The actors played abominably, stupidly. The moral: one should not write plays."

When Stanislavsky read *The Seagull* he found it "monotonous and boring". It seemed to him to be devoid of action. Night after night Nemirovich-Danchenko talked to him about the play, striving to inspire him with his own belief in it. Stanislavsky, unconvinced, went away to the country, "with chaos in my soul", to work out his production of a play which he did not like and did not understand.

One can imagine Stanislavsky's feeling of bewilderment when he pored over the script. He could find in it none of the material upon which he was accustomed to exercise his talents as a producer. He looked in vain for the theatrical climaxes which he could handle so effectively; the play seemed flatly uneventful. Nor could he see any opportunities for the dramatic changes of tone and tempo which were a feature of his productions. These people seldom raised their voices or varied the languid pace of their speech. Their listlessness deprived

Stanislavsky of any chance of displaying his skill in filling the stage with bustling movement. There were no crowd scenes. (But that at least could be remedied: he introduced a crowd at the end of Act III.) The characters seemed dim and colourless. In fact, to Stanislavsky, who delighted in the flaring colours and picturesque effects he was able to use in his productions of histories and fantasies, the whole play appeared to be depressingly drab. And then there were those pauses with which the author had spattered his script. Stanislavsky could not see the point of them: surely most of them were no more than just empty silences. Fortunately the play took place in the country, where birds sing, frogs croak, crickets chirrup, owls hoot, corn-crakes cry, mosquitoes hum and dogs howl. There were all these sounds to fill in Chekhov's pauses, and many others as well—the sounds of a carriage on a nearby road, the singing of a drunken peasant reeling home to bed, the thrumming of music in the distance, the tolling of a church bell, a steamer's siren, the half-heard mutter of thunder. Stanislavsky failed to realise that the silences in *The Seagull* are so eloquent that the producer must step aside and allow them to make their own effect instead of supplying an obbligato of irrelevant sounds. Had he left the pauses to look after themselves and concentrated on the dialogue leading up to them, he would have discovered that each moment of silence in a Chekhov play is so carefully prepared for by the author that it inevitably becomes the sum of all that has been said.

In the end *The Seagull*, the play which everybody associates with Stanislavsky's name, was only partly produced by him. Of the twenty-six rehearsals, Nemirovich-Danchenko took fifteen, Stanislavsky nine, and the other two were taken by Luzsky, who was Stanislavsky's assistant. But it was Stanislavsky alone who planned the production; the other two producers followed the meticulously detailed instructions which Stanislavsky had written against almost every line of his script.

On the first night the theatre was by no means full. The cast were nervous and unhappy. The first four productions at the Art Theatre had failed to draw the public; another failure and the theatre might have to close. The actors had sensed Stanislavsky's lack of faith in the play, and they knew that Chekhov's sister, Maria Pavlovna, had implored Nemirovich-Danchenko to call off the production. Stanislavsky himself, after the dress-rehearsal, had demanded that the first night be postponed. When Nemirovich-Danchenko refused, he asked that his name should be removed from the bills.

The reception of the play that night has been described so often that there is no need to recount yet again the scenes of wild enthusiasm at the end of every act. "A colossal success," wired Nemirovich-Danchenko to the author; "endless curtain calls, we are mad with happiness." But Chekhov, when he eventually saw the play, disliked the production—disliked it so much that for a time he refused to allow the Moscow Art Theatre to have his next play, *Uncle Vanya.* He considered that *The Seagull* had been distorted by the misinterpretation of the part of Nina, and by Stanislavsky's own performance as Trigorin. "It made me sick to look at him," he wrote in a letter to Gorki. He thought the whole atmosphere of the production too sombre, and much of the realistically detailed business irrelevant and distracting.

How was it, then, that the play was such a success in spite of the fact that much of it had been misinterpreted? The answer is that the success on the first night was the producer's rather than the author's. The audience was dazzled and excited by the novelty of the production. The quietness, the intimacy, the complete naturalness of the acting, was something entirely new. There was no trace of theatricality, no sign of the actors playing to the public. We are told that the audience "felt almost embarrassed to be present; it was as if they eavesdropped behind a door, or peeped through a window". Stanislavsky, developing the method he had discovered in *The Sunken Bell,* had provided the actors with settings they could "use", and had related them to their surroundings by means of innumerable touches of realistic business. The settings themselves were no longer mere inanimate backgrounds; by his use of sound and by subtle changes of lighting Stanislavsky kept them always in harmony with the changing moods of the play. One or two critics thought that weather effects and noises-off were too obtrusive a feature of the production. Stanislavsky defended himself on the grounds that "twilight, sunset, sunrise, a storm, rain, the songs of the awakening birds, the trampling of horses over a bridge, the striking of a clock, the chirping of a cricket, are necessary to Chekhov not for the sake of external effects but for the revelation of the life of the human spirit. For it is impossible to separate us and everything that takes place in us from the world of inanimate things, light and sound among which we live and which so much influence our nature".

Another novelty of the production was the daringly slow tempo of the opening act. Chekhov thought it far too sluggish, but the audience was fascinated by the dreamlike slowness with which the characters moved among the shadows of the autumn evening, speaking almost hesitantly, pausing in the middle of a sentence, sometimes lapsing into long silences. Many producers of Chekhov have tried to emulate Stanislavsky in this, but have only achieved a dragging monotony. Stanislavsky avoided it by delicate variations of tone and tempo. But the tempo of the first act was no more than a tour-de-force of technique imposed upon the actors by the producer; it was later that Stanislavsky made it a rule never to produce a scene at a slow tempo until he was convinced that the actors felt the emotion of the scene with exceptional intensity. He used to tell his pupils that most actors wrongly believe that their feelings must be strongest when they are acting "full out". Pace and volume will always hold the attention of an audience for a while, even when the actor is merely simulating an emotion; it is the quiet scene played at slow tempo which demands the greatest intensity of feeling from the actor.

Whatever the defects of that production of *The Seagull*, it proved that Stanislavsky was now a producer of extraordinary range and accomplishment. As he groped his way through the rehearsals of *The Seagull*, seeking to reach an understanding of the play, he had discovered how to work in half-tones, how to make hints rather than statements, how to suggest shadowy half-realised moods and emotions, how to use delicate gradations of tone and tempo to create the effect of quietness and intimacy without monotony. In fact, in the course of a single production he had developed all those qualities which Nemirovich-Danchenko had feared he lacked, and evolved a new technique of production exactly suited to the new kind of play which Chekhov was writing. In his other Chekhov productions (*Uncle Vanya, The Three Sisters, Ivanov,* and *The Cherry Orchard*) he used this technique unchanged except for some slight modifications. For instance, he allowed Chekhov's pauses to make their own effect without always giving them an accompaniment of sound, but he still made so much use of the noises of the countryside to create atmosphere that Chekhov, after seeing *Uncle Vanya*, vowed that his next play would take place "in a land which has neither mosquitoes nor crickets nor any other insects which hinder conversations between human beings". Stanislavsky used the slow, lingering tempo of *The Seagull* much more sparingly in his subsequent productions because he came to realise that Chekhov's characters do not luxuriate in their sorrows but "like Chekhov himself, seek life, joy, laughter, courage. The men and women of Chekhov want to live and not to die. They are active and strive to overcome the frustrations of their life. It is not their fault that Russian life kills initiative and stifles good intentions". But for a while he had to rely upon Nemirovich-Danchenko to guide him to an understanding of the plays. By the time *The Cherry Orchard* was reached Nemirovich-Danchenko was able to write to Chekhov to say that "Alexeyev must be allowed more freedom in *The Cherry Orchard*. . . . He understands you excellently and he has left his whimsies a long way behind".

There is no need to describe all Stanislavsky's productions during the early years of the Art Theatre, because for a time there were no new developments in his methods. Meanwhile, all over Europe symbolism and impressionism were influencing other arts besides painting and sculpture. In Russia the Art Theatre was an obvious target for the anti-realists. They argued that because the art of the theatre is by its very nature unrealistic, it can never convincingly imitate reality, so the Art Theatre should give up laboriously trying to copy life and concentrate on developing a stylised and purely symbolic method of production. These criticisms came at a time when Stanislavsky was beginning to feel that he was leading the Art Theatre down a blind alley. He had perfected his present method of production. His restless, questing mind was seeking new paths along which he could adventure. Hoping that the symbolists could point him the way, he painstakingly studied the work of the most "advanced" painters, and spent hours in front of a mirror solemnly trying to assume the tortured postures of the figures he had seen in their paintings. "My God," he cried in exasperation, "is it possible that we, the artists of the stage, are fated, because of the limitations of our bodies, to the eternal service and expression of coarse realism and nothing else? Are we not called to go any further than the realists in painting went in their time?"

He decided that this was a subject for experiment and research in a theatrical laboratory, and so what came to be known as The Studio in Povarskaya Street was founded. To direct it Stanislavsky engaged Vsevolod Meierhold, who was afterwards to become the leading producer in the Russian theatre during the early years of the Soviet regime. He had been a member of the Moscow Art Theatre company but had left it two years previously when he became a convert to the symbolist movement. Stanislavsky frankly confessed that he could not see how the theories of the symbolists were to be applied to the stage, but he believed that every generation has something of its own which cannot be seen by the eyes of the generation which precedes it, so he gave Meierhold an entirely free hand, never visiting The Studio except when he was invited to do so. Meierhold's method was to abolish scenery and to place his actors against a background of unpainted canvas. Movement and gesture were stylised, made sharp and angular. Any curved or flowing movement or gesture was condemned by Meierhold as naturalistic and had to be suppressed. The actor's speech was drained of all naturalistic inflections until it became cold, hard, toneless and completely impersonal.

After many months of work Meierhold was at last able to show Stanislavsky the completed production of Hauptmann's *Schluch und Jau,* together with some short plays including Maeterlinck's *La Morte de Tintagiles* which was written to be performed by marionettes. What Stanislavsky saw was a dry, precise demonstration of a scientific formula. The actors had been used merely as puppets to illustrate Meierhold's theories. Instead of helping them to create, he had refused to allow them to think or feel for themselves. Consequently, although his groupings and movements were often striking, the performances of the actors were lifeless and mechanical. What shocked Stanislavsky about these performances was their denial of the importance of the actor as an individual.

Meierhold's productions were, for Stanislavsky, a horrifying demonstration of the degrading state of abject and slavish obedience to which the dictatorial producer could reduce his actors. Up to then Stanislavsky had not realised that his feeling of being in a cul-de-sac down which he could advance no farther was due to his rejection of the actor as a partner in production. He left The Studio that afternoon determined that henceforth the actor should be his collaborator instead of his subordinate.

The Studio was closed and shortly afterwards the Art Theatre company set out on its first European tour. When the tour ended Stanislavsky went to Finland for a long holiday which he spent in considering how he could best carry out his resolve. It seemed to him that if the actor was to become a collaborator he must first be trained to develop a creative state of mind. How was this to be attained? In *My Life in Art,* the chapter in which Stanislavsky describes his musing during that holiday in Finland is entitled "The Beginnings of my System". But the evolution of that famous "system" was to take many years, during which Stanislavsky was often to find himself on the wrong path; but always he would set off again in another direction with his determination unabated and his enthusiasm undimmed.

On his return to the Art Theatre he began to try to put his new theory of production into practice by exhorting the actors to "feel" their parts. But he soon found that he was merely attempting to squeeze emotion out of the actor, "urging him ahead as if he were a horse that cannot move a great load from its place". His assistant-producer, enthusiastically taking his cue from Stanislavsky, would shout to the actors: "More, more. Live more strongly. Give me more of it! Live the thing over! Feel it!" Stanislavsky describes how at one rehearsal his assistant, "squeezing emotion out of an actor, suddenly found himself straddling the back of the tragedian. The actor tore passion to tatters, chewed the floor with emotion, and the stage-director sat on him and beat him to encourage it".

This fantastic scene is perhaps a salutary reminder that the Russian actor is temperamentally somewhat different from his English colleague, and that a system devised for Russian actors many years ago may not, in every respect, be applicable to the English actor of today.

From these rehearsals Stanislavsky realised that the actors were merely imitating non-existent feelings, mistaking force for strength and confusing inspiration with mere strain and tension. "The result of our quest for the new," he sadly recorded, "brought us to the oldest and deadest methods that were laughed out of court by Hamlet in his speech to the Players. Instead of naked passion there was bad conventionality, instead of art there was trade. Nature always avenges the violation and the breaking of her laws."

The play that was being produced at this time was Knut Hamsun's *The Drama of Life*. Stanislavsky, in his new-found enthusiasm for subordinating the producer to the actor, made no attempt to compose the intricate pattern of movement and grouping which up to now had been such a feature of his productions. He reduced the scenery to a few frankly un-realistic cut-outs, painted, with a minimum of detail, in primary colours, because he feared that a setting which could be "used" might tempt him to invent elaborate business for his actors.

But they, deprived of the producer's help, and denied the elaborate settings and innumerable properties to which they were accustomed, were incapable of expressing anything except their own embarrassment.

Stanislavsky seems to have been not altogether uninfluenced by Meierhold's "irrealism", for in his next production, Andreyev's *The Life of Man*, the whole stage was hung with black velvet and the furniture painted to match. Doors, windows, tables, and chairs were outlined with rope. The costumes of the actors were black, outlined in the same way as the scenery and furniture. The mood of each scene was suggested by the colour of the rope. In the first scene white rope was used to achieve an eerie, grave-like effect; in the next scene, which had as its theme the youth of man, a more hopeful note was suggested by the use of rose-coloured rope. In the ballroom scene an atmosphere of luxury was indicated with gold rope. It was a method which was justified by the abstract nature of the play, but Stanislavsky's main reason for adopting it was that he hoped it would focus the entire attention of the audience on the actors. Inevitably this kind of setting and costuming compelled the actors to attempt to stylise their movements and speak in "irrealist" tones. And so, ironically enough, Stanislavsky had evolved a style of production not very dissimilar from those productions of Meierhold which had caused him to close down The Studio in Povarskaya Street. Even his intention of concentrating attention entirely upon the actor was not achieved. The "simplicity" of the production was so novel and striking that it most effectively distracted the attention of the audience from the actors who, untrained in stylised acting, merely seemed awkward and amateurish. The production was a success with the public; but once again, in spite of Stanislavsky's intentions, it was a success for the producer rather than the actors.

In his perplexity Stanislavsky sought the help of Gordon Craig. He engaged him to design *Hamlet* and to collaborate in the production. While Craig, in Italy, worked on his designs for *Hamlet*, Stanislavsky began his production of *A Month in the*

Country. He had decided that the Art Theatre must return to realism. Writing to Gurevich, he said, "We have returned to a deeper, more refined and more psychological realism. Let us get a little stronger in it and we shall once more continue on our quest. I do not doubt that every abstraction of the stage, such as impressionism, for instance, could be attained by way of a more refined and deeper realism. All other ways are false and dead."

Stanislavsky had not yet formulated his theory of "inner realism" beyond declarations such as that "it must be sought in the reflection of the life of the human spirit"—which, like so many of Stanislavsky's pronouncements, sounds extremely impressive but is of no practical value either to the actor or to anyone seeking an accurate understanding of his theories. Stanislavsky always had the utmost difficulty in expressing himself in words, as the actors cast for *A Month in the Country* were soon to discover. This was the first production in which he put into practice the beginnings of his "system". The actors were bewildered by his harangues, in which he confused them with jargon borrowed from psychology, science, religion, mathematics, and medicine. Olga Knipper, who was playing Natalia Petrovna, threw up her part in despair. In a letter which Stanislavsky wrote her he said: "I promise not to frighten you with any more technical terms." But it was not only the difficulty of understanding Stanislavsky's theories which brought Knipper to despair. She felt "lonely" because Stanislavsky, apart from lecturing her on his theories, seemed to have withdrawn from her his help as a producer. He had done so deliberately. He had determined in this production to discover "whether it is true that the actor is the prime figure and the prime creator in the theatre". He repeated the experiment made in *The Drama of Life* of giving the actors as few moves, gestures, and business as possible. Once again the scenery was of the utmost simplicity. For instance, it is interesting to compare the garden scene in this production with the garden scene in *The Seagull,* in which the floor of the stage was broken up into different levels by slopes, stumps of trees, hedges, banks, and a bridge over a stream, so that the producer could achieve an infinite variety of movement and grouping. For the same reason the set was scattered with garden seats, benches, and tables. In *A Month in the Country* all that was on the stage was a single seat and a three-dimensional tree set against a painted backcloth. Stanislavsky was determined that neither the actors nor the spectators should have anything to distract their attention from the thoughts of the characters. "Let the actors sit without movements," he said. "Let them feel, speak, and infect the spectator with the manner in which they live their rôles. Let there be only a bench or a divan upon the stage, and let all the persons in the play sit on it so as to display the new essence of the word picture and the spiritual lacework of Turgenev." Having made it practically impossible for the actors to use expressive movement, Stanislavsky went still further in his theory that "inner realism" could be achieved by the abandoning of every kind of theatrical effect. He demanded "hardly palpable intonations of the voice". Once again, he was coming perilously close to Meierhold's methods, but instead of Meierhold's bold, stylised gestures, delicate shades of meaning were to be conveyed by pauses, by the actor's eyes, by minute, barely perceptible movements of their hands, by "some sort of unseen rayings-out of creative will, emotion, longing". In an endeavour to make the actor concentrate on the inner meaning of his lines before thinking of technical means of expression, such as tone and inflexion, no words were spoken during the early rehearsals. The actors moved their lips soundlessly. At a later stage in rehearsal they spoke in a barely audible whisper. I have heard of English producers imitating this method of rehearsal, but it seems to me a dangerous one for English actors. The Russian actor is an extrovert; the English actor is an introvert. I have seen plays in many countries, but nowhere have I seen acting so delicate and so subtle as in the English theatre. The English actor's tendency to underplaying is to a large extent due to the care and sincerity with which he thinks and feels his part, and this often leads to acting which is too inward and insufficiently projected. This method of Stanislavsky's was intended as a drastic remedy for actors suffering from over-production. For years it was he who had done the actors' thinking and feeling for them. (I have been told by someone who saw many performances at the Art Theatre during its early years that it was not unusual for a leading part to be shared by two actors. Both of them would be rehearsed by Stanislavsky with equal care, and it was almost impossible to detect even the smallest differences in the two performances.) When, in *The Drama of Life,* Stanislavsky exhorted his actors to think and feel for themselves, the result had been mere splurgy emotionalism. These whispered rehearsals at least made that impossible.

A Month in the Country was a huge success with the public. At first sight this may seem a complete justification of Stanislavsky's methods, but one suspects that once again the success was largely due to the novelty of the production. Stanislavsky, in one of his letters to Gurevich, admitted that he had deliberately exaggerated his new method of production because he wanted "to force everybody to sit up and take notice of my system". Nevertheless, he did not seem to be sufficiently aware of the dangers inherent in the system. In his search for "inner realism" he was beginning to forget that there are two separate processes in the creation of a part. Feeling and understanding are not enough. The actor has got to communicate his thoughts and feelings to the audience, to project them to the last row of the auditorium. Stanislavsky seems to have convinced himself that this could be done by these mysterious "unseen rayings-out of creative will". But soon his actors, who had so often been praised for the clarity of their speech, were being accused of mumbling and whispering and giving under-developed performances. Stanislavsky's new-found dislike of movement and gesture deprived them of one of their most powerful means of expressing themselves on the stage. He seems to have been converted to this new theory of immobility with remarkable suddenness, as only a few months before he began rehearsals for *A Month in the Country* he argued with Gordon Craig on this very point in a conversation which is recorded at length in

Magarshack's book. "Why," he asked Craig, "do you think we introduce so many movements into Chekhov's plays? . . . We make the actors move about in order to force the audience to take notice and listen. And the most difficult thing in the world is to put two actors on the stage and make them go through their dialogue without moving. This at once becomes theatrical in the worst sense of the word." But perhaps as a result of this conversation Stanislavsky was converted to Craig's theory that "to transmute dialogue into movement is only possible on one condition, namely that there are as few poses and movements as possible".

Soon after the production of *A Month in the Country* Stanislavsky became seriously ill. He was away from the theatre for more than a year. During his absence rehearsals of Craig's *Hamlet* began, with Sulerzhitsky, who was Stanislavsky's assistant, as co-producer.

Stanislavsky's return to the Art Theatre was the beginning of a long period of disappointments and unhappiness. His first disappointment was Craig's *Hamlet,* which seemed in direct opposition to his own new belief that the producer and the designer should subordinate themselves to the actor. It had been agreed between them that the production was to be "as simple and as modest as possible". The simplicity which Stanislavsky envisaged was, of course, an imaginative simplicity, not just the reduction of scenery to bare essentials. "There was very much imagination and simplicity, yet the production seemed exceptionally luxurious, grandiose, affected to such an extent that its beauty attacked the eye and hid the actors in its pomp. The more we tried to make the production simple, the more strongly it reminded us of itself, the more pretentiously it displayed its showy naïveté."

An even greater disappointment to Stanislavsky was the realisation that his company were stubbornly resistant to his "system". One reason for this was that he still could not explain his theories clearly and persuasively. In fact his explanations were more bewildering than ever now that he had become interested in Hindu philosophy and had borrowed from it many words and phrases to add to the confusing jargon in which he strove to express his ideas. The actors might have been more disposed to try to understand him if his own acting had noticeably improved, but ever since he had started to expound his system his performances had steadily deteriorated. His own explanation of his company's reluctance to listen to him sympathetically was that most actors are mentally lazy. Although they are willing to rehearse until they are physically exhausted, they are not prepared to make the mental effort necessary to understand abstract ideas. Stanislavsky was trying to make acting a logical, mental process: but his actors preferred to continue to rely upon their instinct and their imagination. "The poor producer," Stanislavsky bitterly remarked, "must play for ten, sweat for ten, in order that the lazy mind of the actor may react to his desires for at least a moment."

He persisted in trying to put his theories into practice in spite of the hostility of the company. "My obstinacy made me more and more unpopular. The actors worked with me against their wills. A wall arose between me and the company. For years our relations were cold." Inevitably the productions suffered. Although Stanislavsky could not persuade the actors to approach their parts by the devious route advocated in his theory, he could at least put into practice during rehearsals his idea of breaking up a play into what he called "problems and pieces", each of which had to be studied separately. Leonidov complained that in the new productions at the Art Theatre it was impossible to see the play as a whole. "Neither the actors nor the producers seem to think about it. They are all following Stanislavsky's instructions that a play, a part, and a scene must be divided into small pieces, but they forget that Stanislavsky regarded such a procedure merely as a temporary expedient and that having worked on the separate pieces, these must be joined together." But surely it is unfair to put the blame on the actors. It was Stanislavsky who broke the play up into small pieces, and it was his responsibility to reassemble the pieces before showing the production to the public. The real trouble was that Stanislavsky, obsessed by his search for psychological details which would arouse what he called "superconscious intuition", was no longer capable of seeing a play as a whole. For the same reason his own performances became what actors call "bitty". During the last twenty-three years of his life he did not appear in a single new part. He lost all confidence in his own ability to create a character when Nemirovich-Danchenko, during the rehearsals of *The Village of Stepanchikovo*, took his part away from him and gave it to another actor. It was the part in which, twenty-five years earlier, he had achieved his first big success as an actor. This time Nemirovich-Danchenko told him bluntly that he had failed to bring it to life.

Four years before this episode Stanislavsky had founded another studio in order to practise his system with the younger members of the Art Theatre company. The acting in the productions of The Studio achieved great simplicity, reality, and depth of feeling. But The Studio's theatre was no more than a large room seating an audience of only one hundred and fifty, so the intimate atmosphere was ideally suited to the "inward acting" engendered by Stanislavsky's system. When some of the pupils at The Studio appeared at the Art Theatre, their performances seemed dim and shapeless because they were insufficiently projected.

Stanislavsky dreamed of transferring The Studio to the country. He was oppressed by the close, nervous atmosphere of the theatre in which every little grievance and misunderstanding is exaggerated and dramatised. He believed that if the actors met not only in the theatre but got out into the air and the sunlight and worked together on the land it would help to create a deeper unity among them. In the winter they would rehearse and give their performances, in the summer they would farm. When they had gathered the harvest they would return to the theatre until it was time for spring sowing. A country house would be found large enough to accommodate the audience as well as the actors. A ticket for the theatre would include a room for the night. Stanislavsky envisaged the audience arriving long before the performance. "After they had walked in the park, rested, dined, and shaken the dust of the city from their shoulders they would enter the theatre with cleansed and purified souls." A large tract of land was acquired in the Crimea on the shores of the Black Sea, and for three years a group of young actors from The Studio went there each summer to prepare the land for the buildings which had been planned. These included, besides the theatre, a small hotel, barns, stables, and cowsheds. Each actor was to build his own house by the work of his own hands, and it would then become his own property. The outbreak of war in 1914 put an end to the scheme. Whether it was a good scheme is doubtful. Stanislavsky dreamed of creating "a spiritual order of actors who could worship in a theatre as in a temple"; but acting requires a wider knowledge of human nature than can be acquired by actors living in a community of their own, secluded from the rest of the world. At this time Stanislavsky believed that the actor could find all that he needed for his art within his own soul, if only he would search long enough and deep enough.

During the war years the Art Theatre was deprived of many of its actors and it was difficult to cast new productions properly. Then came the Revolution. Stanislavsky, with great courage and integrity, refused to allow his stage to become a platform for spreading propaganda—"for the simple reason that the slightest utilitarian purpose or tendency brought into the realm of pure art, kills art instantly". He concentrated his energies on training the young actors at The Studio. In 1918, at the request of the government, he founded an opera studio attached to the Bolshoi Theatre. In 1920 he produced Byron's *Cain* after one hundred and sixty rehearsals. The play failed, perhaps because of its religious flavour and because the acting of the Art Theatre company was too subtle for the new audience accustomed to the crude, deliberately over-simplified characterisation in the Soviet theatres. The Art Theatre was attacked as "reactionary and academic". Stanislavsky obstinately refused to produce any of the plays by the new Soviet dramatists. He could find nothing in them for the art of the actor. There were only two sorts of characters—good and bad. The good were very, very good, and as for the bad, they were horrid. The following year he produced *The Government Inspector,* which was more to the taste of the Soviet audiences, but he was angrily criticised for "failing to make sufficiently plain the message of the play".

Stanislavsky could find nothing to admire in the Soviet theatre at this time. The official edict was that everything— characterisation, ideas, emotions—should be reduced to the simplest possible terms for the sake of the new audiences, many of them completely illiterate. What this amounted to was a command to the actors to over-act, to abandon all subtleties of characterisation and feeling, to return to the old, crude, melo- dramatic style of acting. Stanislavsky believed that the mission of the Art Theatre was to maintain a standard of acting which the actors in other theatres might attempt to emulate when the first excesses of the revolution had abated. But some of his own company were being influenced by the enthusiasm with which the audiences in the Soviet theatres acclaimed the orgies of over-acting. He realised that he must take his company out of Russia for a while. In 1922 they left for a tour of Europe and America which lasted two years.

When Stanislavsky returned to Russia he had decided that the Art Theatre must to some extent adapt itself to suit the mentality of the new audiences. He produced Ostrovsky's *The Ardent Heart* in bold, sweeping strokes, stressing the melo- drama of the play, emphasising the satire, and enlivening the comic scenes with tricks borrowed from vaudeville. The characters were vigorously outlined and highly coloured. There were no half-tones, no subtleties. But there were none of the crudities and exaggerations of the Soviet producers. Stanis- lavsky had simply returned to his earliest style of production, giving every appearance of doing so with immense relish and vitality. But this was not enough for the Soviet authorities. The Art Theatre could no longer be allowed to avoid its propa- ganda duties. A Communist official was attached to the theatre with instructions to "purify the actors' ideology and stimulate production". The foyer and the greenroom were hung with graphs and diagrams showing the Art Theatre's part in the Five Year Plan. The repertoire had to include plays burlesquing the bourgeoisie and glorifying tractors, power stations, and the heroes of the revolution. "Productivity" was stepped up, so during the four years after his return from abroad Stanislavsky produced seven plays (four by Soviet dramatists) and five operas, delegating much of the rehearsing to his assistants. Work on his system had to be limited to an attempt to inculcate the basic principles. As a producer he let the actors exercise their own initiative to a far greater extent than ever before. He gave them the fewest possible instructions during the early rehearsals, taking great care not to impose his own ideas upon the actors. He waited to see what each one of them would bring to his part. If the actor's conception of a character was faulty, he sought to change it by hints and suggestions instead of offering him a ready-made solution to his difficulties. He took immense care over the rhythms and tempi of the production; but first he waited until each actor had worked out his own rhythms and tempi before he "orchestrated" the production.

At the beginning of 1929 Stanislavsky became seriously ill, and was absent from the theatre for a year and a half. During his convalescence at Nice he prepared the elaborate prompt copy for a production of *Othello* on which he had been working when he was taken ill. He never saw the production which was put on before his return to the theatre and lasted for only ten performances. His notes for this production have been published in an English translation. They show that he had returned to the old style of Shakespearian production. In fact it all reads very like the description of a production by Beerbohm Tree. Magarshack explains this extraordinary old-fashioned production as being due partly to a wretchedly bad translation of the play which gave Stanislavsky no idea of its poetry, and partly to his admiration of David Belasco's lavishly spectacular production of *The Merchant of Venice* which he had seen in New York.

He returned to the theatre still a sick man. He was suffering from an incurable heart disease and had to have a nurse with him for the rest of his life. In 1932 he produced Gogol's *Dead Souls* in his early realistic style after rehearsing it for a year and a half. Even then he was only with difficulty persuaded to allow it to be put on, as he considered it was still far from finished. Another serious heart attack kept him away from the theatre for many months, but he returned at the beginning of 1933 for the celebration of his seventieth birthday. By this time (due, it is said, to the personal intervention of Stalin) the Art Theatre had been relieved of its Communist overseer and allowed to return to producing plays by the pre-revolutionary authors, but the theatre had been renamed The Gorki Art Theatre by order of the government. Lunarcharski, the Minister of Education, who spoke at the birthday celebrations, obviously regretted that he was not allowed to use the Art Theatre as an instrument of propaganda. "How," he asked, "are we to turn this embroidered handkerchief into the banner of our class struggle?"

During the remaining five years of his life, in spite of the fact that he had to spend many months in bed recovering from recurrent heart attacks, Stanislavsky produced two operas and another play. The last production upon which he worked was Molière's *Tartuffe*, but he did not live to see it performed. In 1935 he founded another studio called the Dramatic and Operatic Studio. (The others which he founded had disintegrated during the Art Theatre's tour abroad.) All through these last years he was working on his third book, published in England under the title of *Building a Character*. He lived just long enough to see the page proofs which were brought to him as he lay in bed a few days before he died. On the title page of the book are these words of Stanislavsky's: "An Actor must work all his life, cultivate his mind, train his talents systematically, develop his character: he may never despair and never relinquish this main purpose—to love his art with all his strength and love it unselfishly."

5

SHAKESPEARE: SEVENTEENTH CENTURY TO GRANVILLE-BARKER

The history of Shakespearian production in the English theatre from the Restoration to the present day is mainly the story of the extraordinary ingenuity displayed by managers, producers, and actors in their endeavours to lend a helping hand to Shakespeare. In the eighteenth century the help usually took the form of calling in another author to "reconstruct" the play. When *Julius Caesar* was produced in 1719 it was described on the programme as "written originally by Shakespeare and since altered by Sir William Davenant and John Dryden". Davenant's "reconstruction" of *Macbeth* was so full of songs that Pepys thought it "one of the best plays for variety of music and dancing I ever saw". As *Measure for Measure* seemed to Davenant to be woefully lacking in comedy he imported into the play Beatrice and Benedick from *Much Ado About Nothing* to compensate for this deficiency. To *As You Like It* Charles Johnson added the Pyramus and Thisbe scenes from *A Midsummer Night's Dream* and entitled his version *Love in a Forest*.

In Edward Howard's version of *Romeo and Juliet* the potion proved less potent than Shakespeare had intended; so Juliet revived in time to clasp Romeo to her bosom and the play ended to the sound of wedding bells. Nahum Tate sought to popularise *King Lear* by saving Cordelia from death so that she could live happily ever after as Edgar's wife. Otway, considering it essential that "elevated tragedy" should have a classic setting, removed *Romeo and Juliet* from Verona to

Ancient Rome and renamed it *Caius Marius*. Garrick wrote into *Macbeth* a long dying speech for himself, but by the standards of those days his "judiciously pruned" version was unusually faithful to Shakespeare. Colley Cibber's adaptation of *Richard III*, which was preferred to Shakespeare's for well over a hundred years, was so drastically rewritten that more than half the lines were by Cibber, and a large proportion of those by Shakespeare were taken from his other historical plays. Edward Ravenscroft proudly claimed for his version of *Titus Andronicus* (re-entitled *The Rape of Lavinia*) that "None in all that author's works ever received greater Alterations or Additions". The prologue to Lansdowne's *Jew of Venice* describes it as Shakespeare's play "Adorned and rescued by a Faultless Hand", and goes on to assure the audience that although "The first rude sketches Shakespeare's Pencil drew, All the Master-Strokes are new".

In the nineteenth century there was a gradual return to Shakespeare's own texts. Managers began to advertise performances of the plays "Acted Entirely in Shakespeare's Own Words". But Shakespeare was still far from being allowed to have his own say in his own way. Now it was the turn of the producers and designers to replace the hack playwrights as improvers of Shakespeare. Although only Shakespeare's words were used, by no means all of them were spoken, nor were they always spoken in the order in which Shakespeare wrote them. The texts were cut and rearranged to avoid constant changing of the elaborate scenery that was now being provided for them, and to allow time for the interpolation of tableaux, processions, dances, crowd scenes and "panoramic illusions", such as Daly's "Reconstruction of the passage of Theseus's barge to Athens", a spectacle which Shaw thought "more absurd than anything that happens in the tragedy of Pyramus and Thisbe in the last act".

Nowadays we are very scornful about these interpolations by the nineteenth-century actor-managers, but we ourselves are by no means so guiltless as we seem to think we are. When, for instance, at the Old Vic in 1950 the producer introduced a chorus of dancing Illyrians into *Twelfth Night*, several times interrupting the flow of the play with their irrelevant galumphings, he was doing just what we so sternly admonish Tree for having done. When at Stratford-upon-Avon in 1948 *Twelfth Night* began, for the convenience of the producer and his designer, with the second scene, and then went back to the first, this too was the sort of vandalism for which we condemn the actor-managers. In the production of *Romeo and Juliet* during that same season, the crowd scenes, brawls, fights, processions and dances were so over-elaborated that the momentum of the play was constantly held up by these brilliant but irrelevant displays of production which dragged out the performance for three and a quarter hours in spite of the fact that more than three hundred lines were cut out of the play. In this production the scene between Juliet and Friar Lawrence was omitted for the old, bad reason that it took too long to change an elaborate piece of scenery for the sake of a single short scene.

Tree was not the originator of the style of Shakespearian production associated with his name. He developed and over-elaborated the methods of Irving, who in turn was following the example of Charles Kean. Had Irving chosen instead to continue the tradition established at Sadler's Wells by Samuel Phelps, the history of Shakespearian production in the English theatre might have been a very different story.

Charles Kean was the first of the Shakespearian pageant masters. He employed an army of supers, a troupe of dancers, a company of singers, a large orchestra and a host of "machinists". (One of the busiest moments for these machinists must have been at the end of the third act of *Macbeth*, where the instructions in Kean's prompt book are: "Hecate ascends into the air, the witches disappear, then the mist disperses and discovers A Bird's Eye View of the Island of Iona.") Needless to say, the plays were hewn to pieces to fit the scenery and leave room for the interpolated tableaux, pageantry, dancing and singing. So elaborate were these spectacles that at one time Kean, according to his own statement, was employing nearly 550 people at the Princess's Theatre during the 'fifties.

Phelps, on the other hand, was said to spend only a shilling for every pound that Kean spent. Between 1843 and 1879 he produced at Sadler's Wells thirty-one of Shakespeare's plays. His settings were simple but adequate. His main concern as a producer was fidelity to his author—"to follow the text and order of Shakespeare's scenes, with some few inevitable omissions, but with no alterations". He restored Shakespeare's *Richard III* to the stage in place of the Colley Cibber version; in his production of *The Winter's Tale* "nearly every word of the original text was repeated"; when he produced *Macbeth* the critic of the Athenaeum wrote that "for the first time for nearly two hundred years could a correct view be obtained by an audience of the play in its entirety, and never did its proportions come out more perfectly".

Phelps was still at the Wells when Irving put on his first Shakespearian production at the Lyceum in 1874. Kean had retired from the Princess's fifteen years previously, nearly ruined by the enormous costs of his Shakespearian spectacles. Yet Irving chose to become the successor of Kean rather than Phelps because he believed, perhaps rightly, that the public were not interested in the plays of Shakespeare except as a means of providing an exciting star performance and a lavish display of spectacle. Drastic surgical operations were performed upon the plays to make them fit this theory. Such was Irving's ruthlessness with the texts that Shaw protested in 1898 that "in a true republic of art Sir Henry Irving would ere this have expiated his acting versions on the scaffold. He does not merely cut plays; he disembowels them".

In fairness to Irving and his fellow actor-managers it must be remembered that it was a time when the standard of playwriting in the English theatre was so wretchedly poor that the public had become accustomed to going to the theatre because of the star rather than the play, and they demanded to see as much as possible of the star during the evening. Irving has often been gibed at for cutting the whole of the last act of *The Merchant of Venice* when he toured the play because Shylock does not appear in this act, but I have been told by an actor who was in Irving's company that this was only done because the provincial audiences were restless and inattentive during the final act. They were merely waiting for the moment when Irving would appear to take his curtain calls.

Even if an actor-manager did not think it necessary to cut the play to give greater prominence to his own part, nevertheless there still had to be cuts to make room for the interpolated scenes of pageantry, and because so much time was used up in changing the elaborate scenery. There were at least three intervals, and many long waits between scenes, filled in by actors taking calls and by orchestral interludes. Although more than a third of the play was usually dispensed with, what remained took well over three hours to perform. Tree's heavily cut version of *Julius Caesar* lasted four hours.

Still more barbarous than the cuts were the rearrangements of the text made in order to minimise the number of times the scenery had to be changed. In *The Merchant of Venice* it was not unusual to play all the early Venetian scenes consecutively; then the Belmont scenes were grouped together and played one after the other. In spite of the fact that much of the play was thus reduced to near nonsense, this "arrangement" was for many years regarded as the standard acting text and was still being used by the Benson company when I first saw their performance of *The Merchant*.

Sometimes a set was so elaborately realistic that it was immovable, so willy-nilly most of the play had to be performed in it, except for a few scenes which could be acted before a front-cloth. For instance, there was the famous garden which Tree provided for Olivia in his production of *Twelfth Night* at Her Majesty's. To quote a contemporary critic, "it extended terrace by terrace to the extreme back of the stage, with real grass, real box hedges, real paths, fountains and descending steps. I never saw anything like it for beauty and vraisemblance. The actors were literally in an Italian garden". But this critic was reluctantly forced to admit that "the disadvantage lay in the fact that once put up, this scene could not easily be removed, and it was perforce used for many of the Shakespearian episodes for which it was inappropriate".

But what happened to *Twelfth Night* at Her Majesty's was as nothing compared with the mutilations inflicted upon it by Daly. He began with the first scene of the second act—the landing of Antonio and Sebastian. "This rearrangement," explained one of the critics, "although it destroys all dramatic suspense as to the fate of Viola's brother, has the advantage of allowing the star (Miss Rehan) to enter after the audience is seated." To make things easier for the scene-shifters, the second scene of the first act was played next. Then the sea-coast scene was got out of the way and the Duke's palace was revealed, a fine, elaborate set—so elaborate that there it had to stay for the rest of the act. Daly got out of this difficulty by what one critic mildly described as "a bold rearrangement of the text". The first and fourth scenes of Act I were played consecutively as a single scene; then, after the curtain had been lowered for a moment to denote a passage of time, scenes three and five of Act I were joined up with the second scene of Act II, all run together without a break.

Compared with these "rearrangements", the actor-managers' interpolated scenes seem comparatively harmless. The most famous was the tableau depicting the signing of the Magna Charta which Tree inserted into *King John*. Into *Henry V* he introduced a troupe of singers and dancing girls to entertain the French troops in camp, and a procession of monks singing a requiem after the battle. To *Antony and Cleopatra* he added a scene of tremendous pomp and pageantry showing Antony's return to Alexandria. He cut out of *Richard II* the speech describing Bolingbroke's triumphal entry into London and gave the audience instead a scene showing the actual procession. The play ended with the walls of the dungeon at Pomfret becoming a transparency through which was revealed a tableau depicting the crowning of the new king. In Tree's production of *Macbeth*, Duncan was escorted to the door of his bedchamber by an elaborate procession including singers and harpists. When everybody had at last been got on to the stage, the assembled company sang a hymn, then knelt and were blessed by the King. After the procession had wound its way off the stage, the witches rushed on, cackling malevolently, and executed a grotesque pas de trois.

Another typical instance of how Tree used to spin out a scene for the sake of introducing irrelevant pageantry is described by Ernest Short in his *Theatrical Cavalcade*. "The revival of *King John* in 1899 brings to mind a vaulted state-room, with a throne upon a dais to the left. Noblemen in Plantagenet costume move quietly about the hall and, in answer to a trumpet-call, the Royal Guards march in. The ladies of the court follow, each with her page. Several minutes have thus been occupied, and then the King appears at the head of the stairs on the other side of the stage." Note that all this took "several minutes". No wonder that the plays had to be cut heavily to bring them within the length of an ordinary evening's entertainment.

There was so much music in the productions of the Edwardian era that Sidney Lee described this as "the musicoscenic period of Shakespearian production". The principal characters entered to music, made love to music, soliloquised to music, and died to music. Sometimes, instead of merely speaking a passage to music, they added a touch of variety by actually singing it. In *A Midsummer Night's Dream* it was considered a pretty device to have Oberon (always played by an actress) render "I know a bank where the wild thyme grows" as an operatic aria. Shakespeare having been somewhat sparing in his use of song, it was usually found necessary to enlarge the singers' repertoire by borrowing songs from other of the plays— which explains why in Daly's *Twelfth Night* when Sebastian and Antonio landed on the coast of Illyria they were greeted by a chorus of villagers singing "Come unto these yellow sands". Later in the play Olivia conveniently fell asleep in her moonlit garden so that Daly could bring on Orsino and a male-voice quartet to serenade her with "Who is Sylvia?"—which, of course, fitted very nicely when the first line had been changed to "Fair Olivia, who is she?"

Shaw, in his notice of Daly's *Two Gentlemen of Verona*, describes how "all through the drama the most horribly common music repeatedly breaks out on the slightest pretext, or on no pretext at all. One dance, set to a crude old-English popular tune, sundry eighteenth- and nineteenth-century musical banalities, and a titivated plantation melody in the first act which produces an indescribably atrocious effect by coming in behind the scenes as a sort of coda to Julia's curtain speech; all turn the play into a vaudeville. Needless to say, the accompaniments are not played on lutes and viols, but by the orchestra and a guitar or two. In the first scene the outlaws begin the act with a chorus. After their encounter with Valentine they go off the stage singing the refrain exactly in the style of 'La Fille de Madame Angot'. The wanton absurdity of introducing this comic-opera convention is presently eclipsed by a thunderstorm, immediately after which Valentine enters and delivers his speech sitting down on a bank of moss, as an outlaw in tights naturally would after a terrific shower. Such is the effect of many years of theatrical management on the human brain".

It would be unfair to the managers of the period to give the impression that all their music was, like Daly's, "horribly common". Most of the leading English composers of the time, including Elgar, Sullivan, Alexander Mackenzie, Edward German, and Roger Quilter were commissioned to write overtures, incidental music, and songs. It is an odd paradox that although the actor-managers seemingly had no respect for Shakespeare as a craftsman, little appreciation of him as a poet, and considered hundreds of lines in every play to be unnecessary and uninteresting, they nevertheless had an immense veneration for him as "Our National Bard", so nothing but the best was good enough for Shakespeare. Famous musicians were commissioned to write the music, famous R.A.s (such as Alma Tadema) were engaged to design the scenery, and large sums were spent on fees to well-known archaeologists and historians to ensure absolute historical exactitude in every detail of the production. Geographical exactitude was considered equally important, so much so that William Poel, in *Shakespeare and the Theatre,* published in 1913, offered the following advice to any manager about to produce a play of Shakespeare. "Choose your play, and be sure to note closely in what country the incidents take place. Having done this, send artists to the locality to make sketches of the country, of its streets, its houses, its landscape, of its people, and of their costumes. Tell your artists that they must accurately reproduce the colouring of the sky, of the foliage, of the evening shadows, of the moonlight, of the men's hair, and the women's eyes; for all these details are important to the proper understanding of Shakespeare's play. Send, moreover, your leading actor and actress to spend some weeks in the neighbourhood that they may become acquainted with the manners, the gestures, the emotions of the residents, for these things also are necessary to the proper understanding of the play. Then, when you have collected at vast expense, labour, and research, this interesting information about a country of which Shakespeare was possibly entirely ignorant, thrust all your extraneous knowledge into your representation, whether it fit the context or not; let it justify the rearrangement of your play, the crowding of your stage with supernumeraries, the addition of incidental songs and glees, to say nothing of inappropriateness of costume and misconception of character, until the play, if it does not cease to be intelligent or consistent, thrives only by virtue of its imperishable vitality."

In spite of the fact that the craze for absolute accuracy was carried to ludicrous extremes, it had on the whole a healthy effect on the theatre. It must be remembered that until the nineteenth century little attempt had been made to costume a play with any regard for time and place. Garrick acted Shakespeare in the costume of his own day, sometimes with the addition of a "period" cloak. As Macbeth he was dressed in the uniform of an English general in the reign of George II; his Lady Macbeth wore hoops and feathers. When he appeared as Aegeas in a play set in Ancient Greece, he was dressed as a Venetian gondolier, because he had heard that most Venetian gondoliers were of Greek origin. Talma is said to have been the first actor to appear in a costume which was historically correct. The audience (and the actors too) were deeply shocked because it was a Roman costume which displayed his bare arms and legs. Gradually it became usual for at least the principals to wear costumes which had some relation, however vague, to the period of the play. During the early part of the nineteenth century productions were usually dressed in an extraordinary jumble of costumes from many different periods. Under the repertoire system a large number of new productions were put on in the course of a year, some of them surviving for only a few performances, so it was seldom that a manager went to the expense of having a whole set of costumes specially made for a play. Costuming a new production consisted mainly of a rummage through the theatre's wardrobe. An exception was Kemble's production of *King John* in 1823 for which the costumes were designed (or rather, "faithfully copied from illuminated manuscripts") by J. R. Planché, an antiquary who was a close friend of Kemble's.

Charles Kean was the first producer to insist on absolute accuracy in every detail of production. By nature more of a scholar than a man of the theatre, he had, in his own words, "a sincere desire to convey information to the general public through the medium of refined amusement". His programmes contained long lists of the antiquarians, historians, and archaeologists consulted, the books, prints, and manuscripts which had been studied, the tapestries, paintings, and "monumental effigies" from which the costumes had been copied, the ancient buildings and "specific remains" which had been faithfully reproduced by the scene painters. The programme was also used to instruct the public in such matters as that "Mail is composed of iron rings and bosses sewn upon cloth or leather", and that "Parti-coloured woollens and cloths appear to have been commonly worn among the Celtic tribes from a very early period. Diodorus Siculus and Pliny allude to this peculiarity in their account of the dress of the Belgic Gauls; Strabo, Pliny and Xiphilin record the dress of Boadicea, Queen of the Iceni, as being woven chequer-wise, of many colours, comprising purple, light and dark red, violet, and blue." Information of this sort covered several pages of the programme and was much appreciated by a public which at that time was flocking to popular lectures on any and every subject, gorging themselves with facts under the delusion that they were acquiring knowledge. But one gathers from Kean's farewell speech at the Princess's that the critics did not always approve his scholarly methods of production. He sadly remarked that "in my presentation of *Macbeth* fault was even found in my removal of the gorgeous banquet of gold and silver vessels, together with the massive candelabra (such as no Highlander of the eleventh century ever gazed upon) and with the substitution of the more appropriate feast of coarse fare, served upon rude tables, and lighted by simple pine torches". When he produced *The Winter's Tale* he was much distressed by the fact that Bohemia has no sea coast, so he transferred part of the play to Bithynia and noted on the programme that "The scenes include vegetation peculiar to Bithynia, from private drawings taken on the spot". One of the critics described this as "surely the very ecstasy of accuracy".

After Kean's retirement from the Princess's there were for some years only a few isolated Shakespearian productions, all of them showing signs of Kean's influence. For instance, when in 1875 the Bancrofts put on *The Merchant of Venice* at the little Prince of Wales Theatre in Tottenham Court Road, they were "regretfully unable, owing to the smallness of the stage, to display to the public a sufficiently comprehensive representation of Venice and its architecture", so to make up for this deficiency lantern slides of Venice were shown during the intervals. The smallness of the stage did not, however, prevent the Bancrofts from imitating Kean's elaborate settings, even though it meant limiting themselves to a single scene for each act. This, of course, entailed an even more than usually drastic rearrangement of the play; yet Bancroft honestly believed that he had been exceptionally faithful to Shakespeare's text because "no syllable was altered, transposition of the text alone being necessary for my arrangement".

Meanwhile, the continental theatre had become equally obsessed with the craze for historical accuracy. When in 1881 the Duke of Saxe-Meiningen brought his company to England, with three Shakespeare plays in the repertoire, the public were pleased and flattered to find their taste for irrelevant historical detail confirmed by the example of this ducal management. But Chronegk, the Duke's producer, had a passion for literal truth which sometimes resulted in effects which seemed a little odd to the audience. For instance, when the Meiningen company performed *Julius Caesar* at Drury Lane during a later visit to London in 1891, some of the critics were puzzled as to why the clouds which during the Forum scene gradually veiled the view of the Capitol drifted across the stage only a foot or two from the ground. Chronegk, replying to a critic who assumed that the clouds had got a little out of control, explained that "it must be borne in mind that the Forum Romano, or Campo Vuecino as it is now called, is situated at a considerable elevation and that, therefore, the clouds which lowered and frowned upon Rome on the night preceding the death of Caesar must have been at a very low altitude to obscure the Capitol and the higher buildings of the city from view".

The exaggerated importance Chronegk attached to visual exactitude sometimes had a disastrous effect upon the casting of a play. When he was criticised for giving the part of Caesar to one of the most ineffective actors in his company he defended himself on the grounds that the part had to be played by the actor who bore the closest resemblance to Caesar. Ostrovsky, after seeing the Meiningen company, wrote in his diary: "It is quite sufficient if the scenery and properties do not violate the historic truth of the epoch represented—absolute faithfulness is in fact pedantry, but in the Meiningen company even Julius Caesar is nothing but a property. The first entry of Caesar among the crowd in the Forum, surrounded by his lictors, was very striking: the resemblance was amazing—you could not help feeling you were seeing the real, living Caesar. But the moment he opened his mouth, and all through the rest of the play, this languid and lifeless actor was more like some third-rate provincial schoolmaster than the mighty Caesar." So to Ostrovsky it seemed that what the Meiningen company presented were "not the plays of Shakespeare, but a series of tableaux vivants from his plays".

It is sometimes stated in histories of the theatre that the historical exactitude of Irving's Shakespearian productions was inspired by the example of the Meiningen troupe, but by the time they made their first visit to London Irving had already put on three Shakespearian productions at the Lyceum, with the correctness of scenery, costumes, properties and furniture all vouched for by a long list of experts. Irving did not, however, make such a fetish of accuracy as Kean and Chronegk. Sometimes he would sacrifice historical exactitude for the sake of theatrical effectiveness and distress his experts by insisting on substituting an "incorrect" colour more suggestive of the mood of the scene, or altering a costume to make it more characteristic of the part and less slavishly "in period".

Although Irving was not a good producer of Shakespeare, he was a superb producer of his own arrangements of Shakespeare. He used movement and grouping to compose a series of wonderful stage pictures which were always dramatically as well as pictorially effective. He handled processions, crowds, brawls, with immense skill and zest, but unlike Kean and Daly and Tree, he never interrupted the play to interpolate irrelevant processions or tableaux or song-and-dance scenes. He used music, scenery, lighting, and pageantry to enhance the dramatic effect of a scene, blending them together with the acting into a carefully composed ensemble. This was his chief contribution to the development of the art of production.

As a producer of Shakespeare he had a powerful and wholly beneficial influence on Shakespearian acting. He taught his actors to seek the inner nature of a part. He inspired them with something of his own genius for assimilating a character instead of just impersonating it. At a time when most of the parts in a Shakespearian play were acted as stock figures he insisted that they should be re-created freshly and imaginatively. This resulted in acting which was realistic in the best sense of the word, acting which was not just "natural", but was inspired by what Stanislavsky described as the inner-realism of the imagination. "Concentrated imagination is the quality in a player's mind which enables him to see, as in a picture, what the words mean before they are spoken. The picture goes across *with* the words, as it were." It was Irving who wrote that, but it could easily be mistaken for a quotation from Stanislavsky.

While Irving initiated what was later called "the psychological approach to Shakespeare", Tree on the other hand returned to Kean's mixture of pseudo-romanticism and historical realism. The link between Kean and Tree was the Bancroft production of *The Merchant of Venice* which Tree saw as a young man of twenty-two. Writing about it nearly fifty years later he said : "I do not remember since to have seen any Shakespearian production more satisfying to my judgment. It was the first production in which the modern spirit of stage-management asserted itself, transporting us as it did into the atmosphere of Venice, into the rarefied realms of Shakespearian comedy." He was also much influenced by the visit of the Meiningen company, especially by irrelevancies such as the fact that "the fasces, signa and vexilla were exact copies of antique originals", a detail which he admiringly copied in his own production of *Julius Caesar*.

A more important feature of the Meiningen productions which influenced Tree was their crowd work. The mob in *Julius Caesar* was not just a collection of well-drilled supers. Each member of it was played by a trained actor, produced as an individual; and each individual performance was then fitted, with infinite care, into the general pattern of the scene. Tree adopted this method in his own production with brilliant effect. It is unlikely that we will ever again see crowd scenes as fine as Tree's. Present costs make it no longer possible to employ a big crowd. Nowadays producers are expected to "suggest" a crowd oh-so-cleverly with a few supers and one or two of the understudies, or pretend that the audience in the stalls are the crowd—as happened in Guthrie's production of *Henry VIII* at Stratford when Buckingham's speech to the crowds watching him pass on his way to the Tower was spoken to the audience from an empty stage. Those who are always exhorting us producers to "let the audience use their imagination" may approve of this way of doing it, but I doubt if many members of an audience are capable of imagining anything so convincing as Tree's brilliantly produced mob, one hundred and fifty strong. Myself, I found Buckingham's speech in that Stratford production infinitely less moving than my memories of it in Lewis Casson's production at the Empire in 1925, when the emotional effect of the scene was intensified by the subtly directed acting of the crowd of citizens thronging the stage. It was Casson who produced what were probably the last great crowd scenes we will ever see in a professional production of Shakespeare when in 1938 he directed *Henry V* at Drury Lane with a company of nearly three hundred.

Today we are very scornful about the realism of Tree's productions, but in fairness to him we should remember that they belong to a period when the public demanded paintings in which "everything looked real", so naturally they were delighted with the huge, finely coloured pictures Tree showed them on the stage of His Majesty's, pictures in which everything not only *looked* real but often actually *was* real. We criticise Tree for not realising that Shakespeare's plays can succeed on their own merits without the assistance of all the scenic splendour he lavished on them, but we do not sufficiently consider what chance they would have had with the theatre-going public of that time without Tree's embellishments. He did great service to Shakespeare by re-establishing him as one of London's most popular playwrights. Whether or not we approve the methods by which he achieved this, we must in fairness agree with Tree's claim: "I am at least entitled to maintain that I have done my best to present the works of Shakespeare in the manner which I consider most worthy, and I feel a certain pride in remembering that, be our method right or wrong, we are enabled to give Shakespeare a wider appeal and a larger franchise—surely no mean achievement. Thousands witness him instead of hundreds. His works are not only, or primarily, for the literary student, they are for the world at large. Indeed, there should be more joy over ninety-nine Philistines that are gained than over one elect that is preserved."

Several of Tree's productions each drew an audience close on a quarter of a million, and even *King John,* one of the least popular of Shakespeare's plays, was seen by over a hundred and seventy thousand people. Tree produced fourteen of Shakespeare's plays. All the productions were kept in being and frequently revived. Each year the current production at His Majesty's was interrupted for the annual Shakespeare Festival, which opened on his birthday. There was a nightly change of programme, and as Tree's productions were on a vastly more elaborate scale than is usual in repertoire, these festivals were extremely expensive and arduous undertakings. The first, in 1905, was put on for only a single week. It consisted of *Richard II, The Merry Wives of Windsor, Twelfth Night, Hamlet, Much Ado,* and *Julius Caesar.* Each year the festival grew in length until eventually it lasted three months. Its scope was enlarged to include several guest companies. In 1910, for instance, it included Herbert Trench's company in *King Lear,* H. B. Irving's *Hamlet,* Bourchier's *The Merchant of Venice,* and Lewis Waller's *Henry IV.* There was also a guest whom one would hardly have expected to be invited. He was William Poel with his production of *Two Gentlemen of Verona* "in the Elizabethan manner", for which a large forestage was built out over the orchestra pit. It was typical of Tree's generosity of spirit that he should invite to take part in his festival some-one who for many years had been the most persistently hostile critic of the Shakespearian productions at His Majesty's.

William Poel was the founder of the Elizabethan Stage Society, which aimed "to give practical effect to the principle that Shakespeare should be accorded the build of stage for which he designed his plays". The society began its work in 1881, giving its performances in the halls of the City Companies and the Inns of Court, in the lecture theatre at Burlington House, at the St. George's Hall, and occasionally at one of the smaller West End theatres. These performances proved that the Elizabethan stage was by no means the awkward makeshift it was generally supposed to be—not a very surprising discovery when one remembers that the Globe was built by a syndicate of seven professional actors, of which Shakespeare himself was a member. On a fit-up stage which reproduced the essentials of the Elizabethan stage Poel demonstrated that if it was used as Shakespeare intended, with scene following scene in unbroken succession, and the verse spoken at a fair speed without pausing to interpolate so-called "traditional" business, it was possible to perform a Shakespeare play in its entirety in less time than it took the actor-managers to get through their heavily cut versions.

Unfortunately Poel's productions were not very persuasive examples of his theories. There was a determinedly "educational" atmosphere about the whole proceedings—"a certain rather morbid and inhuman solemnity" which gave the impression that the society regarded Shakespeare as a subject to be "worked at" rather than as a dramatist to be enjoyed. The makeshift platform stage was a bleak-looking affair, the hall was apt to be chilly, and the company, many of them amateur, were usually more earnest than talented. Poel was a scholar rather than a man of the theatre. As a producer he had little sense of the dramatic. His productions were flat and monotonous. He had no gift for teaching inexperienced players how to act. In fact he did not particularly want them to act. He believed "the less Shakespeare's lines are acted the more clearly is the poetry apparent: dramatic emphasis, pauses, facial play are all inimical to the music of the words". Poel regarded the actor primarily as an instrument in an orchestra. When he was casting he always had a very definite idea of the kind of voice he wanted for each part. If an actor had what Poel considered to be the right voice he did not seem to care much whether or not the actor fitted the character in appearance, in temperament, or in acting ability.

He began his rehearsals by "teaching the tunes" to the company. Every line was analysed as a series of musical notes. Then Poel would himself "give the tune" with deliberate exaggeration. The actor had to repeat it with the same exaggeration over and over again until it was firmly fixed in his mind. Only then would Poel allow the actor to speak the lines without exaggeration. All this took time. Usually from two to three weeks were spent with the company sitting in a room concentrating entirely on the music of the verse. The short time that was left for rehearsing on the stage was spent chiefly on arranging very simple moves and groupings while the actor did his best to characterise his part and deliver his elaborately learned "tunes" with an air of spontaneity.

There is no question that Poel had a remarkable understanding of how Elizabethan verse should be spoken. The trouble was that he taught his actors rather than produced them. Fortunately there were one or two young actors and actresses of great talent who occasionally worked for Poel and were able to absorb his teachings and translate them into terms of the theatre. Granville-Barker, Lewis Casson, Esmé Percy, Robert Atkins, Nugent Monck, Ben Greet, Robert Loraine, and Edith Evans all received their grounding in Shakespearian verse-speaking from Poel.

Unfortunately, less-talented actors were able to do little more than deliver the lines exactly as Poel had taught them, concentrating their minds on the task at the expense of acting and characterisation. William Archer, reviewing Poel's production of *The Tempest*, describes as typical of most of the acting "a curate-Ariel mechanically intoning his rote-learnt lines, with his eyes fixed on the ceiling, motionless, expressionless, like one in a dream". In another of his notices Archer points out that Poel failed to realise "that quiet recitation saves for the words their music at the expense of dramatic force, and that the best Shakespearian acting is a compromise between poetry and drama". Max Beerbohm, when he was critic of the *Saturday Review*, challenged the Elizabethan Stage Society's description of its productions as "acted in the manner of the sixteenth century". "Nothing," he protested, "could be more unlike it than the mild and selfconscious recitations of the amateurs who rally round the E.S.S."

It may seem unkind and unnecessary to repeat criticisms made against amateur actors fifty years ago, but it is important to realise the deficiencies of Poel's productions because they explained why for so long the significance of his work was so little understood and appreciated. Poel made the mistake of believing that Shakespeare can succeed on his own merits without any assistance from the actors. He failed to realise that one of Shakespeare's merits is the extent to which he relies on the actor as a collaborator. The desirability of playing Shakespeare uncut is difficult to appreciate when the playing is uninteresting; the dramatic effect of retaining his short, contrasting scenes and playing them in rapid succession in the order in which they were written is obscured and lost if there is insufficient feeling for the dramatic in the acting and the production; the advantages of playing on a bare, platform stage are not very obvious if the producer does not use the freedom it gives him to compose grouping and movement which is both pictorially and dramatically effective. So let us not be too hard on the critics and producers for failing to be impressed and influenced by "Mr. Poel's costume recitals", as they were sometimes rather unkindly described.

I hope I do not seem to belittle the importance of Poel's theories or the courage and persistence with which he continued to demonstrate them in spite of scant encouragement. I am merely pointing out that he was a poor advocate of his own cause. He had a strong case, but, because of his lack of any real sense of the theatre, he presented it tamely and unconvincingly.

Possibly it was as a result of Poel's productions that Benson in. 1895 produced *Hamlet* in its entirety for the first time since Shakespeare's day, playing the first half at a matinée, the rest in the evening. It may have been because of Poel's example that Forbes-Robertson gradually and cautiously restored many of the cut passages in his own Shakespearian productions and was the first producer to bring Fortinbras back into the final scene of *Hamlet* instead of dropping the curtain on "The rest is silence". Otherwise Poel seems to have toiled on for more than thirty years without having any effect on the prevailing method of producing Shakespeare. Then, in 1912, Granville-Barker produced *The Winter's Tale,* the first of three productions which translated Poel's work into terms of the modern theatre and revolutionised English Shakespearian production.

As a very young man Granville-Barker had played *Richard II* for the Elizabethan Stage Society at Burlington House in 1899. He had experienced the sense of intimacy between actor and audience which is made possible by the apron stage, and he had learned from Poel's productions how much the full effect of a Shakespeare play depends on unbroken continuity from scene to scene, and how simply this can be achieved on an Elizabethan stage. When thirteen years later he started to plan his first Shakespeare production he set himself to solve the problem of how the intimacy, speed, and continuity of Elizabethan stage-craft could be reproduced on the modern proscenium stage, and to what extent scenery and lighting could be used to enhance the mood of the play without interrupting the continuity.

He began by building in front of the proscenium at the Savoy a curving forestage extending over the orchestra pit. To light this forestage he installed, for the first time in an English theatre, a row of projectors along the front of the dress circle—a device which is now a normal part of the lighting equipment in all theatres. Most of the critics disapproved of these innovations. The *Morning Post,* for instance, thought the apron stage "a clumsy expedient, altogether unworthy of the ingenuity and resource of modern theatre construction. To say that it provides for quick changes of scene is merely to beg the question. A stage should be of sufficient depth and be fitted with the necessary revolving mechanism to enable one scene to be displayed immediately after another. The argument that there was some such stage in Shakespeare's day is nothing to the point. If that were any justification, it would be as logical to return to the equally primitive lighting effects of the same time. The projection of the characters on the apron stage is radically bad in more ways than one. It is artistically unsound. It is bad for the stage illusion, because the proscenium-line is thrown out and figures come into the auditorium, breaking down their fabled existence by intimacy of contact, and also showing details of make-up and the like that it is the province of art to hide. The apron stage also makes footlights impossible. Footlights are admittedly not a perfect form of illumination, but lights hung from the first tier are so obvious a device and throw such disturbing rays across the auditorium, that one cannot foresee any development of stage lighting on these lines".

Admittedly Granville-Barker's very modified form of apron stage at the Savoy was "a clumsy expedient". It is impossible satisfactorily to combine an apron stage and a picture-frame stage. They represent two utterly different kinds of stage convention. When the actor comes through the proscenium arch on to an apron stage he is literally "stepping out of the picture". Behind the frame of the proscenium he was part of that picture, remote from the audience in a world of illusion. Out upon the forestage he and the audience have to make a rapid readjustment in their relationship. The actor can no longer pretend to ignore the existence of the audience. The audience can no longer remain aloof spectators of the actor. Player and spectator have to come to terms with one another, far more real and intimate terms than when the actor was leading "a fabled existence" in the remote, make-believe world behind the proscenium arch. But when in the next scene he withdraws again into his picture frame, the relationship between actor and audience has once more to be hurriedly readjusted. All through the evening the audience are jolted to and fro between two separate theatrical conventions.

Granville-Barker did much to minimise this by not putting any pictures in his picture-frame. Instead, he used unrealistic, decorative backgrounds. The actor on the main stage was no longer a figure in a realistic scene, so when he came on to the apron he was not stepping out of a picture, although he still had to step out of the picture-frame.

Granville-Barker's three Shakespearian productions (*A Midsummer Night's Dream, The Winter's Tale,* and *Twelfth Night*) were designed by Norman Wilkinson and Albert Rutherston. The settings (Granville-Barker described them on the programme as "decorations") were mainly composed of draped curtains, but the effect was very different from the glum austerity which we nowadays associate with a curtain setting. They were of light, expensive materials, frequently silk, painted with formal designs which were variously described as cubist, futuristic, symbolistic, impressionistic, and sometimes as crude, childish, silly, and vulgar.

In *The Winter's Tale* the settings for the palace scenes consisted simply of white pilasters against a bronze-coloured curtain. The rest of the play was played in curtains painted with gay, formalised designs. Today such décor would seem quite unobtrusive, perhaps rather excessively simple; but *The Times* found it "startling, provocative, and audacious". Most of the critics, accustomed to the historical exactitude of Irving and Tree, were much bothered by the absence of any recognisable "period atmosphere" in the production. But if one is to produce *The Winter's Tale* "in period" one must first solve the problem of when Leontes ruled in Sicily. Seemingly it was at a time when the Delphic Oracle was still consulted and an emperor ruled in Russia—a difficult period for any designer to reproduce accurately. And to add to the designer's difficulties, the daughter of Leontes is cast away on the coast of Bohemia where a very English sheep-shearing festival is being celebrated by shepherds obviously belonging to the Warwickshire of Shakespeare's day. As the play belongs to no specified time or place, there was nothing illogical in Rutherston designing costumes belonging to no particular period or country. Granville-Barker hated the fusty colours and fussy details of the Shakespearian costumes in the Edwardian theatre's wardrobe, so he encouraged Rutherston to concentrate on line rather than detail, and to use pure, brilliant colours. To audiences accustomed to the cautious blending of dull, muddy tints, the boldly contrasting colours of Rutherston's costumes—vivid magenta, lemon yellow, emerald green, bright scarlet—seemed to clash violently with one another. The newspapers sent their art critics to the theatre so that they could trounce Rutherston for his "wilful and foolish disregard for some of the most elementary laws of art"; but P. C. Knody, *The Observer's* art critic, praised Rutherston for using "a palette of unprecedented daring", pointing out that "vivid colours set side by side without intervening passages of neutral colour are not necessarily inharmonious, though it is infinitely difficult to create harmony out of them".

The feature of the production most severely criticised was the pace at which the verse was taken. Judging from what I have been told by actors who were in the Granville-Barker production the speed was not, according to present-day standards, unduly fast; but it must have seemed a breakneck speed in comparison with the slow and ponderous tread of the Shakespearian actors of that time. Irving was notoriously slow and deliberate, and Tree often used to linger over his lines so languidly that the rest of the company had to slow down to a crawl so as not to outpace him. The *Morning Post,* while admitting that it was the fashion to declaim Shakespeare far too slowly, and to slacken speed whenever approaching a beauty spot so that everybody might have a good look at it, thought that the method adopted at the Savoy "not only obscured all the poetry of the verse but made it often difficult to catch the sense". On the other hand *The Daily Telegraph* reported that although certain passages were produced at "a fierce speed", only one or two of the company found it difficult to combine speed and audibility. *The Observer* praised "the substitution of natural human speech for the slow and tedious droning of blank verse". The *Saturday Review* thought the tempo of dialogue and action was admirable. "It varied dramatically with the play's rhythm—the rhythm not alone of the verse but of the play's procedure and emotion." But J. T. Grein, writing in *The Sunday Times,* thought the pace "so fierce that it would beat a hundred-horsepower car scorching on the Portsmouth road; one was benumbed by speed, hullabaloo, cacophony and sundry other features that would make a nightmare of this strange mixtum-compositum of some art, Maskelynic craft, witchery and wilful defiguration. No, indeed, I did not enjoy it".

Replying to these criticisms, Granville-Barker maintained that "all Elizabethan dramatic verse should be spoken swiftly, and nothing can make me think otherwise. My fellow-workers acting in *The Winter's Tale* are accused by some people (only by some) of gabbling. I readily take that accusation on myself, and I deny it. Gabbling implies hasty speech, but our ideal was speed, nor was the speed universal, nor, but in a dozen well-defined passages, really so great. Unexpected it was, I don't doubt; and once exceed the legal limit, as well accuse you of seventy miles an hour as twenty-one. But I call in question the evidence of mere policemen critics. I question a little their expertness of hearing, a little too their quickness of understanding Elizabethan English not at its easiest, just a little their lack of delight in anything that is not as they thought it always would be".

The most convincing evidence against the charge that Granville-Barker made his actors gabble is contained in the short prefaces which he wrote for the little sixpenny editions of the three Shakespearian plays produced at the Savoy. Each preface was written while he was at work on the production of the play, as the editions were intended for sale in the theatre. After reading these prefaces it is impossible to believe that Granville-Barker merely urged his company through the lines at a monotonous gallop. He stresses "the consonantal swiftness" of the verse, but he also stresses "its gradations sudden or slow into vowelled liquidity, its comic rushes and stops, with, above all, the peculiar beauty of the rhythms". In the preface to *The Winter's Tale* he wrote: "As I see it, the verse is complex, vivid, abundant in the variety of its moods and pace and colour, now disordered, now at rest, the product of a mind rapid, changing, and over-full. This is what I have sought to develop in my production." He goes on to examine the musical structure of the last scene. "From the moment the statue is disclosed, every device of changing colour and tune, every minor contrast of voice and mood that can give the scene modelling and beauty of form, is brought into use. Then the final effect of the music, of the brisk, stirring trumpet sentences in Paulina's speech, of the simplicity of Leontes's 'Let it be an act lawful as eating'. Then the swift contrast of the alarmed and sceptical Polixenes and Camillo, then Paulina's happiness breaking almost into chatter. And then the perfect sufficiency of Hermione's eight lines (Oh, how a lesser dramatist might have overdone it with Noble Forgiveness and whatnot!). It all really is a wonderful bit of work."

What is most interesting about the criticisms of Granville-Barker's *Winter's Tale* is not so much the violent division of opinion but the fact that so few of the critics realised the importance of this revival, or foresaw the effect it was likely to have on Shakespearian production in the English theatre. *The Times*, for instance, found the whole production little more than an amusing whim, amiably admitting that "we are as willing to be amused this way as another". J. T. Grein in *The Sunday Times* accused Granville-Barker of having "killed the spirit of Shakespeare and embalmed the body: what we have seen and heard at the Savoy merely made appeal to the clique that bestows its fetish on an 'artistic' management and claims rolled gold as unalloyed 22-carat. . . . It was an orgy of new ideas grafted on classic soil. That is why all the world will run to see it and exclaim in snobbist slavery 'This is the Shakespeare we want'."

The use of a modified form of apron stage was dismissed by most of the critics as a freakish affectation on the grounds that "it could only be a fancy article without the Elizabethan frame of mind in the audience which cannot be reproduced". John Palmer, writing in *The Saturday Review*, was one of the few critics who defended it, pointing out "how gloriously effective upon an Elizabethan stage are the soliloquies and the asides, whether vehemently declaimed full at the spectator or secretively breathed in his ear". He considered Granville-Barker's *Winter's Tale* to be "probably the first performance in England of a play by Shakespeare that the author would himself have recognised for his own since Burbage retired from management".

For weeks controversy raged between the upholders of the old convention and a small, enthusiastic band of reformers. "The strife is serious," declared *The Observer*. "If Mr. Granville-Barker should lose, the birth of the art of the theatre may be delayed for ten or twenty years."

Granville-Barker's next production at the Savoy was *Twelfth Night*. "The traditions of a lifetime have been torpedoed into infinity!" exclaimed the critic of *The Stage*. "Every accepted canon of stage-mounting has been thrown to the winds. And for what! The quaint simplicity of a child's Christmas toy-box." The usual method of staging *Twelfth Night*, with a huge garden for Olivia and a massive palace for Orsino, has been described earlier in this chapter. To Granville-Barker such scenery seemed completely out of key with the mood of the play, so he staged it in a delicate colour-scheme of light, fresh tones. Some of the critics were outraged because the graceful, twisted, barley-sugar pillars in the palace were painted pink and the trees in Olivia's garden were like the trees in a Noah's Ark. But *The Times* thought there was "no flaunting eccentricity, no obvious freakishness in Norman Wilkinson's simple, flat, conventional decoration running much to pinks and relieved by blacks". What *The Times* praised most highly in this production was its speed and liveliness. "It goes slick but not too fast. Though the people say virtually all that Shakespeare set down for them to say, they do not gabble it: they can all be distinctly heard. It is a most agreeable sensation to feel that for once you are listening to Shakespeare as he wrote."

The outstanding feature of this production was the characterisation. Granville-Barker brushed aside tradition and convention and sought for Shakespeare's own intentions. Much of *Twelfth Night* in those days was played as broad farce, but Granville-Barker refused to believe that Shakespeare intended Sir Toby Belch to be nothing but a drunken sot and Sir Andrew to be no more than a cretinous idiot. In Granville-Barker's production Sir Toby became a charming, amiable man of breeding, who was jovial in his cups, but never merely sottish; and Sir Andrew, without being made any less funny, was also allowed to recover his charm and breeding. At that time Feste was always played as a gay young man. But Granville-Barker realised that running through all that Feste says and does there is "that vein of irony which is so often the mark of one of life's self-acknowledged failures", so he gave the part to an actor no longer young, and Feste became a rather touching character instead of the conventional, irritating, hop-skip-and-jump jester. But it was in the casting of one of the smallest parts in the play that Granville-Barker most clearly revealed his method of discovering Shakespeare's intentions about a character simply by reading the play with care and understanding. Fabian in those days was always given to one of the youngest and least important members of a Shakespearian company, but to Barker it seemed that Shakespeare could not have intended Fabian to be a young man. He does not treat Sir Toby as his senior; he is the most cautious of the practical jokers in the play; and he has the courage and authority to speak out very plainly to Olivia at the end. All this seemed to indicate to Granville-Barker that Fabian was not a young man, but an elderly and respected family retainer.

A Midsummer Night's Dream was Granville-Barker's next production. It was criticised on the grounds that it was an incongruous mixture of styles. The palace of Theseus was comparatively realistic—a solidly built affair in black and silver. The forest scenes on the other hand made no attempt at realism, consisting simply of a backcloth, the lower part of it green, the upper part bluish-purple, spangled with stars. Trees were suggested by tall, draped curtains in shades of green, blue, and violet. In the centre of the stage was a mound covered in bright green velvet. Above this was suspended a large terracotta wreath of flowers in which lights were concealed. The two styles of setting were a deliberate attempt to achieve a contrast between the realism of the world of mortals and the unreal fairy world of the enchanted wood, which *The Observer* described as "august and dreamlike and none too exact and earthy for the mysterious gold-faced, gold-robed fairies". These fairies were the most controversial feature of the production. They were dressed in bronze-coloured tights and had gilded hands and faces. Granville-Barker sought to achieve an effect of strange beings from another world, remote from humanity, an effect which was intensified by their stylised movements. Nothing could have been more unlike the pretty, fluffy, skipping fairies of the pantomime stage than these bizarre figures, rather oriental in appearance, with their jerky, angular movements and their glistening, impassive faces. One critic thought they looked "for all the world like an odd lot of brass ornaments that had come to life". Other descriptions of them were: "nickel-plated sprites", "lacquered leprechauns", "peroxidised pixies", "tawny Hindus". For weeks a controversy raged in the correspondence columns of the newspapers. It was an argument without end. One either liked them or hated them. *The Times* summed up in favour. "The mind goes back to the golden fairies and one's memories of this production must always be golden ones."

Another complete break with tradition was the costuming of Puck. He was dressed in vivid scarlet with a huge shock of yellow hair garlanded with red berries. He looked, not inappropriately, rather like Struelpeter. But there was at least one feature of the production of which everybody approved. Granville-Barker swept away all the traditional clowning with which the play scenes had become encrusted. Bottom and his friends were presented as simple, earnest souls, desperately anxious to do their best.

It is extremely difficult to gather from the criticisms a clear idea of the merits and demerits of this production. Opinions differed even more violently than over the two previous productions. Many of the critics changed camps. Some of the sternest critics of the two previous productions found *A Midsummer Night's Dream* wholly enchanting. On the other hand some of those who had staunchly defended Granville-Barker up to now found this production altogether unsatisfactory. John Palmer, for instance, who had been one of Granville-Barker's most appreciative critics, thought that "though it be almost everything by turns and nothing long, it is never Shakespeare's *Dream*. It is the child of Mr. Granville-Barker's perfect sanity—that perfect sanity whose pitiless iron seems finally to have entered Mr. Granville-Barker's soul. I imagine that even those who do not resent Shakespeare being slaughtered to make an intellectual and post-impressionist holiday will find it rather difficult to endure the dissonance of the unharmonic intervals between Mr. Norman Wilkinson's unearthly vision in green and purple, Mr. Granville-Barker's entirely Gallic vision of Shakespeare's comic people and Mr. Sharp's old English music. The production as a whole is more like a battlefield than a collaboration".

Talking to those who saw Granville-Barker's Shakespearian productions one invariably finds that the quality that is most vividly remembered is the air of freshness and spontaneity. Granville-Barker had the supreme gift of a producer: he could arouse and excite the imaginations of his cast. He made his actors forget all the traditional ways of playing the parts and think of them as if they had never been played before. His actors spoke well-known lines which had grown hackneyed as if they were being said for the first time.

Granville-Barker retired from the theatre when he was not yet forty. As a young man he had decided that when he reached middle age he would devote himself entirely to his writing. His retirement came earlier than he had intended because of the war. When it ended Granville-Barker felt little urge to return to producing for the year or two left of that part of his life he had planned to devote to the theatre. Bridges Adams in his essay on Granville-Barker entitled *The Lost Leader* tries to console us for our loss by arguing that the *Prefaces to Shakespeare* are a legacy more worth having than pieced-together memories of what Granville-Barker might have done had he remained in the theatre; but it is hard to believe that Granville-Barker's influence on the theatre would not have been infinitely greater had he continued to put his ideas into practice upon the stage instead of contenting himself with writing about them in his books.

6

SHAKESPEARE: A BREAK WITH TRADITION

In 1916 the tercentenary of Shakespeare's death was celebrated
by a Commemoration Performance at Drury Lane and a Shakespeare Ball at the Albert Hall at which society danced "Shakespeare Quadrilles" dressed as characters from the plays. That
was almost all the West End saw of Shakespeare during those
four years of war. But across the river he found a home at the
Old Vic. It was in October of 1914 that the Vic began to give
Shakespeare regularly on Mondays and Wednesdays ("Tues-
days: lectures; Thurdays and Saturdays: Opera in English;
on Fridays the Hall can be let for Concerts, Meetings, etc.").

I have read that the simplicity of the productions at the Vic
during the war years was the result of the influence of William
Poel and Granville-Barker. In reality it was not inspired by any
theories but enforced by sheer poverty. Nor was it quite the sort
of simplicity which either Poel or Granville-Barker would have
approved. The Vic's own particular theory of staging Shakespeare in these days appeared to be: "Use all the bits and
pieces of scenery you can lay your hands on and then fill in with
curtains." Three of the plays during that first Shakespeare
season at the Vic were produced by Matheson Lang, who
provided scenery from his own store—elaborate, solidly built,
realistic scenery in the Tree tradition. Miss Baylis forgot to
return it ("keeping it for just a few more weeks" was how she
herself put it) and henceforth pieces of it turned up in most
of the plays, mixed up with backcloths from the operas and
remnants of the old Victorian stock scenery. As for the

costumes, the Vic's wardrobe was scanty, so nobody could be too fussy about historical exactitude or mind if the periods got a bit mixed.

During that first season there were productions by five different producers; then from 1915 until 1918 all the plays were directed by Ben Greet. Accustomed to producing Shakespeare under difficulties, he was the ideal producer for the Vic at that stage in its development. For thirty years he had been touring his Shakespeare company all over England and America, playing mainly in schools. Whenever possible he performed in the open air—in a playing field or a quadrangle; otherwise in the school hall or the gymnasium. Under these circumstances he could not rely on scenery or lighting to help him in creating illusion, and his grouping and movement had to be of the simplest so that they could be adapted to stages of every size and shape. He had to recruit his company mainly from young and inexperienced actors and teach them how to capture and hold, under difficult conditions, the attention of an audience unused to playgoing, many of them seeing Shakespeare for the first time. His Vic company was headed by one or two players of experience, but the rest were just the best that could be obtained for a top salary of two pounds a week at a time when the shortage of male actors was so acute that eventually some of the men's parts had to be played by women. Greet taught the company to characterise their parts in bold outline and then rely on clear, vigorous speech and a strict regard for the scansion of the lines. It was as a result of Greet's work that for many years afterwards vigour and clarity were the keynote as of the acting and production at the Vic.

When the war ended it was left to Frank Benson to carry on the tradition of the old actor-managers. Forbes-Robertson had given his farewell performance at Drury Lane in 1913. Tree and Waller both died in 1915. The Benson company had been disbanded in 1916 because of the scarcity of actors, but as soon as the war was over it reassembled. Five months after the Armistice it was back at Stratford to resume the series of festivals which Benson had given there from 1886 until 1914.

Benson was a young man of twenty-four when he first went into management. At that time he was touring with a Shakespearian company which was finding it a hard struggle to keep going. One week there was no money to pay the salaries. Benson borrowed £450 from his father, took over the company, and continued to tour. When it ended he was the owner of a stock of scenery and costumes. Perhaps it was then he recalled a suggestion made by Irving after he had seen Benson's production of *Agamemnon* for the O.U.D.S. "Why do you undergraduates not band together, work, study, and become a company, the like of which this age has never seen? We have the technical skill upon the stage, we have the traditions; the difficulty nowadays is to get a company that has the literary mind and the trained intellectuality which is associated with university students."

The new company which Benson formed was largely composed of university men. In those days a public school and university education meant a classical education. A knowledge of Greek and Latin verse is not at all a bad grounding for the understanding of Shakespeare's rhythms—which was probably one of the reasons why the company spoke Shakespeare so well. Ivor Brown has said that Benson's greatest service to the English stage was that "he put poetry right with the middle classes. In England that is not so difficult: in England you can put anything right with the right-thinking man, even religion, if you mix it up with cricket and physical fitness and a healthy outlook on life". Benson was himself a fine athlete. He gained his running blue at Oxford and reached the semi-final of the All England Lawn Tennis Championships at Wimbledon. He expected his actors to be able to play games. The critics were fond of making good-humoured jokes about the athletic prowess of Benson and his company, but the grace with which the company moved upon the stage and the excellence of their teamwork was probably not unconnected with their skill in athletics. Max Beerbohm described the characteristic qualities of the company as "alertness, agility, grace, and physical strength". Writing about their performance of *Henry V* at the

Lyceum in 1900 he reported that "each member of the cast seemed in tip-top condition—thoroughly fit. Subordinates and principals all worked together. The fielding was excellent and so was the batting. Speech after speech was sent spinning across the boundary and one was constantly inclined to shout 'Well played, Sir!' and then again, 'Well played *indeed*!' As a brand of university cricket the whole performance was, indeed, beyond praise". But Max Beerbohm was not so impressed with the performance as a display of acting. Benson took his company through the play at a sharper pace than usual in those days. It seemed to Beerbohm that "everyone rattled along and bustled about and gave one the impression that he was a jolly, modest, high-spirited, presentable young fellow in private life; and there one's impression of him ended. The whole thing was very pleasant, but it was not Shakespearian acting. It had neither the sonorous dignity of the old school nor the subtle intelligence of the modern metropolitan school".

Benson, as an actor, lacked the voice and the temperament for many of the leading Shakespearian parts, but as a producer he had a genius for developing the talents of other actors. His productions were more notable for vigour than subtlety, but the verse was always spoken clearly, speedily and intelligently. His staging was unimaginative. The settings were in the realistic tradition of Irving and Tree but had none of the splendour of the productions at the Lyceum and His Majesty's. Nevertheless the amount of scenery was such that it necessitated the usual rearrangement of the text. On the other hand, as Benson did not interpolate crowd scenes, processions, and tableaux, he was able to give considerably more of the text than most of the actor-managers. He had no eye for pictorially effective grouping and movement. It was said of his actors that in making their exits they "backed and shunted like a South-Eastern train trying to get into Cannon Street".

During the years immediately after the war there was a reaction against the straightforward methods of Benson and Greet in favour of a more "psychological" interpretation of the plays. Unfortunately this was often achieved at the expense of attack, clarity, and good verse speaking. But it is impossible to generalise about the tendencies of Shakespearian production in the immediate post-war years. There were many influences at work. For instance, Tree's method was revived with much of its old splendour at Drury Lane in 1924 when Basil Dean, who had been Tree's assistant at His Majesty's, produced *A Midsummer Night's Dream*. The settings were elaborately realistic, including a vast palace scene reminiscent of Alma Tadema, complete with a grand staircase down which, Agate remarked, one would not have been altogether surprised to see Cinderella and her Prince and the Brothers This and That making their entrance for the finale. The ballets by Fokine were exquisite, but what with one thing and another, the performance lasted nearly four hours. A production in the same tradition was Casson's superbly spectacular *Henry VIII* at the Empire. The scenery and costumes designed by Charles Ricketts, although realistic, were much more imaginative and less slavishly archaeological than they used to be at His Majesty's. The stage blazed with colour and splendour. I still vividly remember the scene of the coronation of Anne Boleyn as one of the most magnificent stage spectacles I have ever seen.

When Casson in the following year applied the same methods to *Macbeth,* the result was much less successful. This production reproduced some of the worst faults of the old tradition. The play was constantly tripped up by the scenery. The many changes of elaborate sets necessitated the curtain being lowered twenty-two times during the course of the performance, and although *Macbeth* is one of the shortest of Shakespeare's plays, it lasted for nearly three and a half hours. This was the last production in the old tradition. It had finally proved the impossibility of satisfactorily combining an unabridged text with a series of elaborately realistic stage pictures.

Probably nobody was more relieved than Casson himself when the failure of *Macbeth* put an end to these spectacular productions. He had been persuaded into doing this production of *Macbeth* against his own inclinations by the management for whom he was working at the time. The enormous success of Ricketts's settings and costumes for *St. Joan* had suggested the idea of a series of spectacular Shakespearian productions starring the designer. Unfortunately Ricketts thought it did not matter if the audience at a Shakespeare play had to wait while a new stage picture was being got ready for them. "The audience *likes* a bit of a pause after a long scene," he used to argue. "They want to relax for a minute or two, have a chance to look at their programmes, listen to a bit of music." The argument did not convince the worried producer, especially as it was all against his own theories. As a very young man Casson had played many parts for Charles Fry who, at the St. George's Hall, used to give "Costume Recitals" of Shakespeare's plays for those who still did not think it proper for women to go to the theatre. The plays were acted without scenery in a permanent curtain set, with an upper platform at the back. From these performances Casson had learned how effective a Shakespeare play can be when the action is continuous. Then in Paris in 1910 he saw Antoine's production of *King Lear* which combined continuity of action with a certain amount of scenery. Antoine's method was to divide the stage into two halves by curtains. Most of the action of the play took place on the front half of the stage. The back part was used for setting small pieces of scenery, suggestive rather than realistic, which were revealed when the curtains were opened or looped up, not necessarily to their full extent. When the inset scene had done its work by establishing a mood or suggesting a place, the curtains closed while the scene was still in progress so that the next scene could be set. It was much the same technique as is now used in intimate revue when the actors come down to the front of the stage towards the end of a number and the curtains draw behind them while the scene is changed.

In 1912, a year before Granville-Barker's first Shakespearian production, Casson used this method when he produced *Twelfth Night* at the Gaiety Theatre, Manchester. It was what he described as a "mildly spectacular" method of producing Shakespeare without interrupting the continuity. But the action was not altogether continuous. As a concession to the "musico-scenic" style of production then so popular there were sometimes brief musical interludes between scenes, interpolations which were at that time considered essential in order to prepare the audience for the mood of a scene. When two years later Casson produced *Julius Caesar* at Manchester he abandoned music between the scenes and achieved complete continuity by using only a single piece of scenery—a large Roman arch which could be quickly and easily moved to different positions on the stage so as to give some slight indication of the changing locale. In 1923 Casson produced *Cymbeline* in London at the New Theatre according to the methods he had worked out at Manchester. The scenery was described by *The Times* as "more or less futuristic—mitigated by veils—and quite adequate". The stage was hung with curtains of different colours on a semi-circular track so that they could be moved to form various combinations of colour according to the mood of the scene. There was no attempt to suggest ancient Britain. Instead the play was transported to a fairy-tale land, an idea inspired by the fact that the story of the play is not unlike that of *Snow White*. The costumes had the bright simple colours of children's toys. The few small pieces of scenery, mainly rocks, were of the formalised design which in those days was usually described as "cubist".

Meanwhile several producers were working according to what they believed to have been Granville-Barker's methods. Some of the younger producers who had not seen his productions at the Savoy completely misinterpreted his ideas. They urged their actors through the plays at a headlong scamper, believing that they were thus achieving the speed of a Granville-Barker production, not realising that it was variety of tempo rather than mere speed which Granville-Barker advocated. They eliminated scenery and hung the stage with curtains in neutral colours, believing that in this, too, they were following Granville-Barker's example, though the drab austerity of these stages curtained in dull grey or blue had little in common with the decorative simplicity of Granville-Barker's settings.

Nigel Playfair, who had played for Granville-Barker at the Savoy, recaptured the real spirit of the Granville-Barker productions when he produced *As You Like It* in 1920. The text was uncut, traditional business was dispensed with, the speaking was crisp and lively, and the characterisation fresh and unstagey. The settings by Lovat Fraser were based on mediaeval tapestries and illuminated missals, but because of their brilliant colouring and formalised design they were described as "modernistic" and "cubist". Many people found they distracted attention from the script just as much as the elaborate realistic setting of the old days. The same criticism had been brought against Granville-Barker's productions and probably will always be made against any new form of stagecraft, which must inevitably at first seem over-obtrusive simply because of its novelty. I have been told by those who saw Poel's early productions that at first the lack of scenery was far more distracting than the over-abundance of it at His Majesty's.

The attitude of both the audience and the critics towards Playfair's production was a little puzzled and uncertain. *As You Like It* was included in the first post-war festival at Stratford and Playfair recounts that "when Mr. Flower, the Chairman of the Memorial Theatre Committee, was making his closing speech at the end of the festival, he was evidently somewhat at a loss to know what to say about us. 'What shall I say of *As You Like It*?' he asked the audience. It was evidently no purely rhetorical question; he hoped for some sign from them: a boo or a cheer. But no sign was vouchsafed unto him—they waited to hear what he had to say and I think he was rather at a loss."

When Bridges Adams succeeded Benson as director of the Memorial Theatre in 1919 he put an end to the tradition of cut and transposed stage versions. Now that the direction of the plays was no longer in the hands of an actor-manager there was no temptation to use cuts to give greater prominence to the leading part. The settings, which Bridges Adams designed

himself, were an effective compromise between the realism of
the actor-managers and the stylised decoration introduced by
Granville-Barker. They were imaginative and suggestive rather
than detailed. Meanwhile, at the Vic, Robert Atkins, who had
taken over from Ben Greet in 1918, was following much the
same methods. He simplified settings to allow rapid movement
from scene to scene, reduced cuts to a minimum, and maintained
the tradition founded by Ben Greet of clear, vigorous speech.
Atkins recruited a much better company than it had been
possible for Greet to command during the war years, so he was
able to combine clarity and vigour with more speed and in-
cisiveness than Greet could achieve. With only a fortnight in
which to rehearse each play there was no time for subtleties. It
was Shakespeare plain and unadorned, but never in the history
of the Vic has the standard of verse speaking been better, even
though it lacked the refinements of tone and tempo which might
have been developed with further rehearsal.

William Poel's influence was reflected in the work of Nugent
Monck, who stage-managed many of Poel's productions. In
1921 he converted a derelict warehouse in Norwich into a
theatre modelled on the Fortune. But the Maddermarket
Theatre is not an exact replica of an Elizabethan playhouse.
The stage has the balcony, the "study" under it, the canopy,
the middle stage and the exit doors with windows above, all
much as they were at the Fortune and the Globe; but the
acting area gives little idea of the spaciousness of the Elizabethan stage and the small apron is no more than a suggestion of
the great tongue which stretched out twenty feet and more into
the auditorium. Nevertheless, because of the smallness of the
Maddermarket (until recently it seated only 220 with room for
another 20 to stand) and because the side balconies overhang
the stage, there is the Elizabethan sense of intimacy between
actor and audience which enables the plays to be acted at a
speed which comes very near the "two hours traffic of our
stage" which, according to the Prologue of *Romeo and Juliet,*
seems to have been the approximate playing time of that play.
At the Maddermarket *Romeo and Juliet* given with a single

interval of ten minutes and with only a few lines cut keeps the audience in the theatre for only two and a quarter hours—one hour less than it took to get through the far more drastically cut version at Stratford-on-Avon in 1948.

In some respects Monck carried Poel's methods further than he himself did. For instance, Poel's productions did not have an unbroken continuity. Often he would deliberately make a pause of a few moments at the end of a big scene which had worked up to a climax. It was like the pause between the movements of a symphony. Monck, except for a single interval of ten minutes, achieves unbroken continuity. There is literally never a single moment when there is no actor on the stage. It is the actors themselves who draw the traverse curtains, often as they are speaking a line. To take a typical instance from Monck's *Romeo and Juliet*, the scene when Benvolio and Mercutio are searching for Romeo after the dance is played before the traverse curtains which draw across the middle of the stage. As they start to make their exit at the end of the scene, speaking their lines as they move, Romeo appears through the middle of the curtains watching them exit. As he speaks the line "They jest at scars who never felt a wound", he flings back the right-hand curtain, then strides across and flings back the other one. As he does so, he turns and sees Juliet on the upper balcony. The curtains are hung on large wooden rings which make it possible for them to be flung open in a far shorter time than it takes for curtains operated from the prompt corner to move on their tracks. They are not, of course, invariably opened or closed quickly. Sometimes, if the mood of the scene requires it, they are drawn apart slowly and gracefully by pages, but when that happens it is always combined with the speaking of lines so that no time is wasted.

In the London theatre several producers were influenced by Poel to the extent of dressing their productions in Elizabethan costume. This was an inevitable reaction against the historically accurate costuming of Shakespeare's plays from the time of Charles Kean onwards. And yet, after all, to dress the plays in Elizabethan costume because that is how they were dressed in

Shakespeare's day is merely the old passion for historical exactitude in another form. It suits one or two of the comedies well enough, but in the tragedies and most of the histories it is making things unnecessarily difficult for present-day audiences. The argument is that if the Elizabethans could make this effort of imagination, so can we. But once the audience of those days had imagined themselves into another period, the familiar contemporary costumes were no longer a distraction. In some ways they were a help. The audience could tell immediately from the costume of a character the class or profession or trade to which he belonged, whether he was rich or poor, master or servant, officer or private. But to a modern playgoer, watching *Julius Caesar* or *King Lear*, Elizabethan costume is an obtrusive and distracting form of fancy dress, so a double effort of imagination is needed to reach Ancient Rome or Early Britain via Elizabethan England. Even a comedy of Elizabethan life can be made more understandable and enjoyable today by discarding Elizabethan costume, as was proved by Peter Brook's production of *Love's Labour's Lost* at Stratford-on-Avon. The play was dressed after Watteau, which to a modern audience suggested the pastoral element far more effectively than conventional costuming could have done. Writing of this production, Peter Brook rightly maintained that "the producer must be able to discriminate between archaism and the essential living heart of the play—the poet's inner dream—for which it is his job to find theatrical correlatives. In my production of *Love's Labour's Lost* I chose Watteau because the style of his dresses with its broad, undecorated expanses of billowing satin seemed to be the ideal visual correlative of the essential sweet-sad mood of this play".

The logical development from Shakespeare acted in the costume of his time was Shakespeare acted in the costume of our own time. In 1925 Barry Jackson presented at the Kingsway Theatre H. K. Ayliff's production of *Hamlet* in modern dress. Before the first night it was generally regarded as no more than an entertaining stunt. The newspapers heralded it as "Hamlet in Plus Fours", "Ophelia in a Jumper", "A Jazz Hamlet",

"The Gloomy Dane with a Cigarette". But the first-night audience, expecting to be amused and pleasurably shocked, soon found themselves accepting the modern costumes just as easily as eighteenth-century audiences accepted Garrick playing Macbeth in the uniform of an English general in the time of George II, or Lear in black satin knee-breeches and a velvet coat. Hubert Griffith, in his notice in *The Observer*, gave a very fair description of the effect achieved by the producer. "We are quite simply at a little modern Catholic Court—say of Ruritania, say of any small Baltic kingdom. The King and his Ladies and Gentlemen, his secretaries and officials, wear evening dress or morning dress. The younger men from the 'Varsity, Laertes, Rosencrantz, Hamlet himself, show a predilection for tweeds. There is a sprinkling of uniforms at the Court. And that is really all that need be said on the matter of costumes. They are easy, natural, appropriate."

The importance of this production was not just that it was *Hamlet* in modern dress, but that it was *Hamlet* acted as a modern play. The costumes compelled the actors to reconsider the characterisation. They could no longer think of the people in the play as belonging to a world remote from the present. All the old conventional gestures, make-ups, and stage business had to be abandoned. The parts had to be visualised by the players as carefully and exactly as in a modern realistic play. Even more important than the effect of the modern clothes on the characterisation was their effect on the actors' speech. The clothes enforced a naturalism which admittedly entailed some sacrifices. Some of the declamatory passages had to be pruned, others had to be underplayed. Some of the music of the verse and much of its magnificence was lost. But never before had I heard Shakespeare's verse spoken with such directness and simplicity, or the sense of the lines made so clear.

Barry Jackson followed *Hamlet* with a modern dress production of *Macbeth*. He could not have chosen a play better suited to display the limitations of this method of production. Of all Shakespeare's plays, this is the one in which he seems to have taken most trouble to create a sense of period. It is a primitive, barbarous period, when people were intensely superstitious, dreaded the supernatural and saw portents and omens in even the most familiar sights and sounds. But it was not only for reasons of time and place that the modern dress seemed so utterly incongruous in this production. Much of the verse proved to be almost unspeakable in present-day costume. Hamlet survived the change of clothes because most of the verse he speaks is philosophical and reflective. He seldom indulges in rhetoric. But Macbeth is no philosopher. He is a poet who speaks passionately. His speeches demand to be declaimed. They cannot be reduced to the worried thinking-aloud of a khaki-clad general of today. Yet even in this unhappy production there were moments far more effective than I have ever seen them before or since. The Porter's scene, usually so tedious, was for once really funny, played by Frank Pettingell as a drunken Scottish butler. The modern clothes gave added poignancy to the murder of Lady Macduff and her son, who looked like a modern preparatory-school boy, and was much more real and touching than the conventional stage child of the ordinary production. Most moving of all was the scene in which Macduff received the news of the death of his wife and children. Dressed in an ordinary lounge suit, Macduff was able to play this scene with a naturalism profoundly touching. But there are few scenes in *Macbeth* which call for naturalism, and therein lies the explanation of the failure of this production.

Undaunted by the failure of *Macbeth*, Barry Jackson next produced *The Taming of the Shrew* in modern dress. This production differed from the other two in that it did not attempt to reveal merits in the play which had been obscured by conventional costume. Instead, it was quite frankly a joke at the expense of the play. It is a play so tedious and crude that it does not much matter what liberties the producer takes with it if he can mitigate the tedium. The chief amusement in this production was watching the ingenuity with which the producer made new use of old lines. For instance, when Curtis said "There's fire ready", she produced an electric stove, and "Come on, i' God's name" was addressed not by a husband to

his wife but by an exasperated Petruchio to the starting handle
of a battered Ford car. The wedding scene reminded one again
of how much a modern audience can miss because of their
unfamiliarity with the costumes of other periods. The contrast
between Petruchio's outrageous costume and the formal clothes
of the wedding guests is, in an ordinary production, never as
funny as Shakespeare intended because we do not know how an
Elizabethan bridegroom *ought* to look. The rest of the cast do
their best to help by appearing to be extremely shocked, but
these shocked looks had far more point and were far funnier
when Petruchio, dressed in a top hat, a red handerchief round
his neck, morning coat, highly coloured pullover, a pair of khaki
breeches, a riding boot on one foot and a patent leather shoe on
the other, was seen against a crowd dressed with the formal
correctitude of the guests at a fashionable wedding at St.
George's, Hanover Square. Another scene, far funnier than
usual, was the one in which Lucentio's servant, Tranio, dresses
up in his master's clothes. It is difficult for an audience watching
a conventional production to recognise class distinction from
the clothes, but in this production Tranio (played by Ralph
Richardson) was dressed as a chauffeur, so the audience immediately relished the joke when he appeared in a morning
coat and striped trousers, his top-hat at rather too jaunty an
angle, swinging his cane with too ostentatious a flourish, and
speaking in an assumed Oxford accent.

The Merry Wives of Windsor was the next play to be translated into modern dress. In this production by Oscar Asche the
translation was not confined to the costumes; lines were re-
written and interpolated. The play began with Pistol, played
as an old-time ham actor, reciting "Half a league, half a league,
half a league onward", interrupted by a small boy coming on
and yelling, "Get your 'air cut!" Falstaff, excited, shouting
"Taxi! Taxi!" Page's "fallow greyhound" was outrun at
Wembley instead of at Cotsall. Falstaff spoke of young men
who smell like "Piccadilly at closing time" instead of "Butlers-
bury in simple time". The Counter-gate was translated into
Billingsgate, the lime-kiln became a gas-sewer, and a pottle of

sack was changed into a jorum of rum. Shallow made his entrance in a bathchair; Parson Evans, dressed as a shabby little Welsh parson with a speckled straw hat and trouser clips, arrived on a bicycle; there was a monocled Slender; nigger minstrels outside the inn; Anne Page riding pillion behind Fenton on his motor-bike; and Robin the Page as a newsboy shouting all the winners. Mistress Page and Mistress Ford became Mrs. Page and Mrs. Ford, and planned the hoaxing of Falstaff over the telephone. It was not so much Shakespeare in modern dress as a re-dressed revival of one of the old actor-managers' versions of Shakespeare. The play was torn to pieces, much of it discarded, and the rest put together again with little regard for its original construction. The nineteenth-century trick of inventing "good curtains" was revived. For instance, at the end of one scene Falstaff bought an evening paper, scanned the Stop Press, threw it away in disgust, and replaced the Oxford favour in his buttonhole with the Cambridge colours which he produced out of his trouser pocket. In a desperate attempt to make the playwright's technique seem as modern as the clothes, the soliloquies were produced as one-sided conversations. The soliloquiser was always provided with one or two companions who did their best to display an intelligent interest in what was being said by means of nods, shrugs, laughs, and interpolated exclamations. As the whole point of a soliloquy is that it enables a character to tell the audience what he does not want any of the other characters in the play to know, this method of producing the soliloquies was utterly nonsensical.

Herbert Farjeon ended his notice of this production by proclaiming that it was the final defeat of the apologists for modern costume. "Their cause is lost," he wrote. "They have routed themselves. We shall soon be able to look back on all this as just an entertaining little spree that provided a lively topic of conversation in the later nineteen-twenties." Nevertheless, in spite of Farjeon's prophecy, there have been several successful modern-dress productions since then. For instance, in 1939 there was a modern-dress *Julius Caesar*, produced by Henry

Cass as a story of Fascist Italy. There is no garment which more effectively conceals the character of its wearer than a toga, which is perhaps why I remember the Casca of this production, bowler-hatted and carrying a neatly rolled umbrella, far more clearly than any other Casca I have seen. Nor can I remember a more interesting Caesar than Walter Hudd's nervous, dapper, bespectacled dictator, a hypochondriac constantly dosing himself from a box of pills in his waistcoat pocket.

A production in which modern dress made the aptness of the play to the moment all the more vivid was Michael Macowan's *Troilus and Cressida,* which opened the day after the announcement of the Munich Pact. When Thersites bitterly exclaimed: "A burning devil take them all!" he must have been voicing the thoughts of many of those in the theatre that evening. There was an almost embarrassing topicality too about the scene when the Trojans debate what is and what is not worth fighting for. Thersites was played as a down-at-heel embittered journalist in a filthy mackintosh with a cigarette end dangling from the corner of his mouth. Ulysses was a foxy old diplomat with a neat little pointed beard and gold-rimmed eyeglasses on a broad black ribbon. Pandarus reminded one alternately of Mr. Dulcimer in *The Green Bay Tree* and Mr. Douglas Byng. In the first scene of Act III Paris and Helen gave a cocktail party at which Pandarus sang his song accompanying himself on a white piano. It sounded so very much like one of those salacious ditties which were in those days being sung at all the night clubs that one of the critics took the producer to task for interpolating the song. The second scene of Act IV revealed Cressida in bed and Troilus dressing; then Pandarus entered carrying a tray with morning tea for two. The scenery did nothing to stress the modernity of the production. The play was produced on a bare stage with no more than the minimum indications of a room or a camp or a porch against the cyclorama. The debate in the Trojan camp was played round a dinner table, the young men in white mess jackets, Priam, very old, in a velvet dinner jacket.

Timon of Athens is another of the "Ancient Histories" which has been produced in modern dress. Barry Jackson decided to do it this way at the Birmingham Repertory because, he thought: "The play had a good deal in common with contemporary Birmingham"! He cut the play very skilfully and combined several of the small, uninteresting minor parts, mostly servants, into a single character who became the steward of Timon. Willard Stoker, who produced, says that translating the characters into modern dress was not difficult. "They became modern Athenian business men, or servants or soldiers—partisan rebels or the army proper. Apemantus was a rather weedy Clifton Webb sort of person, who was always doing crosswords. It seemed to fit the dry, embittered sage that he is. The play gained, to my way of thinking, because the audience were not bothered by having to think about the relationships of the various classes. They knew instantly who was servant and who was master—and they knew at once what the two camp-followers represented because we got them up as A.T.S. tarts—and had no complaints. With the aid of a constantly ringing telephone during the blackout we were able to make the important point that the house was besieged by creditors. For the second half of the play we decided to have Timon not in the woods but in a little hut beside a bomb crater outside the city. I remember there was a very bleak cut-out of a huge howitzer lying on its side; all very desolate. We took the production to Stratford one Sunday night and played it in the Assembly Hall at the back of the theatre for the annual conference of Shakespearian scholars. No scenery, just a rostrum between two staircases, a telephone, modern dress and some records by Ravel. The impact was astounding."

Much Ado About Nothing was produced in modern dress at the Bristol Old Vic by Hugh Hunt. I asked him why he had chosen to do the play in this way. His answer was: "Because *Much Ado* at the time I produced it had a certain fustiness about it, particularly in the provinces, where it was usually done by Shakespeare Societies in heavy Elizabethan dresses hired from a costumier, lacking the freshness that should be associated with this play; and because I considered the relationship between the soldiers and the girls important. There is a certain glamour attached to the arrival of Pedro and his army which obviously excites Leonato's household considerably. That glamour is largely lost today when we see them dressed in buff jerkins and those dreadful Elizabethan helmets which go up in front and behind, so that much of the romance of the play is dissipated. It was in an endeavour to strengthen the freshness and romance of this comedy that I chose a form of modern dress which was not too strident to clash with the text. The officers were dressed in Italian military costume which is in itself rather dashing; the girls were in long dresses of no particular period which relied on cut for their elegance. I think the play gained in romance, lightness, and in wit by being put into modern dress, but the treatment of Dogberry and Verges as air raid wardens was perhaps a little far-fetched. Leonato was dressed in a frock-coat and white waistcoat, somewhat in the manner of an Italian civil servant. His brother Antonio was dressed in a rather out-of-date officer's uniform. Some of the smaller characters, such as Ursula, were dressed in Sicilian costume. No attempt was made to introduce effective bits of modern business, other than the entrance of Dogberry on a bicycle, of which I am now a little ashamed. The setting was the courtyard of Leonato's house overlooking the Bay of Messina. This could naturally assume a fairly timeless quality and no attempt was made to modernise it. I think the sophisticated wit of Benedick and Beatrice showed up rather well against the romantic background of Sicily."

The most successful of all the modern-dress productions was the Guthrie *Hamlet* in 1938. I preferred it to the original modern dress production by Ayliff because the modernity of the setting and costumes was not stressed. At the Kingsway one's attention was often distracted from the play by aggressively modern touches, such as four members of the Court playing bridge, a jazz band playing offstage, Claudius mixing himself a whisky and soda, the sound of a motor-car drawing up outside the palace, Laertes carrying a suitcase labelled "Passenger to Paris". In Guthrie's production at the Old Vic, the characters wore uniforms or court dress whenever possible. The costumes and settings were more suggestive of Ruritania than of an authentic modern court in the late 'thirties. "It must not be thought," said *The Times*, "that this setting adds the spurious romanticism of popular fiction to the play; on the contrary, it is as if Ruritania were the invention of a consummate artist, for the poetry completely controls the scene and instantly checks every possibility of bathos." A particularly effective scene in this production was the burial of Ophelia. In the ordinary production it is always difficult for the producer to convey that this is a meagre funeral, with only such "maimed rites" as the Church reluctantly allowed Ophelia because "her death was doubtful". In the nineteenth-century productions of *Hamlet* this scene was usually made an excuse for pomp and pageantry. The Priest's inconvenient statement that "We should profane the service of the dead to sing a requiem" was cut, so that Ophelia could be buried with full choral accompaniment. But even when the producer attempts to achieve the right effect of bleakness, he is handicapped by the fact that the unfamiliar costumes of a past age inevitably introduce a note of pageantry. In the Guthrie production it was raining when they buried Ophelia. The little group of mourners muffled up in their overcoats and sheltering under their umbrellas from the rain made the funeral scene pathetically dreary and mournful.

In complete contrast to the discretion of Guthrie's production there was Geoffrey Edwards's modern-dress *Hamlet* at the New Theatre, Bromley, in 1952. Roy Walker's account of it in *Theatre* gives a good idea of the thoroughness of the producer's modernisation. "We start with an air-raid warning and wardens who shine electric torches in each other's faces while they talk. Claudius, apparently gifted with second-sight, breaks off his speech at 'Now follows that you know' to switch on a radio which obligingly delivers a news-bulletin on the Norwegian crisis. Ophelia is discovered in pyjamas and dressing-gown putting away a portable gramophone on which she has been playing crooner records. The Strolling Players bring on placards announcing themselves at the Wittenburg Dramatic Society presented by the Art Council of Denmark, whose production method is to set another portable gramophone in full view of the audience for the sound-effect of recorders. Hamlet, starting off in the same naval dress uniform as Claudius, dons an opera cloak for the 'inky cloak' of his first speech, making nonsense of the references to the mourning he is supposed to be wearing in contrast to the magnificence of the king and queen, and soliloquises while the dance band is playing in the ball-room offstage. Later on, his way of presenting 'the glass of fashion and the mould of form' is to slouch about in slacks and rolled-up shirt-sleeves with his tie loose and collar undone, even in the play-scene where everyone else is in uniform or evening dress: and he is practically a chain-smoker. Gertrude retires in what looks like a funeral parlour where she keeps framed photos of both her husbands on the dressing-table. Hamlet leaves for England by plane and announces his return over a telephone. Ophelia's desire to speak with the queen is announced by a Red Cross nurse with whom Gertrude has been packing first-aid boxes for the front, and at the end of the interview the Queen distractedly pours out tea for Claudius. Hamlet clubs Polonius through the arras with the butt of a pistol handed to him by Horatio at the end of the play scene, in which everyone fell over the chairs and Claudius pulled the curtain down. Hamlet and Horatio change into white flannels in cubicles while chatting to Osric, who is a fencing instructor in a gymnasium where he attaches cables to the belts of the contestants whose hits light up coloured bulbs and send off a noisy 'buzz-buzz'. The rest is silence but for another siren and the drone of Fortinbras' air-borne armada returning from Poland."

A production of *Hamlet* in dress which was modern but not as modern as in the other productions was Michael Benthall's "Victorian" *Hamlet* at Stratford. He had already done a doublet-and-hose production of the play at the New Theatre in collaboration with Tyrone Guthrie, but he felt that "what this fancy-dress style of production loses is the essential realism of the play and its truth for the present time". Rejecting the idea of yet another modern-dress production, he finally selected "a period near enough to our own to heighten the play's realism, and yet far enough distant to give scope for that picturesque romanticism modern life has largely destroyed. I chose the mid-nineteenth century, which would seem close to the audience, almost within living memory and recognizable to many through the photographs of their grandparents in family albums: and I set the play in a mid-European Court where the juxtaposition of crinolines, uniforms, and evening and levee clothes could create the atmosphere of colour and romance associated with royalty of the period. I hoped, in this way, to retain the grandeur of the tragedy without destroying the play's vital contemporary relevance".

On the whole the production very successfully achieved Benthall's intentions, though some of the critics thought Hamlet's frock-coat and narrow, strapped trousers too prosaic a costume for the part. This was the only production I have seen which gave the impression that the king had other matters to occupy his mind besides his family troubles. Seeing him in his study, seated at a handsome desk, surrounded by secretaries and officials, one felt he was a busy and efficient head of the state. Polonius, hurrying about with papers and documents in his hand, was plainly not just an idle busybody but an important palace official with many responsibilities. Perhaps the mid-nineteenth-century costume gave too great an air of respectability to the decadent Court of Elsinore, but, as Harold Hobson remarked, the Queen's opulently discreet costume gave especial point to her shocked modesty at some of Hamlet's less guarded references.

One of the most ingenious translations into modern dress was a naval production of *A Midsummer Night's Dream*. It came about as a result of the producer, Lieutenant-Commander Peter Osborn, reading an account of performances of *Hamlet* and *Richard II* given in the early seventeenth century aboard an East India Merchantman while it was being careened off Sierra Leone. "I had *Hamlet* performed aboard me tonight," wrote the captain in his journal. "This I permit to keep my people from idleness, unlawful games, and sleep." As obviously there was no means of obtaining stage costumes off the West

Coast of Africa, presumably the men performed the plays in their everyday clothes, perhaps borrowing a few cloaks and swords from the officers. So it occurred to Peter Osborn that it might be interesting to present Shakespeare to a naval audience of today in equivalent costumes, and try to show how sailors in the twentieth century would perform a play under limitations similar to those aboard that seventeenth-century merchantman.

So the play of *Pyramus and Thisbe* was presented as a humble but sincere attempt on the part of the lower-deck to entertain their admiral on the occasion of his wedding. Theseus, presumed to be F.O.I.C. Athens, was resplendent in a uniform heavy with gold epaulettes, gold "lightening conductors" (gold lace down the seams of the trousers) and an impressive display of orders and decorations. Hippolyta was a Director W.R.N.S.—the highest rank in the Wrens—while Hermia and Helena were two W.R.N.S. third officers. Demetrius was a lieutenant-commander and Lysander a major in the Royal Marines, his mess jacket providing a fine splash of red. Philostrate was a flag-lieutenant dancing attendance on the admiral and super-vising the arrangements for the wedding. Peter Quince, in charge of the lower-deck concert party, was an elderly, bearded chief petty officer. The costumes for their "most lamentable comedy" were exactly what would have been picked up on the lower-deck for such a performance. Thisbe's skirt was made out of coloured bunting flags and her wig from teazed-out rope. The lion wore a fencing mask covered with rope ends. His "skin" was very obviously a hammock with a bit of rope for a tail. Underneath he was wearing overalls, so that when he made his apologia ("I, one Snug the joiner, am") he pointed to the blue-and-white "chippy's" badge which a naval shipwright wears on his left arm. Bottom was a swaggering sailor in great clumping seaboots wearing a cutlass. Moon of course carried a ship's lantern and was followed by a real dog—the ship's mascot.

The Immortals, in contrast to the blue and gold of the Mortals, were in white tropical rig, with a fairy touch provided by red life-saving lights burning on their hearts—the little portable clip-on electric lights issued during the war so that survivors from a ship which had gone down could be spotted swimming in the darkness. Oberon was the grandest of grand Lord High Admirals in spotless white ducks. Titania was in white W.R.N.S. uniform, Puck in shorts and white singlet—Navy pattern, with square neckline and blue piping.

When Theseus arrived, Philostrate ran up an admiral's flag, a bit of business which was repeated by Puck on Oberon's entrance, but this time it was a fairy flag, filmy and diaphanous, with the anchor sideways—the flag of My Lords Commissioners executing the office of Lord High Admiral. Needless to say, for "the lion tongue of midnight hath told twelve" a ship's bell sounded eight bells. Apart from these two interpolations, the producer firmly resisted all the temptations to raise easy laughs by introducing extraneous business. What was most interesting about this production was that it made the characters and their relationships to one another absolutely clear to the naval audience (most of whom had never seen the play before) because the actors were costumed according to an order and a hierarchy which was perfectly understood by everyone watching the play.

At Stratford, Ontario, in 1953 Tyrone Guthrie produced *All's Well That Ends Well* in modern dress. "Who would have foreseen," asked Robertson Davies in *Renown at Stratford*, "that the Florentine maiden, Diana, and the Widow, her mother, would turn up in the guise of a Canadian keeper of a Tourist Hotel and her daughter? Yet how well it worked! The Widow with her eye to business, her specialisation in pilgrims bound for the shrine of St. Jacques le Grand, her protestations that she is of good family, though in reduced circumstances—we can place her in any part of Canada. In commonplace Shakespearian productions we are too often left in doubt about who is who. The social distinctions of the Renaissance are not familiar to us, and even distinctions indicated by costume may escape us. All Shakespeare's characters, unless they are clowns, are likely to speak in blank verse, which removes them from our ordinary standards of judgment. But in a modern-dress production we have no trouble at all in placing the characters. We see in what way this Florentine Widow differs from the Countess of Rousillon; the difference is approximately that between a woman who looks forward to the Old Age Pension and one who must make provision against the Death Duties. And when Diana at last appears at Court, in her charming frock, we can see at a glance how his frock differs from the gowns of the ladies to whom the Court is an accustomed place."

Guthrie followed this production next year with *The Taming of the Shrew* in modern dress—or, rather, as if it were taking place in California in the high-button boot period at the turn of the century. The Canadian critic Clifford Hulme described it as "a dazzling, side-splitting, rip-roaring, rootin', tootin' romp, compounded from a recipe that includes a pinch of *Hellzapoppin'*, *Annie Get Your Gun*, a Mack Sennett comedy, Charlie Chaplin's *Gold Rush*, the Marx Brothers' *A Night at the Opera*, a smidgem of ballet and of Mortimer Snerd—all this and Shakespeare too". Petruchio was a yahoo cowboy with a ten-gallon hat and a six-shooter, but bespectacled like Harold Lloyd. Christopher Sly looked like one of Walter Trier's hoboes. Here are some descriptions of the other characters taken from E. B. Radcliffe's account of the production : "Kate is a Lautrecan doll right out of the Moulin Rouge. She wears a billowy-sleeved yellow-and-white blouse, dark skirt, and a big floppy picture hat that's the epitome of grotesque elegance. Lucentio is the campus type, mandolin-club model with blue blazer, white trousers, straw sailor, and cane. (He sometimes acts like a refugee from a two-a-day vaudeville song and dance team.) Hortensio is the prissy dandy, in a pearl-grey single-breasted Brooks Brothers ensemble. Bianca reminds you of the little girl in white, blue-bowed, pinafored and straw hatted, in *Oklahoma*. Tranio has buck teeth, bangs, unruly cowlick, and wears white sailor pants (side pressed) and orange-and-blue-striped jersey. Vincentio is right out of a Steinberg cartoon; high grey-topped button shoes, striped trousers, a Hapsburgian velvet-collared box coat (pockets at knees), grey derby, pince-nez, and a big black cigar." Some of the critics thought the production reached an inspired level of ludicrousness; others thought it "more frantic than antic" in its efforts to translate the play into a mixture of circus and vaudeville. Even those who approved admitted that towards the end they began to feel exhausted by the spate of comic effects. "But at that moment," to quote another of the Canadian critics, "Dr. Guthrie is prepared for you. Suddenly he drifts into a passage of pure romance. On come the candles, down come the chandeliers, everybody is smart in black and white, and a banquet worthy of Camille is set up before your eyes."

In 1956 Guthrie returned to the Old Vic for a modern dress production of *Troilus and Cressida,* one of the least popular of Shakespeare's plays. A reason for this is that many of the characters are satirical versions of types instantly recognisable to the Elizabethan audience but unfamiliar today. What made Guthrie's production so entertaining and revealing was that he found the modern equivalent for many of Shakespeare's models. He transferred the play to a period approximately fifty years ago when wars were still regarded as romantic and heroic. The gay, Ruritanian uniforms of the Trojans emphasised their dissolute geniality in contrast to the stodgy correctitude of the Greeks, who were portrayed as arrogant Prussians. Ulysses was dressed as a German admiral, Agamemnon reminded one of Hindenberg. By dressing his production in this way Guthrie accentuated the most contemporory aspect of the play, Shakespeare's anti-heroic attitude to war. But much of the bitter satire of the play was reduced to farcical comedy. Helen was merely a floozie in a tango dress, Cressido no more than a frivolous wanton, Troilus a dolt, and the embittered Thersites, who provides the vitriolic commentary on the play, became a mean, shabby little gossip writer. I doubt if anybody unfamiliar with the play could possibly have realised from this production that there are scenes in which the verse achieves a tragic splendour. As one critic remarked, "All Mr. Guthrie's work seemed to have gone into movement, grouping, business, lighting. In the mere speaking of the lines the cast were left to sink or swim. Few of them could swim."

I doubt if anybody would today maintain that the modern-dress way of producing Shakespeare is the best way, but an occasional modern-dress production is a salutary tonic for producers, actors, and audiences. The importance of the modern-dress performances has been underrated. Much that was worst in the English tradition of Shakespearian acting was purged from the stage as a result of Ayliff's production of *Hamlet* and the other modern-dress productions which followed it. But Ayliff was not, as it sometimes claimed, the first producer to discard what used to be called "the Shakespearian manner". He was, in fact, reproducing, in a more obvious way, many of the theories which Granville-Barker had demonstrated thirteen years earlier. But the almost complete cessation of Shakespearian production during the 1914–18 war had minimised Granville-Barker's influence. When Shakespeare was put on the West End stage again after the war, most of the acting was old-fashioned and conventional. Ayliff, by putting his actors into modern clothes, was simply using a drastic method of forcing them to act Shakespeare according to Granville-Barker—to speak the lines directly, simply, and swiftly, to reconsider the characters without reference to the traditional methods of playing them, to abandon silly, musty business, to pay scrupulous attention to the exact meaning of the lines, to make no thoughtless gestures, to realise above all that the plays of Shakespeare are not just about people who lived in the past, with strange ways of speech and dress, but are about human nature, which, during the passage of the centuries, has changed far less than the ways of speech and dress. If the actors are fully conscious of this, it really does not matter much whether they play Shakespeare in ruffs and doublets or in collars and coats.

7

SHAKESPEARE: SINCE 1940

There is always the danger that a drastic remedy which cures a disease may have after-effects which bring about another kind of illness. So it proved with the antidote to the old style of Shakespearian acting provided by that first modern-dress production of *Hamlet*. The praise given by the critics to the plain, sensible manner of speaking the verse was interpreted as a licence to speak Shakespeare as twentieth-century prose regardless of the period in which the production was dressed. At that time the most admired acting was the seemingly casual, off-hand style of Gerald du Maurier. The younger actors were becoming obsessed by a fear of seeming "ham". They were busily practising the new technique of "throwing away" lines. So they needed little encouragement to reduce Shakespeare's verse to a mumbled prose.

At the Vic this tendency was for a time resisted. Andrew Leigh, who succeeded Atkins as producer, was an old Bensonian, and during his regime he maintained the Vic's tradition of vigorous, straight-forward speech. His successor, Harcourt Williams, had Gielgud to head the company and to set an example of fine verse speaking. It was when Tyrone Guthrie became producer in 1933 that the fashionable gabble was first heard at the Vic.

Guthrie has been the most powerful influence on Shakespearian production since Granville-Barker, but so far as the speaking of Shakespeare's verse is concerned his influence has been a dangerous one. Believing that most of the verse should be spoken "at the utmost speed of which utterance is capable", he drives his actors along at such a helter-skelter that much of the sense and most of the poetry is pounded underfoot in the headlong scurry and scamper. Because he rightly detests the old style of delivery in which the actors broke up the verse into far too many short phrases, he goes to the other extreme and irons out most of those tiny, almost imperceptible pauses which are essential to the proper phrasing of the music and sense of the verse. He is largely responsible for what George Rylands describes as "the pernicious modern practice in verse-speaking of 'jumping the points', of accelerating at the full stop and leaping the line-endings on the supposition that such licence counterfeits natural speech".

Although Guthrie delights in the sensuous appeal of colour and movement, he seems to find little sensuous pleasure in the music of Shakespeare's verse. Perhaps that is why, whenever he arrives at one of the famous speeches, he seems afraid that the audience will be bored by hearing it again. If one takes no pleasure in the music of the verse, then it is certainly a bore to hear once more what one already knows by heart. "You don't *really* want to listen to this all over again," Guthrie seems to say. "No, of course you don't. But I can't very well cut it, so I'll go through it as fast as I can, and meanwhile I'll provide some amusing stage business to distract your attention so that the speech will be over, quite painlessly, almost before you have realised it has begun." Watching a Guthrie production I have often felt the stir of anticipation among the audience as they heard the first words of a famous speech; and afterwards, as the actor flashed past the final line at a furious gallop, I have sensed their disappointment, cheated of the thrill to which they had been looking forward. I am not suggesting that the actor should linger lovingly over every line of a famous speech, but I do suggest that he should have sufficient confidence in it to try to give it its full value by speaking it as well as he can, speaking it as nearly as possible in the way he believes Shakespeare intended it to be spoken instead of either racing through it or cudgelling his brains to find some "fresh approach" which nobody has ever thought of before. The opera singer does not attempt to sing a famous aria in a way it has never been sung before; he simply strives to sing it better than it has ever been sung before. And that, I suggest, is what the actor should try to do with the "hackneyed" Shakespearian speeches.

Nowadays many producers of Shakespeare all too obviously consider that what the audience hears is much less important than what it sees. Their productions are often pleasurable to look at but painful to listen to. These producers are so busy with their groupings, their elaborate patterns of movement, their entertaining bits of business, and their ingenious lighting effects, that they have little time or inclination to give much attention to the delivery of Shakespeare's lines. The verse is spoken out of time and out of tune. Often it is difficult to make sense of what is being said, not only because the actors gabble but because in failing to follow the rhythm of the verse they continually throw the emphasis on the wrong word. It is the producers who are largely to blame for this. Most actors need all the help a producer can give them in the speaking of Shakespeare's lines. The fact that there are only two Shakespearian Companies in England means that few actors are experienced in playing Shakespeare; and at the dramatic schools too little time is given to studying his plays. At the annual public performances given by these schools the briefest item in the long programme is usually the single Shakespearian excerpt, and it is almost invariably the worst performed.

I have heard it argued that students should not be "taught" how to act Shakespeare as it is apt to result in a special "Shakespearian" style of acting. But that is precisely what is needed. Blank verse is an entirely different medium from prose, and requires an entirely different method of delivery—a statement so obvious that it would not be worth making were it not for the fact that many producers and actors seemingly do not realise this. To them blank verse is merely a more involved way of saying something which could just as well have been said in prose. "Blank verse is such a wonderful medium," said George Rylands in a broadcast, "because it can sing and speak; it can sing both high and low; it can speak both slow and fast; it can contract and expand. . . . But to many actors blank verse is blank verse and that is the long and the short of it. There are two things you can do. You can either go to the verse enchanted or you can cling to the word 'blank' and make it blanker and bleaker, transforming it into jerky and incomplete prose." Harold Hobson reviewing an Old Vic production of *The Merchant of Venice* in 1951 gave two typical instances of the second method—one player's "negative attitude of just letting the poetry go by" while another "positively hastened it on its way to oblivion with hearty kicks in the pants, running one line into another, and pausing where no pause should be, apparently with the deliberate intention of destroying rhythm and murdering metre". Milton Shulman gave an example of another favourite variation of this method when he described a leading player in a Stratford-upon-Avon production of *Troilus and Cressida* "delivering lines in monotonous bursts like a drunken machine-gunner who enjoys the noise but has no particular aim".

Too many actors are morbidly afraid of allowing themselves to enjoy blank verse because they believe it is full of temptations. They are afraid they will be mesmerised by its rhythms, fall into a sing-song delivery, take too much pleasure in the sound of their own voices. Admittedly that is what an actor is apt to do if his understanding of blank verse is limited to a vague idea that it is "poetic". Farjeon, reviewing an Old Vic production of *The Merchant of Venice* in the 'twenties, described a Lorenzo who "got going in the moonlight, apparently without any idea of the meaning of what he was saying, just carried away by a hazy notion that beauty is very beautiful, and all this must be beauty, see-saw, Marjory Daw, look at the patines inlaid on the floor". But there is no danger of the actor lapsing into this kind of delivery if the producer insists that the verse is spoken with proper regard for its sense and its rhythm. The two are, in fact, indivisible. In every line the rhythm guides the actor unerringly to stressing the word which makes the meaning plain.

The speed maniacs have a mistaken idea that faithfulness to the rhythm slows down the pace of the production. On the contrary, if an actor follows the rhythm of the verse he can speak it far more swiftly and sensibly than if he converts it into babbled prose. But although much of Shakespeare must be fleetly spoken, some producers seem to have the idea that *all* of it is scored to be taken at the same rapid, unvarying tempo. For a producer to begin rehearsals by saying to his cast "I want this play played fast" is about as sensible as if a conductor were to begin a rehearsal of a symphony by saying to the orchestra "Gentlemen, I want this work to be played presto". Shakespeare was far too good a playwright not to be aware that the deadliest danger in the theatre is monotony, consequently one of the reasons why his verse is so effective is because of its continual variation of tempo. The producer who ignores them wearies the ear of his audience. The Old Vic's two productions of *Love's Labour's Lost* in 1948 and 1954 effectively proved to what extent this play depends for its success upon its verbal music. The second production was played throughout at a hurried, monotonous tempo. But much of the enchantment of *Love's Labour's Lost* is in its languorous grace. There was no enchantment at all in this production. It plainly bored the audience. The reason may have been that the producer felt that Shakespeare's mockery of the "ambassadors of affectation", the fashionable intellectuals and scholastic pedagogues of the day, is incomprehensible to a modern audience, so the only thing to do was to race through the play as quickly as possible in the despairing hope that it would at least seem gay and lively even if it didn't make sense. When Hugh Hunt produced the play six years earlier he, too, was well aware of the danger of an audience being bewildered by its obscurities. In his book *The Director in the Theatre* he says that if we treat the speeches realistically the audience will abandon any attempt to listen to "such apparent gibberish". But his solution was not to scamper through the play. Realising that the play "requires much the same orchestration by the actor as does a symphony by Beethoven or an opera by Mozart", Hunt gave full value to its verbal music, its cadenzas and scherzos, its andantes and largos. The result was incomparably the best production he has ever done. Exquisitely grouped as well as beautifully spoken, it so entranced both the eye and the ear that one cared little about the shortcomings of the plot or the obscurity of the satire. This is one of the few Shakespearian productions of recent years which gave one all the sensuous pleasure which a good Shakespearian production should provide. But in none of his other productions has Hunt relied upon the verse to anything like the same extent. His *Romeo and Juliet,* for instance, was tremendously exciting because it captured the youthful impetuosity of the play, the flash and clash of warring passions, the seething excitement of a town torn by civil strife, but the speaking of the verse was dull and flat. It seems that Hunt is one of those producers who needs to have at least one actor in his cast who can demonstrate how the verse should be spoken. In *Love's Labour's Lost* he had Michael Redgrave, one of the pitifully small number of players in the English theatre who can speak Shakespearian verse as it should be spoken.

If producers appreciated not only the music of Shakespeare's lines but also the musical structure of the plays as a whole, they would be more hesitant about omitting or transposing scenes for no better reason than to make the play fit the scenery. Imagine a conductor beginning his performance of a Beethoven symphony by transposing the first and second subjects of the opening movement. Yet this seems to me no worse than what was done to *Twelfth Night* when it was produced at Stratford in 1948 with the first and second scenes transposed. The opening lines of Scene One ("If music be the food of love, play on") announce the theme of the play. Musically the verse is exquisitely attuned to its purpose, which is to establish a mood. Begin instead with the deliberately utilitarian verse of the second scene and the musical structure is at once shattered. The following season there was a far worse example of such ruthlessness in the production of *Troilus and Cressida.* In this play there is a long sequence of very brief scenes alternating between the political theme of the play and the love story. In order to make things easier for the designer and the producer, the political scenes were played consecutively, as were the love scenes, so as to avoid continually changing the elaborate scenery. The result was the monotony which was precisely what Shakespeare had avoided by going to and fro between two contrasting kinds of scene. It was not only the dramatic effect which was destroyed by the producer's rearrangement; it was equally destructive to the musical pattern of the play, which here depends on the alternation of the rhetorical verse of the political scenes with the lyrical verse of the love scenes. When the scenes were run together to make two large slabs, one rhetorical, the other lyrical, the senses were dulled by the musical sameness of the verse and the audience eventually found it an effort to follow what was being said. In this same production of *Troilus and Cressida* there was another rearrangement for which there could be no vestige of an excuse. The great speech of Pandarus which brings the play to its close was transferred in an abbreviated version to another part of the play, so that the curtain could be brought down upon a dumb-show battle scene invented by the producer.

Misplaced inventiveness has in recent years been one of the most common faults of English Shakespearian production. At the head of what T. C. Worsley calls the "Wouldn't it be fun (just for a change) school of production" is Tyrone Guthrie. A producer with a superb theatrical imagination, a master of pictorial composition, he can enforce the point of a line with a revealing stroke of business, heighten the tension of a scene by unexpectedly dramatic grouping, bring a small part vividly to life by imaginative touches of detail and extract an immense amount of fun from those scenes of comic relief which usually seem so drearily unfunny. But all too often his inventiveness is used not to enhance the author's meaning but merely to surprise the audience or to satisfy his own wayward sense of humour. His much-criticised production of *Henry VIII* at Stratford was an orgy of irresponsible invention. Often the hurly-burly on the stage so forcibly diverted the attention from what was being said that anyone seeing the play for the first time must have had considerable difficulty in making out what it was all about. In the court scene the scriveners sitting at a table along the front of the stage bickered among themselves, made shrill, squeaking noises with their quills as they wrote down the evidence, spilled their papers all over the stage and kept shoving one another off the benches. The pomp of the scenes of pageantry was deliberately and effectively dispelled by choirboys scuttling in late, still struggling into their surplices, by clerics who tripped over their robes, staggered under the weight of a cross, had streaming colds and suffered from impediments in their speech. The Bishop of Winchester was decidedly tipsy, and Cromwell was an agitated little man in a perpetual state of fluster and fuss. In the christening scene the Duchess of Norfolk, who was holding the child, let out a prodigious sneeze during Cranmer's speech prophesying a glorious future for the infant Princess Elizabeth. Cranmer himself was portrayed as a comical old ninny—an innovation which had a shattering effect on the play as a whole and necessitated the cutting of a scene which would have made it all too plain that the producer's conception of the part was completely different from that of the author.

Guthrie's occasional perversities would perhaps matter little compared with the brilliance of his best work were it not for the fact that so many other producers have sought to emulate his inventiveness. Sometimes this has resulted in new business which has revivified familiar scenes and characters without doing violence to the author's intentions. More often it has resulted merely in a dogged determination to be original at all costs, even at the cost of the play. Hugh Hunt, in his *Old Vic Prefaces,* complains that too many critics are "puritan zealots". He argues that audiences are over-familiar with some of Shakespeare's plays, so the producer's job is to "restore their magic. In doing this he knows the puritans will call for less production, but his task is to lead the audience to an enjoyment of the play. If he does this, and remains true to his author, he has succeeded". Nobody could reasonably disagree with so impeccable a definition of the producer's task, but Hunt himself by no means always remains true to his author. Often he seems determined to outplay Guthrie at his own game. Sometimes he takes an idea of Guthrie's and elaborates upon it.

For instance, when Guthrie produced *Twelfth Night* he gave us a youthful Malvolio, a grave, studious young man, very pathetic in the later scenes. Hunt, in his own production of the play, also gave us a young, studious Malvolio, but this time he was made a ludicrous figure of fun, played as a low comedy buffoon. To take another instance, in the Guthrie-Benthall production of *Hamlet*, Osric was made a prominent figure in the earlier court scenes, as a foppish sycophant hovering at the King's elbow. It was an admirable idea which enabled the actor playing the part to establish the character by the time he arrived at his one brief, difficult scene. Hunt very sensibly accepted this innovation, but elaborated upon it by changing Osric from a popinjay into a sly, saturnine figure, a sinister and dangerous accomplice of the king. This new version of the character was, I think, justifiable because Shakespeare's satirical portrait of a foppish Elizabethan courtier has little meaning for present-day audiences; but it would be hard to justify Hunt's treatment of Rosencrantz and Guildenstern as seedy, down-at-heel louts. Some easy laughs were raised from their unfamiliarity with court etiquette, but the effect on the play and some of the other characters was very damaging. It was difficult to believe in the shrewdness of a king who made these stupid bumpkins his accomplices, entrusting them with the treacherous mission to England. Hamlet, too, was reduced in stature by having them as his intimate friends. There is not the slightest justification in the text for playing them as comics. They are suave young courtiers, chosen as fit companions for the prince, "being of so young days brought up with him and since so neighboured in his youth and pleasure".

On the other hand this production was full of examples of how an imaginative producer can legitimately use his inventiveness to refresh and re-illuminate a familiar scene. For instance, the distant howling of the castle watchdogs which heralded the appearance of the ghost; Claudius stumbling from the throne room at the climax of the play scene and, as he passes the player who acted the poisoner, furiously striking him down; at the end of the play another magnificent stroke of invention when

Claudius, as Hamlet advances to kill him, takes the crown from his head and despairingly holds it high as the symbol of the divinity of kings. And it was a pleasant idea to have Laertes and Ophelia, in their scene with Polonius, mockingly but affectionately chorus his last lines as if they had heard that advice from him many times before.

Even the most far-fetched "new interpretations" by English producers seem very mild compared with Akimov's treatment of *Hamlet* at the Vakhtangov Theatre. He produced the ghost scenes as uproarious comedy. The ghost was Hamlet himself, dressed up in his father's armour and a false beard. The ghost's lines were spoken by Horatio, who intoned them into a pudding basin to make his voice sound suitably sepulchral. The idea was that Hamlet and Horatio had faked up the ghost as a means of inciting the people to revolt against Claudius. The king was played as a weak, insignificant little man. In his first scene he was having his portrait painted, and as he was too small for the royal robes they were supported round him on a framework from which he emerged to take a rest, dressed only in his combinations. Ophelia in her last scene was not mad but drunk, and she met her end by tipsily toppling into the stream on her way home from a riotous party.

Although it may seem a safe and sound rule for the producer to strive always to remain faithful to his author's intentions, in doing so he may sometimes end up by producing an effect on his audience altogether different from what Shakespeare intended, because the modern playgoer cannot be depended upon to react in the same way as the audience for which the plays were written. Take, for example, *The Taming of the Shrew*. The Elizabethans, who considered the spectacle of women being publicly whipped at Bridewell one of the best entertainments in the town, obviously saw nothing repellent in wife-baiting. But produce *The Taming of the Shrew* today as it was intended to be produced and we see it as a coarse, brutal, and dismally unfunny play. So producers exercise all their ingenuity to transform it into a gay fantasy or a hearty romp—just jolly good fun, never for a moment to be believed in. Michael

Benthall did a highly stylised production, making it as pretty a
piece as anyone could want to see, with enchanting scenery and
costumes, and exquisite, ballet-like movement and grouping.
George Devine conceived it all as being dreamed by Sly, not
as a nightmare but as a pleasantly ridiculous fantasy. Guthrie
pretended that the company of strolling players were having
great fun making up the sort of play which a drunken tinker
would like to see, an uproarious farce with everybody getting
kicked on the behind, Petruchio arriving at his wedding wearing red-white-and-blue corsets, and Grumio dressed as a clown,
skipping with a rope of sausages. Denis Carey's production was
a nimble, dainty frisk, but, as Milton Shulman remarked: "The
red blood of the play was drained away and replaced by eau
de Cologne." So long as *The Taming of the Shrew* remains
—for no good reason that I can discover—one of the most
frequently performed plays in the Shakespearian repertoire,
producers cannot be blamed for transforming the savage
humours of this nauseous and boring piece into something more
palatable to present-day audiences. On the other hand, it is
arguable that instead of fantasticating the play and decking it
out in every sort of gaily coloured motley it would be better to
drop it from the regular repertoire and give an occasional production of it played as Shakespeare intended it to be played.

Although *The Taming of the Shrew* is an extreme example of
the difficulties of reconciling the tastes of modern audiences with
a play written three-and-a-half centuries ago, the difficulty crops
up here and there in many of the other plays. One of the
reasons why *Macbeth* is today the least popular of Shakespeare's
major tragedies is because we are no longer fascinated and
horrified by the supernatural as the Elizabethans were. When
Komisarjevsky produced *Macbeth* at Stratford he decided that
the play would seem much more convincing to the audience
if they were not asked to pretend to believe in the supernatural
element, so the witches became old crones who at the beginning
of the play were plundering the slain on the field of battle, and
foretold Macbeth's future by reading his palm. What Macbeth
believed to be Banquo's ghost was his own shadow on the wall.

Instead of the visions being conjured up by the witches, they were presented as a nightmarish dream of Macbeth's as he lay tossing and muttering in his sleep.

Every innovation must be judged on its own merits; but we must be satisfied that the motive behind the innovation is a sincere one—an honest desire to bridge the centuries or a genuine belief on the part of the producer that his new way with a scene or a character is a sincere attempt at interpretation. What the playgoer has a right to expect is that every time he returns to a play there will be something in a performance to surprise him into a new appreciation of the familiar. Agate, in a notice of Gielgud's performance as Macbeth at the Old Vic, defined a good performance of a Shakespearian play as "recognisable by the fact that it arouses fresh shock at something which one knows so well that one takes it for granted—to each spectator his own shock, of course". Agate's own occurred not because of some elaborate ingenuity on the part of the producer but simply "when Macbeth came away from the murder carrying with incredible clumsiness both daggers as witnesses. To experience this shock is to believe in the murder, and this again is to believe in the actor".

The argument that audiences have grown so familiar with the plays that they must be startled into considering them afresh is a poor excuse for far-fetched readings and irrelevant inventiveness. Anyone so familiar with a play that he is bored by it should stay away from it and let it be produced for those for whom it has not yet become stale and unprofitable. The most important members of the audience at any Shakespearian performance are those who are seeing the play for the first time. These are the people the producer should have in mind all through his rehearsals. As for the playgoer who has seen the play many times before, he may be mildly amused or intrigued by the innovations which the producer thinks up for his entertainment, but these ingenuities will not help him to recapture the magic of the play. To take an instance from the ballet: *Les Sylphides* is given so often in the repertoire that after sitting through it innumerable times one despairs of ever again recapturing its first enchantment. Then one evening there is a performance in which one miraculously experiences once again all the old magic, not because there are any innovations or because there is a new and strikingly "different" backcloth, but simply because the performance is exquisitely attuned to the mood of the ballet.

The great orchestral conductors continually prove how unnecessary it is to have "a fresh approach" to even the most familiar masterpiece. Bernard Shore, who used to be the principal viola in the B.B.C. Symphony Orchestra, describes in his book *The Orchestra Speaks* how Toscanini would take a hackneyed piece and make it sound completely fresh, "much of it as though unheard before"—though remaining resolutely faithful to the score and the composer's tempi. "In no great music did he seek to impose his mind on that of the composer, but was always tirelessly trying to interpret with the utmost truth. In lesser works he allowed his creative powers more scope —not arbitrarily, but by making them sound like masterpieces." The final sentence of Shore's chapter on Toscanini might profitably be pondered upon by many producers of Shakespeare. "His crowning glory was the presentation of a work with such divine simplicity that it suddenly appeared in a new and fresh light—but, incredibly, only as the composer left it."

It is an ironical fact that although the more prankish producers protest they are only trying to make the plays more interesting to the audience, the public shows a marked preference for the work of producers who seek to give interpretations which are sincere rather than novel. Supreme among these producers is John Gielgud. He has what so many Shakespearian producers lack—confidence in his author. The distinctive feature of his productions is an affectionate appreciation of all that is best in the plays, a belief that if these are given their full value there is no need to attempt to surprise and intrigue the audience by doing something nobody has ever thought of doing before. When he experiments with fresh business it is to emphasise something already in the play, not to put in something new. Glen Byam Shaw's productions have the same virtues.

He made a poor beginning as a Shakespearian producer with *Antony and Cleopatra* at the Piccadilly Theatre in 1946, an awkward, often clumsy production, ill-phrased and badly spoken. His second production of the play seven years later showed that he had gained an understanding second only to Gielgud's of how Shakespearian verse should be delivered. The verse in *Antony and Cleopatra* is often extraordinarily intricate; a single sentence sometimes extends to eighteen or twenty lines; but in that Stratford production, for the first time in my experience, the phrasing of the verse made it possible to follow the play without having to make a continual effort to sort out the sense from a tangle of smashed and twisted rhythms. Glen Byam Shaw lacks the flourish which Gielgud can give to a production, but his work has more warmth and humanity. He does not highlight the dramatic moments as sharply as Gielgud, nor do his productions have the glittering vitality of Gielgud's work—a vitality which sometimes becomes too taut and nervous—but his touch is lighter and more graceful. His *As You Like It* had a lovely romantic quality. It was gay, tender, and charming, and equally graceful to the eye and the ear.

A very much younger producer who has already given us two superb Shakespearian productions is Peter Brook. He began with frisky-tricksy productions in the "*must*-think-of-something-new" style, obviously delighting in his own cleverness. He was hardly out of his teens when he was producing at Stratford, and although much of his early work was exhilarating, one often had a feeling that young Master Brook was skipping about in the wings gleefully exclaiming: "Oh, what a clever boy am I!" Then suddenly he reached maturity with his production of *Measure for Measure*. The presence of John Gielgud in the cast and his dislike of producers who indulge in exhibitionist caperings no doubt had a sobering effect on Brook. There was none of the irrelevant, dragged-in business which was a tiresome feature of his earlier productions. His only inventions were Pompey eagerly seizing upon every opportunity to distribute cards advertising Mistress Overdone's establishment, and the grim procession of prisoners shuffling through the hall of the gaol. Both innovations were entirely appropriate to the mood of the play. In this production Brook proved himself genuinely imaginative instead of just inventive. He vividly re-created the period in which the play takes place, not by obvious "period touches" but by playing it at the emotional temperature of the age so that its violence, its lustiness and ferocity of feeling became completely credible. Technically the direction was masterly, particularly in the way the drama and tension of the play were given their utmost effect by means of variation of tempo, the handling of the climaxes, and the use of sudden, boldly sustained pauses. Although visually the production was more dramatically effective than anything Brook had yet done, for the first time he had lavished as much care on what the actors said as on what they did. Here again the salutary influence of Gielgud was obvious. When a little later Brook produced *The Winter's Tale* with Gielgud in the leading part, he used, except in the Bohemian scene, the barest minimum of movement and gesture, introducing no business that was not absolutely essential to the action. T. C. Worsley, remarking that in its first and last acts this was the quietest and most straightforward Shakespearian production we had seen for some years, described it as "a production designed, so to speak, vocally not visually".

The success of this production must have startled those producers who seem to believe that a Shakespearian play degenerates into a mere recitation unless the verse is given a continual accompaniment of movement. Most Shakespearian productions are far too restless, the actors are always on the trot, there is too much scuttle and scamper, too much rowdy romping, too much fuss and fantastication. Agate, reviewing one of Guthrie's productions, was driven to protest that "the thing is after all a poem and not a mindless hop-skip-and-jumpery".

A producer whose early work was particularly strongly influenced by Guthrie is Michael Benthall. As a young actor he was produced by Guthrie at the Vic, and later was co-producer with Guthrie for the Vic's production of *Hamlet* at the New

Theatre in 1944. At first it was Guthrie's vices rather than his virtues which Benthall copied, so his early productions were marred by distracting movement, irrelevant and sometimes silly business, and small parts transformed into buffoons and grotesques. But nowadays Benthall rarely introduces anything into his productions which distracts attention from the play itself. "If he adds decorations," wrote Lionel Hale, "it is like a man putting diamonds round the neck of a woman—not to conceal it, but to enhance it, because it is beautiful and because he loves it." Like so many other Shakespearian producers he has been influenced by the ballet. (Farjeon once drily remarked that perhaps the reason for the Shakespearian producers' fondness for ballet is because it has no words.) But in Benthall's work this has not merely resulted, as so often happens, in self-conscious posturing and prancing. His knowledge of ballet is considerable. (He is the author of *Adam Zero* which used to be in the repertoire of the Sadler's Wells Company.) He uses his knowledge to compose lovely, formalised patterns of movement and gesture. His carnival scene in *The Merchant of Venice* was a wonderful, glittering swirl of movement, the entrance of the Prince of Morocco and his suite was enchantingly and stylishly executed, and throughout the production the lightness and grace of the movement gave the play an air of freshness, gaiety and romanticism.

One of the characteristics of Benthall's productions is the impetus he gives to the plot of the play. His production of *Macbeth* in 1954 achieved an extraordinary atmosphere of intensity, of mounting suspense and horror. The story became a tumultuous stream of events sweeping Macbeth frenziedly towards his doom. But what should be the background of the play—its barbaric violence, the shedding of blood, the atmosphere of the supernatural—was in Benthall's production the theme of the play. He converted it into a gory melodrama, seemingly oblivious to the fact that next to Hamlet, Macbeth is the most introspective of all Shakespeare's characters. The poetry was swept aside in the onrush of the physical action, the music of the play was lost in the clamour.

Benthall's chief contribution to Shakespearian production is his bold return to the pictorial setting. He believes that beautiful and elaborate settings are essential "to satisfy the craving for magic in every true theatregoer". If only he could be persuaded that in the theatre there can be magic in what is heard as well as in what is seen, what a wonderful producer of Shakespeare he would be.

He has his own theory of how Shakespeare should be spoken. He argues that "verse in the modern theatre has become divorced from realistic scene and character; it is no longer an accessory in the most vital contemporary drama. But for the Elizabethan playwright and actor it was the normal instrument of dramatic expression—as normal as the racy, clipped dialogue of a Noel Coward comedy to the actor of today—and instinctively they use it for its true and natural purpose, the revelation of character and the heightening of the play's dramatic effect. A return to this perfectly normal and unselfconscious attitude towards the verse seems to me an essential on the part of modern producers and actors if Shakespeare's plays are to attain their maximum effect in the theatre".

The obvious fallacy in this argument is that the dialogue in a Coward comedy is a reflection of everyday speech, but to the Elizabethan blank verse was no more "normal" a form of speech than it is today. A modern comedy is essentially realistic. Shakespeare was not a realistic playwright: however hard Benthall tries he will never succeed in making Shakespeare's verse sound "perfectly normal".

In the article from which I have just quoted, Benthall goes on to declare that "to treat Shakespeare's plays principally as vehicles for the verse is to destroy their vitality in the theatre; concentration on the verse at the expense of other factors is admirable at a poetry reading, but it has nothing to do with the theatre, the prime function of which is to stimulate, excite, amuse, or exhilarate an audience". Yes, but who wants "concentration on the verse at the expense of other factors"? Verse was Shakespeare's means of expression, and it is the "other factors" which suffer when the verse is not allowed to make its full effect. "Verse and prose were Shakespeare's sword and dagger," said Granville-Barker. "Let these rust or let them be ill-wielded, and no defensive armouring of a performance by scenery, costume, or even by well-thought acting will avail."

The visits to the Old Vic by the companies from the Bristol Theatre Royal and the Birmingham Repertory gave the audience an opportunity of seeing something which had long been lacking from the Vic's own productions—first-rate team work. These companies displayed that unity of style which it is impossible for a producer to create at the Vic with a company assembled for only a single season and working under several producers, each with his own ideas about how Shakespeare should be acted. Although *Henry VI*, which the Birmingham company presented in its entirety, is the most unfamiliar of all Shakespeare's plays, with an intricate plot and verse (much of it by other hands) which is often clumsy and awkward, the audience nevertheless had no difficulty in following the play because Douglas Seale's production kept the outline of the story bold and clear, with the sense of the lines always sharply pointed, though the speaking was swift and vigorous. This was an exhilarating production, acted with confidence, zest and attack —qualities which are difficult to achieve except when a company is well accustomed to playing together under their own producer, with whom there exists a mutual feeling of confidence and understanding.

Denis Carey's production of *Two Gentlemen of Verona*, brought to the Vic from Bristol, displayed all these qualities which make him so likeable a producer of Shakespeare's comedies. What was particularly attractive about this production was its warmth and charm, its unselfconscious gaiety, its light and lively sense of humour. It was a beautifully lucid production, easy to listen to, delightful to watch. When Carey produced *Twelfth Night* with the Old Vic company his work lacked the air of happiness and confidence so characteristic of his Bristol productions. The Vic company, unaccustomed to his method of rehearsal, seemed far less responsive than his own company to his delicacy of touch. He failed to evoke the lightness and gaiety with which he obviously intended the play to be acted, with the result that the comedy scenes were curiously muted, a little flat. His production of *The Merchant of Venice* at Stratford was far more successful. It was interesting to compare this with Hugh Hunt's very enjoyable production of the same play. Hunt throughout held it firmly on the line of high comedy. The Trial Scene had an unexpected gaiety. One felt that Portia was a mischievous young woman who thoroughly enjoyed dressing up and playing tricks of this sort. Her comic byplay with Nerissa made it plain that she thought it was all immense fun. Shylock was carefully produced so as not to conflict with the comedy, and any suggestion of pathos on his exit at the end of the trial was avoided by making him cringe and whine on the line "Give me my capital and let me go", thus re-establishing his nastiness. It was a production which deliberately made no attempt to take the story of the play seriously, presumably because Hunt thought it too familiar and too absurdly improbable. Denis Carey, on the other hand, courageously produced the play as if nobody had ever seen it before, treating the plot with the utmost care and respect. He restored the balance of the play by giving the parts of Antonio and Bassanio their proper prominence. When a production is centred entirely on Shylock the emphasis of the play is misplaced and the last act seems a trivial anti-climax. Carey created an extraordinary atmosphere of emotional tension during the trial. Although we in the audience knew what the outcome would be, he succeeded in forcibly reminding us that Portia and Bassanio and Antonio did not. The scene was produced as though everybody on the stage believed that Antonio was in desperate danger of being killed, holding their breath in their excitement, praying that somehow all would come right in the end. Bassanio was tortured by a feeling of guilt, he spoke with a lump in his throat, often he was near to tears. Because one felt that the chief characters in the scene were suffering an agony of suspense it was possible for Peggy Ashcroft as Portia to speak with a depth of feeling such as I have never heard before in this part. The ending of the play was a good example of the grace and humanity Carey brings to his productions. The lovers wandered away into the shadows of the moonlit garden in couples, hand in hand, absorbed in one another, until only Antonio remained: there was a moment's pause, he looked round, realised he had been left alone, gave a half-smile to the audience, a slight shrug of his shoulders, and walked slowly off, swinging his cane. It was a kindly, worldly-wise comment on the whole story.

Among all the conflicting opinions held by the producers on how Shakespeare should be produced there is one point on which they are nowadays in complete agreement. It is that nothing must be allowed to interrupt the continuous flow of the play from scene to scene. The most valuable and sincere experiments in Shakespearian production during recent years have been to find the best way of achieving this. It seemed for a time that the solution was the single, all-purposes, unlocalised setting, a frankly unrealistic composition of steps, arches, rostrums and balconies serving for both Venice and Belmont, Egypt and Rome, indoors and out-of-doors. This kind of setting provides equivalents of the Elizabethan main, inner, and upper stages. It can be varied by making slight rearrangement of the set pieces while a scene is played in curtains drawn in front of the set, and for the more intimate scenes the lighting can be concentrated on a small acting area leaving the rest of the stage in darkness. These functional "architectooralooral" settings, as Agate called them, rapidly found favour with the producers, not only because the play could move swiftly from scene to scene without interruption, but also because the various levels provided opportunities for strikingly effective groupings and movement. Some producers became so obsessed by the idea of having innumerable levels on which to group their actors that the sets became a confused clutter of platforms, stairways, and ramps. As the rostrums grew more numerous, they of necessity grew smaller, until the actors were often playing scenes perched perilously on a high platform of such inadequate size that the audience feared for their safety. In one of Guthrie's productions of *Hamlet* steps and stairs occupied so much of the acting area that the king and the queen were ignominiously obliged to sit on the bottom steps to watch the play.

Alec Guinness, who had clambered about these built-up settings in many Shakespearian productions, staged his own production of *Hamlet* on a flat, bare stage. "Rostrums," he protested, "apart from cluttering up the stage, tend to produce a one-foot-up, one-foot-down sort of acting which I find peculiarly dispiriting. I hold very few conversations on the stairs in my own house, and see no reason for making God's gift to the actor—a flat, square stage—into something like the entrance to the Athenaeum. I wanted a suggestion of reality here and there, and came to the conclusion that each scene should be played round, or influenced by, one or two specific real things; for instance the battlement scene round a Tudor cannon, the Polonius household a table with a globe and papers, the main Court scenes dominated by a large Renaissance classical doorway, and for the rest blackness and open wings." But as Guinness himself admitted in this article in *The Spectator* from which I have just quoted, the experiment was not a success. The groupings and movement became monotonous and undramatic. In most of his plays Shakespeare visualised certain scenes as being dominated by an actor in a higher and more commanding position than the rest—on the balcony of the Elizabethan stage. Unless the back of the stage is raised it is impossible for the producer to fulfil Shakespeare's intention.

The built-up, unlocalised setting is more helpful to the producer than the audience, who are apt to feel lost and bewildered in this never-never land of strange, jutting shapes, giving no suggestion of natural surroundings, where slopes and stairways lead nowhere in particular. There is, of course, the argument that Shakespeare did not demand realism, so these settings are the modern equivalent of the Elizabethan stage. But the Elizabethan audience saw the same setting every time they went to the theatre; they were so familiar with it that they took it for granted. Besides, there was nothing odd about it. It was not unlike the architecture of their inns and houses, and provided a passably realistic background for most of the interior scenes.

In an attempt to make the formalised setting more acceptable to audiences, producers began to add a few recognisably realistic features to the permanent set—a great doorway, battlements, richly painted curtains which could be draped in various ways to indicate different interiors. But this only made it all rather more confusing. As soon as any suggestion of realism was introduced the audience tended to associate certain features of the set with a definite locale, and were puzzled when the same doorway or stairway was used several times during the course of the play for altogether different purposes. Agate, reviewing a production of *Hamlet,* protested that so far as he could gather, Ophelia was buried in the middle of Gertrude's bedchamber, and I remember another production in which the audience were surprised to see a grave being dug at the foot of what they had hitherto believed to be the main stairs of the palace.

Gielgud and Guthrie, who were the first producers to use permanent built-up architectural settings in the English theatre, were the first to tire of them. Both found the most unsatisfactory feature of this sort of setting was that it necessitated playing a number of scenes before a front curtain while behind it furniture was changed and draperies rearranged. The narrow, shelf-like strip of space in front of the curtain made it impossible to compose grouping and movement which were anything but flat, repetitive, and undramatic. Guthrie, in his Stratford production of *Henry VIII,* achieved unbroken continuity without a front curtain by using the minor characters as furniture removers, but this resulted in the end of one scene and the beginning of the next being frequently lost in the scurry and bustle of chairs and tables being carried on and off the stage. The semi-realistic set was recognisably a hall in a Tudor palace, but as it remained completely unaltered throughout the performance, scene following scene without the smallest pause, without even a change of lighting to indicate a change of locale, the audience were often confused into thinking a scene was happening in the same place as the preceding scene when the action had moved to Kimbolton or to York Place or to the queen's apartments, or to a street in London. The Elizabethan audience had no difficulty in realising when the scene had changed because the four clearly defined acting areas of Elizabethan theatres—forestage, main stage, inner stage, balcony stage—made it possible to indicate a change of place simply by using another part of the stage. This Stratford production proved that if a set remains unchanged throughout the play it must not remotely suggest any particular place but must be simply a neutral platform.

Peter Brook, in his Stratford production of *Measure for Measure,* proved by means of a setting he designed himself that a permanent structure can, with a few slight variations, make it easy for the audiences to follow the changes of locale. This set was a beautifully composed perspective of arches. For some scenes they were open to the sky, for others they were filled in by flats which unobtrusively slid into position without interrupting the flow of the play. Thus the audience were never in any doubt about whether the scene was indoors or out-of-doors. By the occasional use of a significant touch of detail and by lighting which was skilful and imaginative, the setting easily and unmistakably became a palace or a prison, a street or a monastery. This is the only permanent set I have ever seen which was equally helpful to the producer, actors, author, and audience, vividly suggested the period and the country in which the play took place, stimulated the imagination and delighted the eye.

Hugh Hunt in his Old Vic production of *Hamlet* at the New Theatre sought, in collaboration with his designer Laurence Irving, to overcome the drawbacks of the permanent setting without interrupting the flow and without resorting to a front curtain by mounting parts of the scenery on small turntables which could revolve during a blackout. For instance, what had been part of the battlements became, when swung round, part of the interior of the palace, with a throne or some other piece of furniture already in position. The experiment was not altogether successful. The blackouts, brief though they were, jerked the play to a stop between scenes, and the method of staging did not allow for sufficient variation of the semi-realistic décor to cover all the scenes in the play.

Gielgud's production of *Much Ado About Nothing*, first given at Stratford and later brought to the Phoenix Theatre, was a much more successful solution of the problem of changing pictorial décor without blackouts or a front curtain. The lovely and elaborate settings by Mariano Andreu were most ingeniously designed so that they could be swiftly changed by pages during the action of the play. Some of the briefer scenes were played in graceful little pavilions set on either side of the proscenium arch.

When in 1951 the Histories were given at Stratford in chronological order they were all produced in the same permanent setting embodying most of the features of the Elizabethan stage. The front curtain of the theatre was not used, not even at the beginning and end of the performance, thus making it possible to build the setting out beyond the usual line of demarcation between stage and auditorium dictated by the proscenium curtain. This abolition of any barrier between actor and audience gave some suggestion of the intimacy of Shakespeare's theatre. But the setting did not attempt to be a faithful copy of Shakespeare's stage. In some respects it was an improvement on it. For instance, curving stairs led up to the balcony at the back, greatly increasing its usefulness. The inner stage underneath the balcony was put to much more varied use than in the Elizabethan theatre. Sometimes it was left open to the cyclorama so that it made an effective centre entrance, often different backings were used to indicate the scene, at other times it was closed by massive doors. Set permanently on one side of the stage was a throne, on the other side a penthouse. Occasionally some small touch of detail suggested the locale—a wattle fence for the orchard scene, ropes and tackle for King Henry's embarkation, foliage for the garden of the French Court, banners and golden hangings for the Coronation. But the set itself was unnecessarily bleak, giving no suggestion of the splendour of the Elizabethan stage, which was richly decorated in scarlet, blue, and gold. At Stratford the stage looked like a newly restored Tudor barn.

The advocates of "Shakespeare's stage for Shakespeare's plays" urged that henceforth all the productions at Stratford should be given in this setting, but Anthony Quayle wisely ignored this clamour. It had been extremely interesting to see the plays performed somewhat in the Elizabethan manner, and the use of the same setting throughout gave a sense of unity and continuity to the Histories. Nevertheless, many of the audience who saw all the plays that season missed the variety of scene to which they had become accustomed at Stratford. But a far more disappointed audience were the Old Vic's regulars who during the 1953–4 season grew very weary of the uninspired permanent setting, mainly consisting of three huge arches, which was used for all the plays—a setting as boring to the audience as it was obstructive to the producers.

It was interesting to compare the Stratford *Henry V* with Glen Byam Shaw's Old Vic production of the play during the same year. At the Vic, Motley's setting owed nothing to the Elizabethan stage. The simple but decoratively pictorial scenery was so ingeniously designed that it could be frequently changed while the play flowed on without interruption. In fact it flowed rather more easily than at Stratford where, because of the way the set was designed, the exits were apt to become overcrowded when, after a scene with a large number of characters, the producer needed to clear the stage rapidly for the next scene. That Vic production was an important one, because it showed that in a theatre without any mechanical devices such as Stratford possesses and without much money to spend, it is possible to dispense with a permanent set and make frequent changes of scene without halting the progress of the play. On the other hand Michael Benthall's production of *Antony and Cleopatra* at the St. James's, designed by Roger Furse, demonstrated that the revolving stage is an admirable means of combining continuity with a rich variety of scene.

The ingenuities of producers and designers bent on giving us more decorative and pictorial productions of Shakespeare seem sheer waste of effort to those who believe that the only satisfactory way of acting the plays is on an open platform stage with the audience partially surrounding the actors. This much-argued theory is discussed later on in a chapter dealing with the various kinds of stages. Those who want their Shakespeare unadorned persistently attack any producer who uses pictorial settings, accusing him of smothering the play in the scenery. But surely this betrays a curious lack of faith in the power of Shakespeare's writing. Lesser playwrights than Shakespeare have no difficulty in being effective on stages where the scenic designer has made full use of his opportunities. Obviously in a Shakespearian production the scenery must be subordinated to the play, but that is an elementary principle of good scene design which applies to any play of the slightest worth—though it does not necessarily mean that the scenery should humble itself to the play. "But Shakespeare doesn't *need* scenery," protest the purists. "He did his own scene-painting, using words to conjure up in our imagination scenes far more lovely than anything a designer can create." This picture of Shakespeare as a scene-painter has been much exaggerated. The passages in which he gives a detailed description of a scene are comparatively few, and some of the most famous, such as the description of Cleopatra's barge, and the stream in which Ophelia drowned are scenes not shown upon the stage.

Most of Shakespeare's so-called scene-painting consists of no more than a bare word or two in the dialogue indicating to the audience the place in which the scene is happening. Of course, Shakespeare does not *need* scenery. It is the ordinary, everyday theatregoer who needs the scenery if he is to be persuaded to accept Shakespeare's plays as a normal and thoroughly enjoyable part of his theatregoing. It is no use arguing that if the Elizabethan audience could do without scenery the modern audience can do likewise. We have not got the highly developed visual imagination of the Elizabethans. It was not only in the theatre that they exercised it. They had to picture for themselves places and events which to-day are depicted for us by the camera. When we read in our morning paper about an earthquake or a flood or an atom bomb explosion we have probably already glanced at a photograph sent by radio showing the havoc wrought. So as we read the report it needs no effort of imagination to picture the scene. Besides, we will see it all in much greater detail an evening or two later on the newsreel. The Elizabethans did not even have paintings and drawings as an aid to their imagination. In those days there were no English landscape painters and drawings were still crude and unrealistic. The Elizabethan had to piece together in his imagination his own picture of foreign lands from a traveller's tales; his idea of what a great battle must have been like depended on how vividly his imagination reacted to the stories he heard in the taverns from the soldiers, boasting over their drinks.

Too many producers dither half-heartedly between the pictorial and anti-pictorial conventions instead of firmly making up their minds either to depend upon Shakespeare and the actors to create their own illusion, or frankly to rely upon the assistance of pictorial scenery. In an article on *Style in Shakespeare Production,* Peter Brook says : "A production cannot toy with illusion—it must either go all the way or none of it. If the producer tries to compromise by allowing the play to be semi-formalised, instead of going all the way pictorially, the audience will feel cheated. It will neither have the satisfaction of exercising its own imagination, nor will it have the thrill of yielding to a continually imaginative and convincing stage illusion. The great percentage of Shakespeare productions one sees today are dull simply because they make this compromise: sometimes through fear, sometimes through modesty, sometimes through lack of ability on the part of the producer."

That article from which I have quoted was written in 1948. Since then producers have become bolder, there have been fewer compromise settings: but they are still too frequent—for instance, that permanent setting at the Old Vic during the 1953–4 season. Dull and bewildering sets of this sort are, I believe, one of the reasons for the declining popularity of

Shakespeare in the theatre during recent years. It may seem odd to talk about a decline in popularity when almost every season the attendances at Stratford set up new records, but it is the increasing number of tourists visiting England rather than an increasing interest in Shakespeare which accounts for the size of the Stratford audiences. At the Old Vic there is a "repeater audience", most of whom see all the plays, so the total number of people who go to the Vic during the course of a season would not be sufficient to keep a play running for more than a few weeks. And yet, to make certain of an audience, the Vic has to engage at least one or two players whose names have been blazoned across the front of cinemas. No longer dare it rely on Shakespeare and young, comparatively unknown players of promise as it used to do. In the provinces a professional production of Shakespeare is now a rare event. In the old days there used to be four Shakespearian companies on the road— the companies of Benson, Henry Baynton, Ben Greet, and Charles Doran. Martin-Harvey included three Shakespeare plays in his touring repertoire, the Compton Comedy Company gave at least two, and the provincial towns were also visited by Shakespearian productions from the London theatre where Shakespeare was far more frequently performed than he is today. During the theatrical season of 1953–4 there was not a single production of Shakespeare in the West End. During the 1949 season a few Christmas matinées of a very modest production of *A Midsummer Night's Dream* was all that the West End saw of Shakespeare, and the Vic that season gave only two of his plays.

Some of the reasons for the decline in the number of Shakespearian productions, especially in the provinces, are financial. Rising costs make Shakespeare's plays, most of which have large casts, expensive propositions. But this would not matter so much were it not for the fact that he is nowadays considered to be "bad box-office"—and for that the producers and actors are largely to blame. I do a considerable amount of lecturing, and during the question and discussion following a lecture I hear a great deal of dissatisfaction expressed, by people who are keen playgoers, over the way Shakespeare is presented and played. Lecturing to a course on the drama organised by the Army Education Corps I found that the majority of the audience, most of them still in their teens, frankly admitted that as a result of what they had seen of Shakespeare in the theatre they preferred to go to any passably good modern play. They apologetically blamed themselves for this. Shakespeare, they said, was "too difficult" for them, because the language and the blank verse made it hard to understand the sense of what was being said on the stage. But a young man more theatrically sophisticated than some of the others indignantly denied this. The previous evening they had all been to the Old Vic. He maintained that those who blamed themselves for not being intelligent enough to follow the play were doing themselves an injustice. It was the producer and the actors who were to blame. The verse had been so badly babbled that he himself, who knew the play well, often had difficulty in understanding what was being said.

Here we have the fundamental reason why the audience for Shakespeare is not larger than it is. The young playgoer goes once or twice to a Shakespeare play and unless he is fortunate enough to have picked on one of the rare, well-spoken performances he is apt to decide that Shakespeare is "too difficult" and perhaps never see another of the plays for the rest of his life.

For years the critics have been complaining of the inaudibility which is the inevitable result of maltreating Shakespeare's rhythms, but with little effect. The problem is not just how to teach actors to speak the verse properly, but how, in the first place, to convince them of the necessity for doing so. One might begin by persuading them that the verse is not, as most of them believe it to be, the enemy of characterisation. In any play an actor inevitably—and rightly—begins by devoting all his thought to the characterisation of his part, but in a Shakespeare play he is apt to think that unless he plays tricks with the verse to make his lines sound more "characterised" his performance will seem dull—as if he were "just saying the lines". G.B.S. had something to say about this: "Shakespearian delineation of character owes all its magic to the turn of the line, which lets you into the secret of its utterer's mood and temperament, not by its commonplace meaning, but by some subtle exultation or stultification, or shyness, a delicacy, a hesitancy, or what-not in the sound of it. In short it is the score and not the libretto that keeps the work alive and fresh."

Even if one could persuade all actors to speak Shakespeare's verse rhythmically, with the stresses rightly placed, with all the variations of tempo, the crescendos and diminuendos, that would still not be enough. The verse cannot be fully effective unless it is spoken by actors who have well-trained and well-exercised voices. The English actor is thoroughly alarmed if he is told he has a "voice". He takes it not as a compliment but as an accusation. He is morbidly afraid that if he uses the full range of his voice he will become "ham". So he deliberately makes no effort to develop the compass of his pitch and tone, he monotonously repeats the same cadences and modulations, always carefully listening to himself to make certain that he is not speaking "musically". The consequence of these inhibitions is that most Shakespearian performances offend the ear. The voices are dull and heavy, or hoarse, and rasping, or thin and sharp, dismally lacking flexibility, delicacy, and colour. A play such as *A Midsummer Night's Dream* which needs to be spoken lyrically is today vocally beyond the range of most English actors. Harold Hobson, reviewing the Stratford production of *The Dream* in 1954, described how "some of the sweetest verse which Shakespeare ever wrote was spoken in tones that recalled lemons, slate pencils, and the whinnying of horses: everything was sour, shrill, and tart". The tragedies and the histories demand a vocal magnificence which only a very few of our actors and actresses can achieve. Most of them do not even attempt it. The great climaxes, the final swell of passion, what Trewin describes as "the thunder-arched fury of the breaking wave", need actors who can produce the sheer glory of sound which Shakespeare relied upon for his crescendos.

It is not the fault of the producer if the range of his actors' voices is narrow and cramped. The fault is in the actor himself, in the way he has been trained. But at least the producer can begin by persuading the actor to find a sensuous pleasure in Shakespeare's words—in their colour, their richness, their flavour.

When I was on a "Brains Trust" with Edith Evans I remember her complaining that most actors reduce Shakespeare's language "to grey, pallid *little* words. But they have the most *glorious* colours", protested Dame Edith, "and they are not little words but great *big* words, so big and full of meaning that sometimes, when I am tired, I find them almost too big to lift up and send winging on their way to the audience". I went home after that and re-read in Herbert Farjeon's *The Shakespeare Scene* the passage where he describes Dame Edith as "that rare thing", "an actress who can bring out the full literary flavour of every word. To those who know their Shakespeare before they see him on the stage, how maddening it is to find word after word misunderstood, slurred over, debased, diminished, or subjected to the ignominy of substitution by the performer. But Edith Evans quickens every syllable, recognises in a choice epithet something as three-dimensional as a living being, reveals new wonder unspoiled, never to be forgotten. . . . She illuminates the text, revealing beauties undreamed of by the reader—which is surely the business of the Shakespearian theatre".

8

THE PRODUCER AND THE PLAYHOUSE

On an evening in 1906 the Berlin first-nighters arriving for
the opening performance at Reinhardt's newly built Kleines
Theatre gazed around in astonishment. It was all so unlike the
kind of theatre to which they were accustomed. Gone was the
traditional elaborately ornamented proscenium arch; instead,
the stage was framed in a narrow strip of the same dark wood
with which the auditorium was panelled. The orchestra pit had
been abolished and the stage joined to the auditorium by a
shallow flight of steps. All the usual lines of demarcation
between actor and audience had been smoothed away. Stage
and auditorium merged almost imperceptibly into one another.
"It seemed," wrote one of the critics, "that when the curtain
rose the players and the spectators were together in the same
intimate, discreetly decorated room rather than in a theatre."

The building of the Kleines Theatre initiated a movement
which has been steadily growing in strength during the past
fifty years. Its aim is to break down the separation of stage and
auditorium into two compartments, to restore the old intimacy
between actor and audience. Reinhardt, in his endeavours to
rescue the players from their isolation behind the proscenium
arch, often took them out of the theatre to play in places which
in those days seemed odd and eccentric settings for a theatrical
entertainment—a piazza in Venice, the ballroom of a palace in
Vienna, the Boboli Gardens in Florence, the Domplatz in
Salzburg, and inside the cathedral itself. He produced *Oedipus
Rex* in a circus, and it was as a result of this experiment that he

built the Grosses Schauspielhaus, the colossal "Theatre of the Five Thousand" in which the stage was like a vast circus arena with one end used for gigantic architectural settings unframed by any kind of proscenium. For his production of *The Miracle* in London in 1911 he transformed Olympia into a cathedral so that the audience became part of the congregation—with results that were perhaps not altogether happy. Komisarjevsky, for instance, thought "the gentlemen in Savile Row tails and the ladies in Worth creations sitting in the middle of a papier mâché cathedral looked quite funny to me".

Reinhardt's most successful experiment in abolishing the division between actor and audience was the series of productions he staged in Maria Theresa's ballroom at the Hofburg in Vienna. Here there was no proscenium, no curtain, just a platform set at one end of the ballroom in front of the great double staircase leading to a balcony. To emphasise the unity of player and spectator Reinhardt kept all the seven huge chandeliers in the ballroom alight throughout the performance so that not even the lighting would give any impression of isolating the actors from their audience—though actually the actors were cunningly emphasised by means of spotlights concealed in the chandeliers nearest the acting area.

Recently I read an article in which one of the advocates of what is nowadays called "the open stage" described Reinhardt as "the modern theatre's first and most powerful opponent of the picture-frame stage". He himself would have vehemently denied this. In one of the very few articles he ever wrote, he said: "It would be a theory as barbaric as it is incompatible with the principles of theatrical art, to measure with the same yardstick, to press into the same mould, the wonderful wealth of the world's literature. The mere suggestion of such an attempt is a typical example of pedantic scholasticism. There is no one form of theatre which is the only true artistic form. Let good actors today play in a barn or in a theatre, tomorrow at an inn or inside a church, or, in the Devil's name, even on an expressionistic stage: if the place corresponds with the play, something wonderful will be the outcome. All depends on realising the specific atmosphere of a play, and on making the play live . . . Therefore, do not write out prescriptions, but give to the actor and his work the atmosphere in which they can breathe more freely and more deeply."

Today there are many who believe that the actor can only breathe more freely and deeply if he is rescued from his confinement behind the proscenium arch and reinstated in the freedom of the open stage with the audience seated either all round him or at least on three sides, while he acts upon a bare platform where there is no place for the paraphernalia of the realistic theatre.

There are three kinds of open stage. The most extreme form is the Arena Theatre, sometimes called Theatre-in-the-Round, in which the players are encircled by the audience except where two aisles on opposite sides of the acting area enable the actors to make their entrances. America already has over forty of these theatres, both professional and amateur. London has no professional theatre of this kind since the closing of the Pembroke, Croydon, but Paris has Le Théâtre en Rond, which opened in 1954 with a production of *The Importance of Being Earnest*. Another professional arena theatre, the luxurious Teatro Sant' Erasmo, was opened in Milan the same year.

The term Arena Theatre is also often used inaccurately to describe the Amphitheatre, in which the audience is seated on three sides of the acting area. The Intimate Theatre Group have been touring England since 1949 with a theatre of this sort, housed in a circus tent. London used to have two very small Arena Theatres—The Cockpit Theatre in Westminster and The Theatre Centre in St. John's Wood.

The third kind of open stage is a near approach to the Elizabethan platform stage. During the Festival of Britain a stage of this kind was built in the Royal Exchange for Bernard Miles's Shakespearian productions, and in the 'thirties Robert Atkins converted the Ring at Blackfriars into something approximating to an Elizabethan theatre. But the most interesting and successful example of an open platform stage can be seen each year at the Edinburgh Festival, set up in the Assembly Hall. It has been used for Guthrie's productions of *The Three Estates* and *The Highland Fair,* for the Old Vic's productions of Shakespeare and Ben Jonson, and for a huge musical production with a cast of a hundred and seventy entitled *Hail Caledonia!* Guthrie's experience of producing on this stage has made him a fervent believer in the principles of open staging, so that when he became director of the Shakespeare Festival at Stratford, Ontario, he designed for it a stage on much the same lines as the one built for the Assembly Hall at Edinburgh.

Within a few years there are likely to be a considerable number of open-stage theatres in England, if only because they cost a fraction of what it costs to build an ordinary theatre today. An open stage, unlike a picture-frame stage, does not need a building specially designed for it. A touring company using an open stage can give performances in towns where there are no proper facilities for ordinary theatrical performances, setting up their stage in the town hall or drill hall or in the swimming baths, in fact in any building of suitable size which has a roof and four walls. During the Edinburgh Festival of 1954 the Oxford University Players effectively demonstrated this with their amphitheatre production of Marlowe's *Edward II* in the great hall of Heriot's School. The only construction entailed was an oval rostrum with steps leading down into the main acting area. This fine production, which had a cast of over forty, would have been a cramped and makeshift affair if it had been crammed onto an improvised picture-frame stage rigged up at one end of the hall. The Theatre Centre in St. John's Wood provides another example of how a group of young professionals without the money to convert a building into even a very small picture-frame theatre are able to have an open stage theatre of their own.

The extremists declared that there is no play which cannot be better performed on an open stage than inside a picture frame. They prophesy that if the National Theatre is built with a proscenium stage it will be hopelessly out of date within a few years. So let us examine in some detail the advantages and disadvantages of the different types of open stage, beginning with the Arena Theatre.

The Producer and the Play

In this theatre—the Theatre-in-the-Round—the stage is at floor level, circular or oval in shape, with the front row of the audience seated round the edge of the acting area except where an aisle on either side of the stage allows for the actors to make their entrances. The obvious advantage is the intimacy between actor and audience. The equally obvious disadvantage is the fact that the actor's face can never be seen by more than half the audience at the same time. The usual answer to this is that the actor must learn to make his back as expressive as his face—which is an impossibility. An actor can droop his shoulders to express depression; he can brace them to express determination; he can twitch them to indicate that he is laughing and he can shrug them—that is all. With his back he can suggest none of the subtle shades of emotion which the face can portray. The more reasonable advocates of the arena stage admit this, but point out that the actor is on such intimate terms with his audience that he does not need to rely on facial expression to "put it across" to the extent that he does in an ordinary theatre.

Obviously acting in such close proximity to the audience requires the actor to revise his technique. An American actor describes how on making his first appearance on an arena stage he was "conscious of nothing but a sea of leering, peering faces, often closer to you than the nearest actors. . . . Far better try lying to your own mother than attempt to give a false performance before the eyes of such a proximate audience. The actor, as though seeing himself under a microscope, improves his technique with many refinements". This actor considered himself well rewarded for the pains he took to master the art of playing to the "proximate" audience when he was told one of them had been heard to remark: "I felt as if I had been inside that guy's head." An American critic, describing how at an arena performance he saw an actor's lighter fail to work and a member of the audience instinctively offer his own lighter, enthusiastically ended his notice by declaring that "when such contact is established we have achieved the kind of theatre for which we all search". Perhaps it would be more true to say that it is *one* of the kinds of theatre for which *some* of us search.

The chief disadvantage of the arena theatre is that the size of the audience must be severely limited. If an actor plays with sufficient intimacy and delicacy to appear completely natural to the audience in the front row, who may be only two or three feet away from him in some of his scenes, his performance becomes ineffective a few rows back, particularly to those of the audience who are behind him. It is no solution to move the front row farther away from the acting area to enable the actor to give a more projected performance which will be effective in the further rows without seeming over-acted to the front row. The intimacy between actor and audience is dissipated and most of the advantages of acting in what one critic has called the "theatre-in-the-lap" are lost. Glen Hughes, director of the Penthouse Theatre, the pioneer of such theatres in America, maintains that the audience should not extend to more than three rows. "If you add a fourth row they no longer feel they are *in* the play." The Penthouse seats an audience of 172 round an acting area 14 ft. × 15 ft. By extending the size of the acting area one can, of course, increase the size of the audience without increasing the number of rows, but there is the danger that in a large acting area much of the action of the play will take place too far from most of the audience for the feeling of intimacy to be maintained. Margo Jones, who founded the first professional arena theatre in America, believed that the acting area could be extended to 28 ft. in diameter. Her own theatre at Dallas, Texas, seats an audience of 195 round an acting area 24 ft. × 20 ft. Il Teatro Sant' Erasmo in Milan seats 240 round a circular acting area 18 ft. in diameter. Le Théâtre en Rond, with an acting area approximately the same size, seats 300, which is about as large as a theatre of this kind can be without sacrificing most of the advantages of acting "in the round".

For big, spectacular productions an arena theatre can, of course, be very much larger. The Music Circus in Lambertville, New Jersey, which puts on Broadway musicals, has 900 seats. There are several of these Music Circuses in Canada, some of them with a capacity of fifteen or sixteen hundred. The average size of the acting area is 30 ft. × 22 ft. The disadvantage of staging a musical in an arena is that during the ensemble numbers the cast have to face towards the conductor, so the part of the acting area round which the orchestra is placed tends to become the front of the stage, and those on the opposite side of the arena are apt to get less than their fair share of the show.

A spectacular Broadway musical performed without scenery in a tent may sound rather a bleak affair, but according to all accounts the proximity of the audience has a tremendously exhilarating effect on the players. The great value of these Music Circuses is that they are taking live entertainment to places where it would be impossible to stage a big musical in the ordinary way.

In England the Conesford Players, an amateur group, effectively converted the Royal Hall at Harrogate into the larger type of arena theatre for a production of *A Phoenix Too Frequent* by using the space normally occupied by the stalls as their acting area and seating part of the audience on the stage, while the rest of them overlooked the players from the circle and the boxes. Only a very few amateur groups in this country have made any attempt to experiment with theatre-in-the-round, although it provides the solution to many of their difficulties. Most amateur companies have to perform on appallingly awkward makeshift stages in halls where the flat floor of the auditorium makes it impossible for most of the audience to get a clear view of the stage; yet how simple it is to mark out an ample circular or oblong stage on the floor of such a hall, surrounding it with a few rows of seats, improvising means of slightly raising the back rows. The fact that the scene of the play has to be left entirely to the imagination of the audience is a decided advantage, as it is rarely that an amateur company is able to manage the solid and convincing realistic setting required for most of the plays they perform. The incongruous mixture of real doors and windows mixed up with curtains serving as walls, which is the usual amateur "realistic" set, is more of a hindrance than a help to the imagination of the audience.

It is much easier for the inexperienced amateur to act "in the round" than on a picture-frame stage because he is not troubled with the technical difficulties of projecting his performance to distant rows of audience. He can rely upon sincerity to a far greater extent than in the ordinary theatre. The producer, too, has fewer technical problems. Movement can flow much more easily and naturally than on a picture-frame stage where the producer has to achieve the effect of people moving about a room in a normal way while keeping them facing as much as possible in one direction—in the direction of the audience. Nor does he have any troubles about his actors masking one another because, as Guthrie put it, "If the audience sits around the stage, actors cannot fail to mask one another and that's that." But he considers this is more than compensated for by the fact that the actors' physical relation to one another can be completely natural.

One reason why many amateur producers hesitate to experiment with theatre-in-the-round is the fear that their actors may be acutely nervous when acting in the middle of a ring of peering faces; but Frances Mackenzie, the head of the British Drama League's Training Department, who has done several productions with amateurs in-the-round, says that "none of them appeared to be embarrassed by the proximity of the audience, but rather stimulated by it; probably because of the quality of concentration that this proximity demands. Even an actor playing a small part, or a member of a crowd, feels that he cannot for a moment relax his imaginative concentration on his character". Watching an arena production one's own concentration is far greater than in an ordinary theatre, which perhaps explains why the audience opposite so quickly become unnoticeable, provided the lighting does not spill over the edge of the acting area.

Although it is often claimed that any play can be performed in-the-round, there are practical difficulties which make some plays ineligible for this sort of production—for instance, if a staircase or a window is an essential part of the action, or if it is necessary to have a high piece of furniture, or an upright piano, which would obscure the view of the stage from a part of the audience. And there are plays so dependent on their realistic setting that they cannot be divorced from it. It would be impossible, for example, to produce *Street Scene* on an arena stage.

Frances Mackenzie, after seeing arena productions in several countries, considers that costume plays are least suited to the arena stage. "Watching a good and lively *Twelfth Night* production, I felt rather as if I were at a party where the hosts were in fancy dress but not the guests. Viola, in an aside, came right up to me and spoke with her face close to mine, but with her eyes looking just over my shoulder at someone in the row behind. I was rather embarrassed and felt that I ought to make a polite and sympathetic reply, but was handicapped by my lack of fluency in Shakespearian blank verse. I wanted to recoil in my seat and pretend not to be there, but then, of course, I should have been failing in 'audience participation'."

If a play belonging to another age is produced in an arena theatre it should, it seems, be given in modern dress. Richard Southern, in his book *The Open Stage*, describes a modern dress production of Vanbrugh's *The Confederacy* at the Cockpit Theatre. "It was remarkable," he says, "to see how, with no 'picture' to sustain, the 'picture' costumes of the period were not in the slightest degree missed, but one had for the first time a sense of the contemporariness of the play through seeing it performed as it was intended—that is in the dress of the audience. The language offered not the slightest anachronism. The open stage endowed all with an actuality and a zest for life."

At present the chief value of the arena theatre is that it can give new life to old plays by revealing details of characterisation and nuances of feeling too delicate to survive the passage from stage to auditorium in an ordinary theatre. But a play can only be seen to best advantage in the theatrical convention for which it is conceived, so to assess the true value of theatre-in-the-round we must wait until we have seen plays specially written for it.

It used to be possible to see such plays at the Realistic Theatre in Moscow, directed by Nikolai Okhlopkov, a one-time pupil of Meierhold. Here the audience did not just surround the actors, often they sat among them. For instance, in *The Iron Stream* the whole auditorium was converted into a rocky, un-even, mountainous terrain, and the audience were seated scattered among the rocks. The mingling of actors and audience

began before the start of the play. The doors of the auditorium
were closed until a minute or two before the advertised time of
starting, then a bell rang, the doors opened, and the audience
surged into an auditorium already seething with life. André van
Gyseghem vividly describes the scene in his book on the Soviet
theatre :

"Babel. A theatre more full of sound than the crowded
foyer. Women shrilling across at one another—babies crying—
men shouting orders—lovers quarrelling—a group of men singing to a harmonica. The savoury smell of cooking assails our
nostrils as we stagger dazedly into this hubbub, looking for our
seats. Seats, did I say? We can't see any seats—anyway, they're
looking the wrong way, surely? Pardon, madame, was that
your child I stepped on? There are some seats, but a rocky
promontory has first to be navigated; we dodge under the
muzzle of a gun that is being cleaned by a young man singing
lustily as he polishes, only to find our heads entangled, as we
come up, with a mass of washing hanging out to dry. The
young woman doesn't thank us for spoiling her work. We are
sorry, but you see—don't argue, comrade, did you or did you
not spoil my washing? Yes, we did, but quite accidentally——
Very well, you spoilt my washing, now that's enough, go away
and let me get on with my work! Perspiring and muttering our
apologies to an inattentive ear, we pass on, see a seat number
—no, ours is in the next group. Here we are—careful—mind
that loving couple at our feet—if you would just move your dress
a little—thank you. We throw ourselves into what we hope are
our seats, first taking care to remove the frying-pan left there for
a moment by the young man attending to the camp-fire at our
side. But having got to our seats that is not the end of it—nor
the beginning, for others have not been so quick as we and the
long auditorium is still a shouting, gesticulating conglomeration
of audience and actors, uniforms and mufti, make-up and sweat-
ing faces. Only gradually do they disentangle themselves; only
after a great deal of searching, chattering, mistakes, shouted
advice from the few attendants and vociferous comments from
the actors do the spectators settle themselves into the irregularly

225

placed seats—the clamour dies down and lines of dialogue begin to emerge which are obviously part of a text and not extemporary. The bald, general lighting fades and spotlights pick out the costumed actors. The play begins—or should I say continues at the point interrupted by our entrance?"

The Iron Stream is about an isolated group of partisan fighters in the north of Russia during the civil war and their long trek across hostile country to find and link up with the main body. Van Gyseghem describes the final scene when at last the partisan army is sighted. "The excitement mounts as the news spreads, the whole company pour onto the rocky steps, shading their eyes, peering into the distance. Yes!—it is our friends, our comrades—and crying and laughing they rush forward to greet—US! We, the audience, represent their comrades, and the actors flood the theatre, the iron stream breaks over us, our hands are clasped by the gnarled hands of bearded peasants, woman greets woman with a warm embrace and the children dart in among the seats, throwing themselves at us with cries of delight. Actors and audience are still one—and we applaud one another."

In Okhlopkov's production of a dramatisation of Gorki's *Mother* there was a scene in which the old woman, having heard her son is to be released from prison that day, excitedly begins to get ready a meal for him. "She produces a cloth, and food, and drink, but she can't stop talking—she must tell someone what a great day this is and what a great boy he is. She talks to the people sitting nearest to her—chats with them about the ways of boys and about her Pavel; but her hands are full, she can't do everything herself, so she gives one of the audience bread to hold while another spreads the cloth. Chatting away all the time she thanks you for helping her, the cloth is spread, the food and drink laid out ready for him. She has played the whole scene alone, yet we feel she has told all her neighbours about it, we share her delight and envy her happiness—those members of the audience that have been included in the scene have in some way stretched the veil of illusion to include us all."

It is difficult to imagine an English audience overcoming their inhibitions sufficiently to become participants in a performance, nevertheless it is impossible for anyone to remain an altogether passive and aloof spectator in an arena theatre. One finds oneself participating mentally and emotionally to a far greater extent than in the ordinary theatre. The pleasant custom at the Realistic Theatre of the actors applauding the audience at the end of the play might well become the custom in all arena theatres as an acknowledgment of the extent to which the actors in those theatres depend upon the collaboration of their audience.

Halfway between the arena theatre and the proscenium theatre is the semi-circular amphitheatre which allows for the fourth side of the acting area to be used for a modified form of theatrical setting. The Intimate Theatre Group's tented travelling theatre seats an audience of five hundred rising tier upon tier round the acting area so that no member of the audience is more than forty feet from the stage. Before the performance begins the stage is concealed by a curtain running on a semi-circular track around the whole of the acting area. This curtain is drawn during the intervals to conceal any necessary changes of furniture and setting. In the production of a modern play the fourth side of the acting area is often used for a solidly realistic background. In fact, the impression one gets when the curtain opens is of an ordinary box set from which not only the fourth wall has been removed, but the sides as well, so that the audience looks in upon it from all sides but one. The Intimate Theatre Group has produced realistic plays such as *Little Foxes, Candida, Still Life,* and *The Paragon,* but although these plays have been enjoyed by the audiences, the most successful productions by all accounts have been Goldoni's *The Servant of Two Masters* (which was never intended for the proscenium stage), *Our Town,* and *Alice in Wonderland.*

The amphitheatre is an admirable stage for Shakespeare— better, I think, than the Elizabethan stage. It can provide the Elizabethan balcony and inner stage, and a spacious forestage surrounded by the audience. The fact that this forestage is the floor of the theatre, not a raised platform as in the Elizabethan theatre, seems to me an advantage. It is far easier for the actor to speak a soliloquy on floor level, with the audience banked up in tiers around him, than to speak from the platform stage to an audience many of whom are below him.

We have become much too reverential about the Elizabethan theatre. It is spoken of as the perfect theatre. It was far from being that. For instance, the lines of sight were poor. Scenes played on the inner stage were invisible to at least a third of the audience, and the stout pillars supporting the roof of the stage obscured the view from some parts of the auditorium. The groundlings round the edges of the forestage had to stretch their necks to an uncomfortable angle to see the face of an actor standing above them. Many of those on the sides of the theatre saw more of the back of an actor than his face. We are told that on the forestage the Elizabethan actor played to all parts of the house in turn, but it is more likely that he spoke his big speeches "out front", aiming them at the best seats where sat the wealthy noblemen upon whose patronage the actors were financially dependent. No doubt the Elizabethan play-house seemed an ideal theatre to those who could afford the best places, but the groundlings who paid their penny to stand where they could find room may have been more critical of it.

Those who clamour for a theatre to be built in which Shakespeare's plays can be performed under exactly the same conditions as in the Elizabethan playhouse are demanding the impossible, because there is one essential condition which cannot be re-created—a huge audience in the closest possible proximity both to the stage and one another. At least two thousand people (some estimates put it as high as three thousand) were crammed into a space about a quarter the size of a modern theatre with a similar capacity. The closer an audience is packed together the more intense is the excitement which can be generated—which is why a crowded gallery is the most responsive part of the house. At the Globe six hundred people stood jammed shoulder to shoulder round the three sides of the stage, while the most distant spectators in the galleries, which almost overhung the stage on three sides, were no more than 40 ft. from an actor on the front of the forestage. Tyrone Guthrie argues that if today people are prepared to stand wedged in a crowd to watch a football match or a royal procession they can do so to watch a play by Shakespeare. But they would not be allowed to do so. A building so densely packed would never be licensed because of the risks in the event of fire.

There should be at least one replica of an Elizabethan play-house in England to demonstrate how Shakespeare used his stage, but as the auditorium could contain only a fraction of the audience which packed themselves into it in Shakespeare's day, the actor-audience relationship would be a tame affair compared with what it must have been at the Globe. To build a larger auditorium, seating a thousand or so, would destroy the relation-ship. It may be argued that in a theatre of this size, built on the Elizabethan plan, the farthest seats would still be closer to the stage than in an ordinary theatre, so the actors could play far more intimately than on a proscenium stage. Actually they would have to deliver their lines much more loudly and unnaturally than in an ordinary theatre seating the same number of people because it is easier for an actor to project his voice from a stage set at one end of an auditorium than it is to speak in the middle of an open space, especially where part of his audience is behind his back.

On the open stage at Edinburgh the actors either shout them-selves hoarse or are seldom completely audible to all the audience at the same time. Nevertheless the Assembly Hall stage is the most important theatrical experiment made in this country since Terence Gray built the Cambridge Festival Theatre in 1926, a theatre with no proscenium (the width of the stage was the width of the auditorium itself) and a roomy forestage merging into a great fan-shaped flight of steps extending to the feet of the audience seated round it. The stage at Edinburgh is Elizabethan in character, but not in detail. It is a "fit up" designed for the great square hall where the Church of Scotland holds its Assembly—not unlike a Parliament house, with deep galleries round the four sides, and in the centre the Moderator's Chair in the same position as the Speaker's Chair at Westminster, with rows of pews for the clerks facing him. Raked benches, seating fifteen hundred, face inwards on three sides. The long, high apron stage, its length about twice its width, is built jutting out over the clerks' pews, stretching like a peninsula into the centre of the auditorium. The front half of the apron is a step down, making two clearly defined acting areas and giving opportunities for groupings on different levels. Running round all three sides are steps reaching to floor level. At the back, on either side, curving stairways lead to an upper stage built out from the balcony. Because of the architecture of the hall it is not possible to have an inner stage under the balcony, so the back of the forestage is a solid wall reaching to the upper stage. For *The Three Estates* narrow galleries were built against this wall. For *Hamlet* a wide flight of steps rose from the forestage to the upper stage. Other producers have preferred to leave the back wall as it is so as to be able to make full use of the flat forestage. Flanking it, on floor level, there are entrances from which steps lead up to the forestage. The main entrances are through four aisles in the auditorium, and there are also entrances on either side of the upper stage.

This stage is, I think, an improvement upon the Elizabethan model in spite of having to dispense with the inner stage—which anyway would have been invisible to a large part of the audience in the Assembly Hall. In Shakespearian productions the upper stage has been effectively used for scenes written for the inner stage. It also serves, of course, for the balcony scenes, but as it is wider and more spacious than the Elizabethan balcony it can be put to more varied use, especially when the stairways joining it to the main stage are employed. The eight entrances enable the producer to bring on his actors from many different directions—suddenly and dramatically through the entrances on the upper stage and those flanking the forestage on floor level, or in slow procession through the aisles—which serve equally well for the excited entrances of a surging crowd. When I produced *Hail Caledonia!* I found it was possible to pour a hundred and seventy people onto the stage from all directions in less than half a minute. The steps round the fore-stage greatly increase its usefulness as large numbers of people can be grouped on them, either sitting or standing, without masking the players on the stage itself.

It has been possible to get some idea of the advantages and disadvantages of this stage by comparing performances of the same play by the Vic company at Edinburgh and in their own theatre. The crowd scenes, the brawls, the duels, and the battles have proved to be infinitely more exciting out among the audience on the open stage. The soliloquies have been more effective at the Vic where the whole of the audience has been able to see the actor's face. Broadly humorous scenes, especially those dependent on comic business, have gone better on the open stage, but verbal humour is much less effective. Watching a play at the Assembly Hall one realises how much an actor relies on facial expression to point a comedy line. Often I have heard a laugh come only from the part of the audience towards which the actor was facing. Sometimes the laughter would come from the rest of the audience a moment or two later because they had tumbled to the point of a line on hearing the reaction of the other half of the audience. Unexpectedly, in *Macbeth* the banquet at which the ghost of Banquo appears was, on the open stage, genuinely horrifying for the first time in my experience. In an ordinary production one gets no impression of a great hall where a huge gathering of people are feasting. The·group round a single table suggests no more than an intimate supper party. But at the Assembly Hall the table set in the middle of the audience became in one's imagination the "high table" and oneself one of the guests crowding the rest of the hall. One was "in" the scene, a part of it, intensely experiencing the same emotions as those upon the stage. At the Vic one became merely a spectator of the scene.

On a stage viewed from three sides the producer has an exciting sense of freedom. He is no longer limited to two-dimensional grouping, he is given a whole new dimension in which to work. Guthrie rightly claims that "in scenes of action and excitement the big wheeling and spinning movements which can be made offer a choreographic freedom that is quite beyond the range of the proscenium theatre". He is "convinced that the plays of Shakespeare demand that the actors must be grouped in circular positions to face one another, not the audience". But it is Shakespeare's theatre rather than Shakespeare's plays which demand this, or at least make it the most convenient kind of grouping on a stage where it is never possible for the actor to face the whole of his audience. The defect of this "inward grouping" is that in a scene between two or three characters there is no way of ensuring that the audience seated round the stage all see it in the same way. The emphasis is different from various parts of the house. The character dramatically the most important at a certain moment in the scene inevitably has his back to a section of the audience, so their attention is diverted to a less important character whose face happens to be visible to them.

Guthrie describes how when he is producing on an open stage he "keeps all the grouping very fluid and mobile, so that each actor, during a scene, is continually on the move, continually revolving in the centre of his audience like the hub of a wheel". What this amounts to is that the producer is displaying the scene to best advantage to each part of the audience in turn, rather like someone walking a horse or a dog round a show ring. It does not solve the insoluble problem of how to group a scene on an open stage so that it makes a simultaneous impact on the whole audience.

This diffusion of visual emphasis matters less in Elizabethan and Jacobean plays than in modern plays, which rely to a far greater extent on subtleties of facial expression. Strindberg's *The Stronger* provides a good example of the sort of scene which cannot be properly produced on any of the three kinds of open stage discussed in this chapter. It is a brief one-act play which Strindberg wrote for an actress renowned for the subtlety of her facial expression. There are only two parts, both women, one of whom remains silent throughout the entire play—but it is the silent woman which is the leading part. The two characters are sitting at a table in a café. There is no movement. Strindberg wrote the play to be produced with the talkative one seated downstage, almost with her back to the audience, so that visually the attention of the audience is concentrated on the face of the woman who listens but never speaks. On an open stage half of the audience would get an impression of this play which would be literally the reverse of what the author intended.

In most plays there is a climatic movement when every member of the audience needs to see the expression on the face of a certain actor. Frances Mackenzie, writing about an arena production of *The Glass Menagerie,* says: "In the Gielgud proscenium production I shall always remember the look of mortification on Helen Haye's face at the moment when she realizes that 'the gentleman caller' is not interested in her daughter. This poignant pause held the whole audience for several seconds. In the arena production the expression of the mother's face was inevitably lost to a third of the audience, and the silence, without movement, could not hold for long. Again, at an arena production of *St. Joan* I was unlucky enough during the trial scene to have only a back view of the Inquisitor when he told Cauchon that he believed Joan to be innocent. I badly wanted to see his face, as well as the reaction on Cauchon's face on hearing this."

Only on a stage set at one end of the auditorium can actor and producer be reasonably certain of making the same effect simultaneously on the entire audience. This need not necessarily be a proscenium stage—though it generally is. Nowadays so many hard things are said about the "peep-show theatre", as it is often contemptuously described, that one marvels how it has existed for nearly three hundred years and that so many masterpieces have been written for it. But during those three hundred years the design of the proscenium theatre has steadily deteriorated. At first the proscenium arch was no more than a frame at the back of the stage to display the pictures painted by the scenic artists. The actors stayed outside the frame on a deep and ample forestage. Much of the Elizabethan intimacy between actor and audience was still preserved by the circles curving round to the edge of the forestage and by the rows of boxes overlooking it. But as scenery became increasingly elaborate the scene painters demanded more and more room to display their art, so the space behind the picture-frame was increased at the expense of the forestage. Bit by bit it was nibbled away until it became a mere ledge and the actor was forced to retire behind the proscenium arch to become part of the picture in the frame. He was compelled to withdraw still farther when lights were installed behind the proscenium arch, forcing him upstage so that his face could be properly illuminated. It was then that actors began to talk about "putting it across"— across the no-man's-land between themselves and the audience.

Meanwhile, the old horseshoe type of auditorium had become unpopular because from the ends of the circles it was no longer possible to get a good view of the actors. It had never been easy from these seats to see the whole of the picture set inside the picture-frame, but in the days when the play was acted out upon the forestage the actors were visible from every part of the house. New theatres were being built in which the circles no longer converged in a graceful curve towards the stage but were straightened out to become distant balconies parallel to the stage. Finally the actors were deprived of their last link with the audience when theatres were built without boxes, so that on either side of the proscenium was a huge expanse of blank wall which made the picture-frame and the actors within it seem still more than ever isolated from the audience. Sadler's Wells, built in 1931, is a typical example of this sort of theatre. It was never intended that it should be used only for opera and ballet. The plan was to interchange the Vic companies between the two theatres, but when plays were transferred from the Vic to the Wells they failed to "get across" because of the difficulties the actors experienced in projecting their performances past these great blank walls and over the moat of the orchestra pit. Eventually it was decided to use the theatre exclusively for opera and ballet, which do not require an intimate relationship between stage and auditorium.

There are still theatres in England where the relationship between stage and auditorium is easy and intimate, but most of the newer theatres are appallingly badly designed. Many of them, particularly those in the provinces, are more like huge

cinemas than theatres. The resemblance is not always accidental. Some of them were built with the intention of converting
them into cinemas if they failed as theatres. In London the
Dominion Theatre, the Carlton and the Leicester Square
Theatre all became cinemas soon after they opened.

I have three times had the experience of transferring a
production during its London run from one of the oldest theatres
to a badly designed modern theatre. The most noticeable result
in all three cases was that a considerable number of laughs
were lost and never recovered, however much we rehearsed
and experimented with the lines. These were not, of course, the
big "safe" laughs but the quick ripples of laughter which
depend upon an easy relationship between stage and auditorium.
The running time lengthened by several minutes because the
reactions of the audience were slower, and because the actors had
to broaden their performances as light, quick touches of detail
no longer made their effect. Yet the seating capacity of the
theatres to which the plays were transferred was much the same
as the theatres in which they had originally been produced. The
difference was that the audience, instead of converging towards
the stage, stretched away from it, row upon row, in a long,
rectangular block, as in a cinema, so that the most distant seats
were far farther from the stage than in the older theatres.

While the general trend of theatre architecture in England
has been to increase the separation of actor and audience, the
continental theatre has been seeking to bring them together in
an increasingly intimate relationship. In the many new theatres
now being built in Germany a pattern for a new type of
proscenium theatre seems to be emerging. The front of the
stage is no longer a straight line firmly defining the division
between stage and auditorium; it curves slightly outwards, and
this curve is repeated in the arrangement of the rows of stalls.
The circles, too, converge towards the stage, but the relations
of stage and auditorium is so planned that it is possible to get
a good view of the stage from the sides of the circles. There is
a movable forestage. When it is not in use the space is occupied
by extra rows of stalls. So that the actor does not appear to be

"stepping out of the picture" on to the forestage, the proscenium merges into the walls flanking the forestage, which are designed so that the décor can be changed to harmonise with the scene on the main stage.

But this kind of theatre, in the opinion of some producers, is still far too rigid, and likely to be as obstructive to the theatre of the future as hard and fast aesthetic theories. These producers believe the theatre of the future must be an adaptable, all-purposes theatre. A theatre of this kind is about to be built in Ealing by that most enterprising of all amateur companies, The Questors. In consultation with a panel of professional producers, plans have been completed, and a model built, for a theatre so flexible that it can be used as a picture-frame theatre, as a Restoration proscenium theatre with forestage, as an open-stage theatre, as an arena theatre, or as a theatre-in-the-round. So far as I can tell from a very careful examination of the model and plans, the scheme is workable. Surely here is the pattern of the theatre of the future? I very much doubt it. The Questor's theatre is planned for an audience of only three hundred and fifty. The scheme would not be practicable for a larger theatre because of the problems of adapting the sight-lines to five different kinds of stage. For instance, the two balconies in the Questor's plan have only two rows of seats. If a third row were added the occupants would be unable to see the stage when the theatre was being used as a theatre-in-the-round or as an open-stage theatre. Admittedly it is perfectly possible to build a theatre with a large seating capacity designed in such a way that everybody has a view of the central arena. The Grosses Schauspielhaus in Berlin and the London Hippodrome, which was built for spectacular water shows performed in a central arena, are examples. But in these theatres, in order to ensure a view of the arena from all parts of the house, the balconies have had to be withdrawn far from the stage, and steeply raked, so that there is nothing of the intimacy between actor and audience for which we are striving today.

Personally, I am very doubtful if it is possible to build an adaptable theatre without sacrificing many of the advantages of each kind of theatre. I agree with André Villiers who, in his contribution to a symposium of opinions on the theatres of the future published by *World Theatre*, said: "I have the deepest distrust of adaptable theatres. It is so important in any work of architecture that it should express even in its slightest details its precise intentions. We have to do, in the theatre, with visual impressions that are very subtle but are profound and essential—and which only too easily upset the technical ingenuities of 'all-purpose solutions'. I reject—however hopeful they seem in their intentions—deliberate schemes for multiform halls and adaptable theatres which, as I see it, only betray a culpable in-decision." Gordon Craig expressed much the same views in a letter in which he amiably refused to reply to *World Theatre's* questionnaire. "I feel strongly that all these questions somehow don't do. Open stage, frame stage—why not both?—and twenty more. It's all too fussy for us to 'or' about it. 'And' is the right word I feel. For whatever we build or do, one stage will be all right *if very well done*. If not—then not."

Whatever the form of the theatre of the future, it seems unlikely that in London, apart from the long-promised National Theatre, any more theatres of the conventional sort will be built because of the enormous increase in the value of sites in central London. Already several existing theatres are in danger of being pulled down and rebuilt as blocks of offices which can be let for far more money than could possibly be charged for a theatre. If we are going to have any new playhouses they will have to be open-stage theatres which require far less space than an ordinary theatre, are far less expensive to build and can often be fitted into an existing building. The success of these theatres will largely depend upon the playwrights providing plays specially written for them. At present we have too little experience of writing and acting plays for the open stage to say with any certainty what are its advantages and disadvantages, but the one thing that is certain is that it will force the play-wright to abandon the old realistic formula and use in ways that are as yet unpredictable his release from the confines of the picture-frame stage.

9

THE PRODUCER AND THE PLAYWRIGHT

We producers are constantly being told that our task is faithfully to interpret the author's intentions into terms of the theatre. But in practice the producer's responsibility towards his author is by no means so simple and straightforward. If the producer is dealing with a new script of any depth and subtlety he will probably find that what the author has achieved is rather different from what he intended, though he may not himself realise this. "If the author is a wise man," remarked Tyrone Guthrie in one of his lectures, "he will admit that he does not know what his play is about. . . . The more important the work of art, the less he knows what he has written." This happens, of course, not only in playwriting but in any form of imaginative writing. "How strange," remarked Thomas Hardy, after reading the reviews of *Tess of the D'Urbervilles,* "that one may write a book without knowing what one has put into it." When *A Mummer's Wife* was published, George Moore was astonished to find it praised for qualities he did not know it possessed. "No critic," he said, "seemed cognisant of the merits and demerits I saw and which in turn delighted and tortured me. As the public verdict continued to affirm itself, to realise itself, the book I knew of was changed, metamorphosed, disappeared, and another bearing no more than a distant family resemblance to my *Mummer's Wife* was gradually forced upon me. I have since forgotten the old, and have accepted and am content with the *Mummer's Wife* of the critics and friends."

Guthrie tells how Bridie used to say: "I am the last person you should ask about the play. I am only the author. I have written an armature, inside which possibly are the deepest ideas which have never quite formulated themselves in my conscience. If, as I hope and believe, I am a poet, there will be something in these, but I am the last person to know what it is." Chekhov detested being questioned about his plays by his producer or his actors. "I wrote it down; it is all there," he would reply. "Why don't you read my play?"

The producer should begin his work with the author by patiently seeking to discover what were his original intentions. Frequently the producer will find passages in the script where the author has failed to convey his intentions in the dialogue, but it may be that they can be made plain by the addition of a few more lines, or the producer may be able to convey them to the audience in his production by means of a pause or a glance, a gesture or a significant piece of business. But often the producer will find that his task is to convince the author that the play he has written is not the play he first dreamed. Otherwise time will be wasted during rehearsals in arguments with an author who still wants to see upon the stage something as near as possible to his first conception of the play in spite of the fact that, without him realising it, his conception has altered considerably during the writing.

During the preliminary work on the script a producer need seldom take much notice of the author's stage directions. Nowadays most of them are just popped in here and there, not so much as instructions to the producer and actors, but simply to make the scene more vivid to someone reading the script. And the someone whom the author has in mind is generally the theatrical manager to whom he has to sell his play before it is worthwhile thinking seriously about the mechanics of its production. But I have found when producing a Pinero play that one must faithfully follow the author's stage directions. While he was writing his plays Pinero worked out the moves on a model theatre with the result that the dialogue and the movement are so closely related that the production simply does not work if the grouping and movement are not exactly as the author envisaged them. The reason why authors today take so little trouble over the mechanics of their plays compared with the older authors is probably because of the position the producer now holds in the theatre. Most contemporary authors would probably agree with T. S. Eliot when he says, "I have always felt that stage directions were an interference by the author in the domain of the producer, and that every stage direction I found myself obliged to insert was an admission of some flaw in the play." But I think Pierre Fresnay is right when he says that the production is in every case latent in the author's mind and that the producer's job is to elicit it. "Scene by scene, page by page, he must oblige the author to search his memory for what he saw as he wrote—the positions and movements of his characters at each moment, and the relationship between them. According to the degree of the author's visual imagination the producer will obtain more or less numerous points of reference. Sometimes they will be so numerous that the complete successions of positions is established, but in all cases they will be sufficient to indicate the general outline."

Pierre Fresnay's method of working out the moves in collaboration with the author was the custom of most of the actor-managers. A. E. W. Mason describes how a few weeks after his play *The Witness for the Defence* had been accepted by George Alexander he was summoned to the boardroom of the St. James's Theatre where on a model stage were a set of draughtsmen labelled with the names of the characters in the play. For two days author and producer worked together arranging and marking in the script every move throughout the play. At the same time Alexander analysed the dialogue, sentence by sentence. "Every now and then," says Mason, "he would turn upon me with a quite disconcerting abruptness and say: 'What did you mean by that?'—disconcerting because—and I had noticed it before—suddenly out of a pair of familiar and friendly eyes a complete and rather hostile stranger seemed to look at me."

Shaw in his famous and much-quoted essay on production

declares that the most desirable producer of a play is the author. This may be true if the author is a widely experienced man of the theatre and his play is of no particular depth or subtlety; but if he dispenses with a producer he is depriving himself of his first critic. An author is too close to his own work to see it in perspective. Usually certain scenes are overwritten, others under-developed. The good producer is the advance guard of the audience, able to sense when the audience is likely to become bored, or when they might be a little uncertain of the author's intentions; and he must do more than just point out the weaknesses in the script, he must be able to indicate to the author how they can be put right.

All Shaw's later plays would have been improved if he had placed any reliance on the judgment and critical faculties of his producers. These plays are stuffed with unnecessary lines and speeches which go on reiterating the same point long after it has been made plain to the audience. Shaw's producers itched to prune away the dead wood from the dialogue, but Shaw, as he disarmingly described himself, was "a pigheaded, arrogant, obstinate, domineering man of genius, deaf to reason, and invincibly determined to have my own way about my own works".

He distrusted most of the producers who directed his plays because they tended to try to produce them too subtly for his taste. He would turn up at rehearsal assuring everyone that he had come merely to watch, not to interfere. After an hour or so he would come on the stage to give what he described as a few notes, which often amounted to a complete re-direction of the scenes he had been watching. Hesketh Pearson, who played in Granville-Barker's production of *Androcles and the Lion*, describes Shaw arriving "like an avalanche" at the dress-rehearsal and completely upsetting Granville-Barker's instructions, transforming the play in the course of four hours from a comedy into an extravaganza, "while Granville-Barker, who had retired from the contest, looked on at the destruction of his month's work with a face that registered amusement and annoyance in about equal degree".

Shaw had no patience with producers who laboured to make the grouping and movement and business as realistic as possible. I have seen him break up a neatly composed piece of grouping and re-arrange the four actors in the scene until they were ranged almost in a row, parallel with the footlights, delivering their lines not to one another but out to the audience, rather in the manner of an operatic quartette. On another occasion he stopped a scene between two actors and said to one of them: "Don't keep repeating that speech to *him*. He knows all about it, he's been listening to it for the last two weeks. Say it to the audience. They'll be hearing it for the first time." He had a musician's ear for tempo. Most producers believe that Shaw's plays should be taken at a terrific speed, but he himself, while demanding that certain scenes and passages should be played very fast indeed, constantly varied the tempo. He would tell the cast to mark passages in their scripts with musical terms—andante, largo, presto, and so on.

To return to the preliminary stages of rehearsal—the work on the script—it is essential that the producer should be very much aware of the dangers of attempting to impose his own ideas upon the author. "The profession of the producer," said Jouvet, "suffers from the disease of immodesty and even the most sincere do not escape it. Their licence to work freely with the plays of other people, to dabble with them and make them over, is an established and accepted convention, and a man must have a steady head and a firm foothold to resist the dizziness in which, convinced of what he would like to believe, he approaches the conclusion that his author understands nothing of the theatre."

Jouvet, who was the humblest of producers, used to say that the essential qualification for his profession was "docility of mind, absence of imagination". But it is too sweeping an assertion. Most of the plays which Jouvet handled were of superb quality. Sometimes he did a disservice to the author of a less good play by being too uncritically faithful to the text, too unwilling to allow his imagination to play upon the more barren patches. His production nakedly exposed the weaknesses of the play as well as its merits. A producer must find the right balance between criticism and appreciation. While keeping his enthusiasm for the play as a whole, he must also remain conscious of such weaknesses as it may have and do his best to mimimise them by touching on them as lightly as possible in his production, hurrying the audience past the duller passages which it has been impossible to eradicate from the script, giving the fullest possible value to all that is best in the play.

There is a danger, however, that the producer, when deciding whether to stress or to minimise, may be allowing his own personal likes and dislikes to distort his conception of the play. A producer with a fondness for an extremely naturalistic style of acting is apt to be too afraid of a long speech, which may not be nearly so effective when pruned to a more natural length. A producer with a lively sense of comedy may tend to emphasise the humour in the play at the expense of its emotion. Another, with a bias towards sentiment, may over-stress sentimental passages which may already have been too heavily emphasised by the author. A producer with an itch to create may seize upon certain incidents in the play because of the opportunities they give to exercise his inventiveness, elaborating and embellishing them until they assume an exaggerated importance and throw the whole play out of proportion.

The creative producer can often turn a thin play into a rich entertainment, but he can be a menace to a good play. He is apt to be less interested in the merits of a play than in the scope which it offers for a display of his own virtuosity. I once asked one of our leading producers why he had turned down a new play which was later produced with considerable success. He shrugged his shoulders: "There was nothing for *me* in it. There was really nothing I could *do* with it." Jouvet records a conversation he had with a producer who confided in him that he was in despair because he had been working for two months, without any result, on *Le Malade Imaginaire*. "When I expressed astonishment, he said: 'Yes, I have just spent my whole summer at it. I have tried lighting it from above, from below and from the side; I have experimented with settings and movement.

There is nothing, nothing, to be done. It's the perfect play. It is a work of genius.' "

Copeau defined the relationship of author and producer as a "friendly conflict between creator and interpreter". It is essential that the author and the producer should like and respect one another, and have an appreciation and understanding of each other's quite different problems. If the relationship ceases to be friendly, if the conflict becomes real, the cast sense a divided control and lose confidence in their producer. Then they are apt to ask the author's advice when they can get him alone, so their performances tend to be an uneasy compromise between the conflicting ideas of author and producer. In self-defence the producer may be driven to keep the author out of the theatre during some of the rehearsals, but this is a confession of weakness. It is the producer's job to try to persuade the author to his own point of view. If he is a sensible producer he may eventually be persuaded to the author's point of view. This is "the friendly conflict" to which Copeau refers. But on all important matters the conflict should take place before the rehearsals begin. After that, to use a phrase of Jouvet's, "they should move through the rehearsals hand in hand". Naturally many minor points will crop up during rehearsals; adjustments will have to be made to suit the personalities and techniques of the actors, and even the most experienced producer cannot be certain that all is right with the text or his own ideas of production until they have been tested during rehearsal.

During these early stages of rehearsal an inexperienced author often maddens the producer by constantly interrupting to make small points, breaking into the producer's concentration. The author has long ago visualised the play in performance and does not realise how slowly and painstakingly that performance has to be built up during rehearsals, or how slow and devious is the route by which the producer brings his cast to the final rehearsal. It often seems to the author that the actors are being allowed to make far too many mistakes without being pulled up. He does not understand that the producer is at first simply outlining the production and the performances, deliberately not worrying the cast about details, however important, until the later stages of rehearsals. The inexperienced author will, for instance, mutter in the producer's ear: "This scene is far too *slow*; can't you get them to take it much faster?" —not realising that the tempo of a scene must be left until the actors know their lines.

I do not think that any author should speak directly to the cast except when the producer has asked him to do so and then only in the presence of the producer. Actors cannot take guidance from two people, even if these two are in agreement. I remember one instance of a moment or two's conversation between an actor and an author on a bus going home after the dress-rehearsal having a shattering effect on the actor's performance. He was an excellent actor apart from one fault: he had a tendency to be slow. During the last week of rehearsals I had been making him play the part rather faster than I actually wanted it to be played, knowing that once he got in front of an audience he would slow down. But I knew that if he had become accustomed during rehearsals to a fast tempo he would probably not slow down to his usual crawl. During that bus ride the actor asked the author what he thought of his performance. "Excellent, excellent," said the author. "You've got the character to perfection. My only criticism is that you are perhaps taking it a little bit fast. If I were you I should take your time over it." Needless to say he did—even more time than he usually took over a part, with disastrous effects not only on his own performance but on those of the other actors.

The author of a first play showed me a letter from an experienced playwright whose advice he had asked about how to behave at rehearsals. "Remember," wrote the experienced author, "that when rehearsals begin *you* have done ninety per cent of your job—and you probably think you have done one hundred per cent—but the producer is only beginning on his job, and it is one which needs intense concentration. If you want your play done with all the interest, skill and enthusiasm which you believe your producer has for it, then you must sit quietly at the back and let him find out for himself how it is unloading off the pages of the script. You must be prepared to criticise your own work, and be ready to alter it if the producer has sound reasons for wanting you to do so. A good producer will find the right way of telling you immediately *why* he is worried—and ask your help in straightening out a line or a scene. A bad producer may consider you a damned nuisance for being there at all. But if you are a sensitive author you will choose your moment to give your opinion and do so privately, *not* in front of the cast. You will always get a good producer's attention to your own point of view provided that you choose the right place and the right moment to express it."

As a successful production depends to a large extent upon an understanding collaboration between author and producer, the author should be consulted on the choice of his producer and the two should meet before the producer is finally engaged. Nowadays in the English theatre the management frequently cast leading parts before considering who is going to produce the play, and the producer is often the choice of the star rather than the author of the play. Naturally, leading actors and actresses have their preferences about producers but it does not follow that the producer chosen by a star because he or she likes working with him is the best producer for that particular play. A leading actor or actress will give an effective performance irrespective of who produces the play, but if the producer has been miscast there is a danger that he will allow, even encourage, performances which distort and spoil the play. A producer can do a technically brilliant production which ruins the play by misinterpreting it—and he can do so without incurring any blame from the critics who can only judge a new play in the form in which it emerges from the production.

A year or two ago I saw at a weekly repertory theatre a play which was a gay and charming fantasy. It was bought by a West End management and eventually arrived in London directed by a different producer, and with an entirely different cast. When I read the notices I was astonished to find them all bad, although the cast were praised. But when I went to see the play again I found it bore little resemblance to the play I had seen at that repertory theatre. The script, so far as I could tell, had been very little altered but the production had changed the play from a lightly comic fantasy into a clod-hopping farce festooned with extraneous comic business. The repertory production, simple and straightforward, had exactly caught the mood of the play. The restrictions imposed by the inadequate time for rehearsal in weekly repertory allow the actors to do little more than learn the author's lines and to say them as intelligently as possible. There is no time for invention, elaborate characterisation or detailed business. The result is that sometimes, if the company is a talented one, and the play is a fairly easy one, it exactly conveys the author's intentions without the slightest distortion, even though the performance may be underdeveloped.

When a producer turns from contemporary plays to directing a revival, faithfulness to the author may easily become a fault rather than a virtue unless the play is a masterpiece. The reason why so many of the classics are rarely performed is because they belong too exclusively to the age in which they were written. They lack the timeless qualities which enable the major plays of Shakespeare to span the centuries. If a play is worth reviving it must have at least some qualities to which a present-day audience is immediately responsive, but unless it is a masterpiece much of it will inevitably seem pointless and dull, even silly, except to those who have a considerable knowledge of the period in which it was written. So it is the producer's task to make the most of the scenes and characters which age has not withered and to use the rest as material out of which he re-fashions something to the taste of his audience. What he cannot profitably use, he must, whenever possible, discard.

The most audaciously successful operation I have ever seen performed upon a play was in Nugent Monck's production of *Doctor Faustus*. He cut out of it almost everything except the superb opening and closing scenes, then neatly stitched them together to make a one-act play. Anyone in the Maddermarket audience who had already seen the play in its entirety must have been profoundly grateful for being spared the moribund humours, the silly conjuring tricks and the flat-footed verse of the rest of the play. When Monck produced *Pericles* at Stratford he omitted the whole of the first act on the grounds that it does not seem to be by Shakespeare and because the scenes of incest have nothing to do with the tale of a prince who strangely found a wife and then strangely lost her. At the Open Air Theatre Robert Atkins produced *The Comedy of Errors* and *The Two Gentlemen of Verona* as a double bill. I, for one, have never enjoyed either of these plays so much.

Another revival which owed much of its success to bold and ruthless cutting was Guthrie's compression of the two parts of *Tamburlaine* into a single play of reasonable length. *Tamburlaine* owes its overblown reputation to one or two magnificent speeches, the only examples of "Marlowe's mighty line" in the whole play, which for the rest degenerates into a monotonous tum-tum. There is no dramatic conflict, no plot, the characterisation is crude, and many of the scenes are ludicrously over-written. It might be argued that the only point of this revival was that it proved the play not worth reviving, but paradoxically enough, although it did prove that, it nevertheless provided a memorable evening in the theatre. Guthrie produced the play with an almost demoniac zest, aided by a tremendous performance from Donald Wolfit. The lurid orgies of sadism, torture, and lust which could so easily have seemed ludicrous or just dully brutal—as indeed they are—were transformed by the splendour of his imagination into scenes of genuine horror. The savage colours of Leslie Hurry's scenery and costumes matched the ferocity of the production. The play became an exotic pageant of barbarism. With a huge cast at his command Guthrie used them to compose surging, feverish patterns of movement, macabre, horrifying groupings. Again and again he exercised his genius for theatrical invention to give excitement to scenes where the writing completely lacked it—for instance, the scene where the dying Tamburlaine calls for a map so that he can retrace his conquests. Marlowe aims at pathos in this scene but fails to achieve it, for there can be no pity for the death of this bestial monster whom we have seen committing

almost every conceivable kind of cruelty. In Guthrie's production six slaves dragged on a gigantic map of the world
painted on a cloth which they spread over the stage. The dying
Tamburlaine, wrapped in a huge cloak of rough shaggy fur,
because he was already deathly cold, staggered across the vast
map following the trails of his conquests, until growing weaker,
he fell upon his knees and crawled on all fours from place to
place on the map, like some huge, loathsome brute beast. Thus
Guthrie created an effect of horror and repulsion instead of the
pathos which he knew could not be evoked.

Nigel Playfair's production of *The Beggar's Opera*, which
during the 'twenties ran for nearly fifteen hundred performances, was yet another revival which owed much of its success to
the cutting and rearrangement of the text and a deliberate and
justifiable perversion of the author's intentions. When Playfair
first read the play he found it "a pretty indigestable dish". In
The Story of the Lyric Theatre, Hammersmith he describes
"the Herculean task of reading it through—a task which, I can
assure you, took a great deal of faith, hope and trust in the
judgment of critics dead and gone. I can claim the merit of
recognising the plums; but I came very often very near to being
choked by the suet. I'm not quite sure what a colander is, but I
felt that some such implement must be wielded at once to
reduce its density".

With the help of Arnold Bennett the script was analysed,
dissected, and put together again, and the score was rearranged
by Frederick Austin to fit the new version. Playfair's theory
was that in reproducing old plays "one is out, I maintain, not
so much to give a replica (which is impossible) as to furnish a
sort of review and criticism— a *parody* if you like, but a parody
which expresses admiration and not contempt". What Playfair did in his production of *The Beggar's Opera* was quite
frankly to laugh at the play a little—not with condescension but
with affectionate amusement. The "suet" which he removed in
huge chunks was mainly the scurrilous political satire which
was no longer comprehensible to a modern audience. What he
made of the rest was an entertainment full of gaiety and charm.

Gay would hardly have recognised his work, nor would he have recognised the London of his time in the neat, trim, clean-as-clean-could-be settings of Lovat Fraser. In fact, what Playfair did was to disinter a work long dead and use the bones to fashion a delightful entertainment of his own devising.

The German production of *The Beggar's Opera* (entitled *Die Dreigroschenoper*), although inspired by the success of Playfair's revival, had nothing in common with it except that it was equally well suited to the taste of the audience. The Playfair version would inevitably have failed in Berlin. It was far too dainty—which was one of the reasons for its success in England at a time when the women's pages were full of advice about dainty ways of preparing food, dainty frocks, dainty curtains, dainty presents, and dainty ways of arranging dainty little flowers. There was nothing dainty about the taste of Berlin in the 'twenties. Brecht re-wrote the text and the lyrics, the original score was scrapped and replaced by music which had much in common with the lewd husky ditties of the Berlin nightclubs. The predominant flavour of the production was that peculiarly German mixture of sadism and sickly sentiment.

When Playfair revived *The Way of the World* he was dealing with a play which was a failure when it was first produced and had never been successfully revived. He decided that its persistent failure, in spite of the eulogies heaped upon it by the literary critics, was largely due to the "jungle of passionless intrigue" which makes the plot so bewilderingly complicated. By means of skilful cutting he simplified the plot as far as possible and frankly burlesqued what was left of it. He made it plain to the audience that they could treat it as a joke and need not bother their heads too much about the tangled threads. His next problem was to find a way of ensuring that the licentiousness should not seem gross and offensive to a modern audience. There is a passage in *The Essays of Elia* in which Lamb ingeniously justifies his enjoyment of Congreve's plays in spite of their grossness because he could "never connect these sports of a witty fancy in any shape with any result to be drawn from them to imitation in real life. They are a world of themselves, almost as much as fairy land. . . . They break through no laws or conscientious restraints. They know of none. They have got out of Christendom into the land of—what shall I call it?— of cuckoldry—the Utopia of gallantry, where pleasure is duty, and the manners perfect freedom". It was into Lamb's "Utopia of gallantry" that Playfair removed the play. The satire and cynicism were touched on as lightly as possible. The emphasis was all on the grace, the gaiety and the wit. Doris Zinkeisen's scenery and costumes in fresh, gay colours charmingly fantasticated the period. It became a Restoration fairyland, where the audience could feel, like Lamb, that they were "taking an airing beyond the diocese of the strict conscience" in a realm from which "our coxcombical moral sense is for a little transitory ease excluded". Although for two centuries the critics had been fulminating against the immorality of Congreve's plays, Playfair's production of *The Way of the World* completely disarmed the moralist critics, although the script had not been bowdlerised.

When in 1943 Gielgud gave a much more realistic production of Congreve's *Love for Love* it was attacked by some of the newspapers as an obscene and improper play. In Gielgud's production the characters were no longer living in the world of fairyland. They were real people living in a real world, subject to the laws of morality. Gielgud's direction was far closer to Congreve's intentions and much closer to the spirit of the Restoration than Playfair's, but it is doubtful if such a production would have been enjoyed or even tolerated at the time when Playfair produced *The Way of the World*. Moral standards deteriorate during a war, and the morals of wartime London at the time when Gielgud produced *Love for Love* had a good deal in common with those of the Restoration. Both productions were successful with the public because the producers, whether consciously or unconsciously, had attuned their methods of presentation to the mood of the moment.

Playfair's fondness for elegantly fantasticating a period sometimes misled him into imposing his style of production upon a play ill-suited to it. When he produced *She Stoops to Conquer*, he obscured the simple good humour of the play with too many airs and graces, and settings and costumes which were too stylishly sophisticated. Michael Benthall, when he produced *She Stoops to Conquer* for the Old Vic in settings and costumes "after Rowlandson", erred in the other direction, making the play into a bumpkin farce, transforming many of the characters into grotesques, whipping up the humour until the play's robust jollity was transformed into hectic high spirits. It was often brilliantly done and often hugely entertaining, but in the frisking and romping much of the enduring, lovable qualities of the play were lost—its warmth, its charm, its humanity and its essential realism. Benthall lavished so much invention on the production that he obviously had little faith in the ability of this sturdy old play to stand squarely on its own legs. There are few classics of the English theatre which need less assistance from the producer than *She Stoops to Conquer*.

The School for Scandal, on the other hand, has not weathered the passing of the centuries quite so successfully. There are scenes in it which time has withered—the scenes of scandal and tittle-tattle. The tittering gossips who call at Lady Sneerwell's are no longer recognisable types, the subjects about which they gossip have long ago lost their topicality, and nowadays we are accustomed to back-biting much more sharply and amusingly written by Coward and the authors of intimate revues. When Laurence Olivier produced the play he was obviously well aware of the danger of these scenes becoming tedious to present-day audiences, so he stylised them, giving them an exaggerated artificiality, making the characters pose and posture like ballet dancers. The gay patterns of movement certainly enlivened the duller scenes, but as the rest of the play was acted realistically there was an irreconcilable clash of styles, especially in the second half of the play when the minor characters turned up at Sir Peter's and continued to caper like characters out of the Commedia dell' Arte.

When Willard Stoker produced *The Rivals* at Birmingham (the production was later seen at the St. James's for a limited season) he put it into modern dress. While he was reading the play he suddenly recognised Mrs. Malaprop as a Memsahib he had once met in Calcutta, and as it seemed to him that none of the characters had dated at all, he thought the play might seem more real and enjoyable to his audience if the characters were presented as contemporary figures. He ingeniously solved the problem of how to get away with the duel in modern dress by starting the play with an old sandwich-board man standing in the middle of the stage advertising a fancy-dress ball at the Assembly Rooms, so that some of the earlier scenes were played with the characters trying on wigs and unpacking boxes from the costumiers; then in the last scene but one all the principals were dressed for the ball in the costume of Sheridan's day, so it was perfectly natural for the men to be wearing swords. In this production, Faukland, played in a manner slightly reminiscent of Coward, seemed a much more vivid character than usual. Acres was played as a tweedy, huntin'-shootin'-fishin' type. Captain Absolute, in khaki, proved to be the charming, cheerful, slightly bumptious young officer who is as much a product of Sandhurst as of the eighteenth century. The audience the night I saw the play got immense enjoyment from nudging one another and pointing out resemblances to people they knew. "My dear," said an old lady sitting behind me, "they are all just like my cousins in the North"—a remark which was a tribute to the agelessness of the play and the success of its translation into modern dress.

Melodrama, because it often rides perilously close to absurdity, is particularly difficult to revive successfully. Melodramatic situations, because they are contrived rather than real, soon begin to look shabby and rather ridiculous after they have been used for a while, so audiences are no longer prepared to take them seriously. When Michael Benthall produced *A Woman of No Importance* he wisely treated it as a comedy instead of the drama which Wilde intended it to be. The melodramatic scenes were pruned in the script, and toned down in the production, so that the emphasis of the play was entirely on Wilde's wit. But he boldly produced Webster's *The White Devil* as a melodrama, relying upon the tremendous vigour of the verse and the blazing colour of the language to give an air of splendour to the melodramatic scenes of sadistic vengeance. If he had handled the melodrama more cautiously it is unlikely that this revival would have succeeded, for there is little in the play apart from its melodrama. The character drawing is weak and unsubtle, and only rarely does the verse become poetry.

Apart from great tragedy no form of play revives more easily than a good farce. The drolls, the gulls, the buffoons of farce belong to no particular period; they live in a cloud-cuckoo land of their own. Two of the best revivals of minor classics during recent years were Guthrie's *The Country Wife* and Anthony Quayle's *The Relapse*. Both productions abounded in the comic invention so essential to farce and were directed with tremendous gusto and genuine high spirits. But because it is easy for an inventive producer to enliven what seems dull and dated by making it farcically funny, in some revivals the humour has been broadened so much that the whole character of the play has been distorted. When *The Alchemist* was produced by John Burrell, and *Bartholomew Fair* by George Devine, both producers changed these sardonic satires into hurly-burly farces— but they had every justification for doing so. The producer's difficulty with Ben Jonson's plays, apart from *Volpone,* is that few of the contemporary types he portrays exist today, so the satire no longer has much point—probably the only way to make the characters entertaining to modern audiences is to caricature them. The fault of these lively, vigorous productions was not in their exaggerations but in the fact that neither of the producers seemed to appreciate that what is the most enduring quality in the plays is the eloquence of the language, its glowing, gleaming richness, its wonderful variety. The words were seldom allowed to make their own effect. Even during the play's most splendid speeches the attention was distracted from the words by the continual flow of comic business.

The most straightforward revival of a classic in recent years was Peter Brook's production of *Venice Preserved*. William Archer described the play as "a clumsy, blundering, coarsely

bombastic work". That it never seemed so in Brook's production
was to a large extent due to the tact and skill with which he cut
and rearranged the text so that the improbabilities of the plot
were by-passed and the construction of the play made more taut
and dramatic. Making no attempt to produce it in the operatic
style of eighteenth-century Heroic Tragedy, he pruned away the
more over-blown lines and speeches. Having eradicated so far
as was possible the weaknesses of the play, Brook developed to
the utmost the qualities that remained—the humanity, the
pathos, the intensity of the dramatic conflict. He added nothing that was obviously his own to the production, relying upon
a magnificent cast to give the virtuoso performances which
the play demands, without the aid of those clever, inventive
bits of business which at one time he was so fond of introducing.
Because of its simplicity and dignity and power, this production achieved a tragic grandeur such as is seldom seen upon
the English stage.

During the past thirty years or so, a time when there has been
an ever-increasing shortage of good new plays, the English
theatre has owed much to its producers for reviving so many of
the lesser classics in productions which have never been merely
dutiful but have always sought to re-create the plays as lively
entertainments. But most of these productions have had in
common the same fault—a lack of any real sense of style. Too
many producers seem to believe they will achieve a stylish
production if they encourage their designers to emphasise the
period by over-exaggerating its extravagances and affectations,
and keep their actors busy bowing and bobbing and curtseying,
fluttering fans, flourishing handkerchiefs, tapping snuff-boxes,
twirling canes, and tripping about the stage with mincing steps.
The style of a play is not in its period fripperies but in the
words. It is dependent upon the rhythm and phrasing of the
dialogue, the relishing of the language. Yet one can hardly
blame the producers for attempting to achieve an air of period
elegance almost entirely by visual means when they are working
mostly with actors untrained in the style of acting which
classical comedy demands. The Old Vic's unhappy attempt at

The Producer and the Play

The Way of the World all too convincingly proved how completely the English theatre has lost its traditional skill in playing high comedy. Only two members of the company were able to deliver Congreve's lines with the necessary grace and elegance. The rest were unable even to speak the dialogue clearly, intelligently, and rhythmically. While they strutted and posed and flounced with a great show of elegance they were blundering their way through the lines with such clumsiness that much of the play was unintelligible. Producers surely have a right to expect that actors who have spent two years at a dramatic school should have been taught how to speak the prose of eighteenth-century comedy instead of being sent out from these schools imagining that they have learned to act "in period" because they have been taught how to bow or to curtsy, how to manage a fan or a snuff-box.

10

THE PRODUCER AND THE PLAYER

In the theatre of today the relationship of producer and actor is very different from what it was when I went on the stage during the middle 'twenties. Those were the last years of the reign of the dictator-producers. The autocratic Dion Boucicault, at the age of sixty-five, was still the most consistently successful producer in the English theatre. He dictated to the actor every move, every intonation, every gesture. He acted all the parts himself and the cast had to copy him down to the minutest detail. He would demonstrate some small, meticulously-timed piece of business over and over again until he was sure that the actor had absorbed every detail of it, then he would send him away to practise it in front of a mirror in a dressing-room.

In Hector Bolitho's book on Marie Tempest there is a description by her of Boucicault at rehearsal. "Like all little men, he was eager to impress one with his personality. His chief weapon was irony and he was never charming until he had first impressed you with his power. This was deliberate, and effective. He never shouted. He waited for silence and then he spoke in a voice which was calm and deadly. He would spend an entire morning over one scene of ten minutes. He insisted on definite movements, never varying, definite inflexions and perfect timing. An actor took out a cigarette as he was standing upon a definite flower in the pattern of the carpet. He took two steps and, as his foot came to the carpet again, he tapped his cigarette on his case. He spoke a line, took one more step, and struck a match. A few more words, a step, and the match was blown out. Then the phrase was finished. The same method was used for the lifting of a fan . . . one never toyed with it, at will. One's coffee was drunk, at a given second, one's gloves were taken off, 'by numbers'. Every look and gesture was drilled into me by 'Dot' Boucicault. He said of me that I swallowed everything he gave me, digested it and brought it up in my own fashion."

Not all actors and actresses were as amenable as Marie Tempest to Boucicault's methods. Lilah Macarthy protested that he turned her into an automaton. Gladys Cooper in her autobiography describes his method as "old fashioned". But Marie Tempest said that all she knew about acting she learned from Boucicault. "I was a blank page upon which he was able to write at will, and if he ever created anything, Dion Boucicault created me as an actress." She simply did not believe actors and actresses who told her they could visualize their parts from the start. "That's all eyewash," she used to say. "I only begin to know the character I am to play after two or three weeks of rehearsal when the producer has given me everything."

Boucicault had learned his method of rehearsal from his father, the author-producer, and from Pinero, another author-producer for whom he had acted. Actors used to say of Pinero that he would have been happier with a cast of performing parrots. W. S. Gilbert was another of the author-producers who demanded unquestioning obedience. Before the first rehearsal he would spend day after day working out the moves on a model stage with blocks of wood representing the actors —three inches high for the males, two-and-a-half inches for the women. At rehearsal he pushed and dragged the cast about the stage like live chessmen upon a board, giving them every inflexion and gesture as he did so.

Although he was moody and irritable, often flying into violent rages, he would suffer fools gladly provided they were docile enough. Hesketh Pearson has described how he would stand on the stage by the side of an actor or an actress and repeat words and gestures over and over again, without the least sign of despair or irritation, until he had achieved the exact intonation and gesture he wanted. "He could be extremely tactful provided he was always having his own way. To one well-meaning girl who kept putting the accent on the wrong syllable of the word 'indubitably' he remarked that hers was a Parisian pronunciation and though, of course, it would be understood by the stalls it might not be understood by the gallery." But with anyone who betrayed the slightest reluctance to obey him unquestioningly he could be viciously caustic. "Never mind," he said to an actress who showed signs of having a mind of her own, "you can't help it; it needs a lady to get it the way I want it." There were frequent clashes between Gilbert and George Grossmith who often had suggestions for effective bits of business. The more effective they were the more they infuriated Gilbert, who hated to believe that anyone but himself could contribute anything to the production.

Hesketh Pearson describes Gilbert as being at his best and his worst when drilling the chorus. "Then the military-looking gentleman became military in manner. He issued his words of command as if he was on parade, and when they were not obeyed he stormed and shouted. Sometimes he would even seize the leader of the chorus and shake him into a Gilbertian view of his duties. He seemed to be possessed of demons. When the dancers failed to put sufficient vigour into their performance he would show them how to do it by twirling up and down the stage, his coat tails flying, his square sporting hat jammed hard on his head, his feet moving at a most unmilitary speed and his body gyrating in a manner never seen on the drill ground. Even though he could not sing a note in tune, he would instruct the chorus in rhythm and pronunciation. However rapidly uttered, every word had to be given its full value, every syllable its proper inflexion."

Another of the dictatorial producers who allows the actor very little freedom to create for himself is Robert Atkins. He is not a particularly inventive producer. Most of the business in his Shakespearian productions is traditional. He accepts what he calls the "tried and true" readings of the characters. Even though he produces the same play three or four times he never varies his conception of it and he imposes upon each actor the same business which he has used for the actor who played the part in his first production of the play, without taking into consideration differences of personality and physique. But for an actor to argue with Atkins would be as unthinkable as a private questioning the orders of his commanding officer. Yet in spite of having to assimilate some outworn clichés of production, the actor gains from Robert Atkins a sound knowledge of the Shakespearian traditions, and learns that many of them are to be respected.

When Atkins is producing Shakespeare he is infuriated by any actor who distorts the metre of the line. Sometimes he will literally howl in agony or bellow like an enraged bull. He bangs out the rhythm like a teacher of dancing. I have seen him rehearsing at the Open Air Theatre in Regent's Park, clapping his hands in time to the rhythm of the verse, banging it out on the backs of deckchairs and even bashing the bushes and shrubs if nothing else was handy. He is apt to frighten and fluster his actors so that they retire into their shells and long for rehearsal to end. But I have never known an actor who has worked with Robert Atkins who did not understand and respect the rhythm of Shakespeare's verse.

During the 'twenties Basil Dean was achieving a series of brilliant productions by methods which had much in common with the ferocity of the old author-producers. John Gielgud, who worked with him in *The Constant Nymph,* says that although he got good results from the actors in the end, it was usually after a great deal of heartburning. "He would not allow people to think for themselves or develop their characters freely, and his meticulous method of giving them every inflexion and tone, before they had experimented themselves, made them feel helpless and inefficient." Noel Coward in *Present Indicative* describes what a nerve-racking experience it was to be produced by Basil Dean, how he tore himself and the actors to shreds. Myself, I only know Dean as a charming and amiable member of my club. Talking to him it is difficult to believe the many stories of how he terrifies his actors. Noel Coward suggests that the explanation is that Dean's "genuine passion for perfection of detail, his technical thoroughness, and his tireless energy as a rule completely shut him off from any personal contact with his companies. I don't think it ever occurred to him that actors' feelings are notoriously nearer the surface than average people's; if they weren't they wouldn't be good actors. Every good surgeon knows that no operation, however swift and brilliant, can ultimately be considered a complete success if sensitive membranes and organs and viscera have been handled carelessly in the process. A first-rate theatrical producer should learn early on in his career that most actors wear their intestines on their sleeves. Basil's only real failing in the theatre was a lack of psychological perceptiveness".

Coward is today the only playwright of any note in the English theatre who still produces his own plays. Like Dean, he dictates every inflexion, demonstrates every bit of business in exact detail—and at times he can be every bit as scathing. He begins by reading the play to the company, portraying every part so vividly that some of the cast are apt to be reduced to a state of gloom because they doubt their ability to give a performance anything like as good as the author's own reading of their part. During rehearsals the actor never has that encouraging moment when he makes the rest of the cast laugh by neatly timing a line or a bit of business: Coward has got all the laughs in advance during that first reading. He insists on the cast reproducing exactly his own inflexions. Most actors and actresses willingly submit to this because they realise that Coward knows better than anyone else how to time his own laughs, how to point his own lines with absolute precision. His sense of audience is so unerring that he is quite confident that lines and bits of business which do not seem amusing during rehearsals will nevertheless get their laughs. He will say to an actor: "On the first night you will find your part is full of laughs where you didn't think there were any"—and the first night will prove Coward to have been right.

Coward's rehearsals are virtually a series of dictation lessons. In theory this should result in an atmosphere of dullness at rehearsal because the actors feel they are being deprived of all initiative, but Coward is so electric a personality that he keeps his actors alert and eager. One of his cast told me that when Coward arrives for rehearsal in a chilly, dimly lit theatre on a dreary, wet morning, "you feel as if all the lights have suddenly been turned on and a glass of champagne put into your hand".

A peculiarity of Coward as a producer is that he insists on the cast knowing their lines at the first rehearsal. Engaging an actress for a part he will end the interview by handing her the script and saying: "Now, go home and learn your lines, duckie; that makes practising a pleasure"—advice that is usually followed up by a note from H. M. Tennent Ltd., politely intimating that "Mr. Coward would be very pleased if you would know your lines by the first rehearsal". Of course no actor can really be word-perfect until he has become accustomed to hearing the other actors and actresses speaking his cues, so for the first two or three days of Coward's rehearsals the cast are so busy trying to remember strings of words that they have no time for interpretation or characterisation. Presumably this is Coward's intention. All he requires from the actors is that they should present him with the skeletons of their parts to which he himself adds the flesh and blood.

Not all actors and actresses are able to adapt themselves altogether happily to Coward's way of rehearsing. No cut-and-dried method of direction can be equally suitable for every member of a company. Gladys Cooper, for instance, on the one occasion she acted in a Coward production, disliked his method as much as she disliked Boucicault's—and for the same reasons. She is an actress who likes to fit herself very gradually into a part and is incapable of learning a line until she knows exactly what she is going to do with it. Her ideal producer was Gerald du Maurier. She describes him as "just letting you go your own way, understanding and seeing what you are trying to get at, and the consequence was he achieved a production over which there was the stamp of reality and naturalness".

Daphne du Maurier's biography of her father contains a detailed description of his methods. "Try and remember it's your own drawing-room," he would say, "and there's no one there but yourself, and you're tired after a long day, and all you want is a drink and a couple of aspirins. Perhaps I am entirely wrong, but what about trying something like this?" Then, after he had demonstrated what he meant, he would say: "Don't necessarily do that, but something like it. You see what I mean?"

He hated any kind of stage cliché, especially in love scenes. At that time there was a conventional, stagey way of playing these scenes. "Must you kiss her as though you were having steak and onions for lunch?" he would say. "It may be what you feel, but it's damned unattractive from the front row of the stalls. Can't you just say 'I love you', and yawn and light a cigarette and walk away?" Or he would say, "Be playful, be like puppies, be fond of one another, but don't go to the extremes either one way or the other. Strike some sort of medium between afternoon tea in a cathedral town and supper in a flat in Paris, for Gawd's sake." He was exceptionally tactful as a producer, taking immense pains not to hurt anyone's feelings. Although he often did what is so dangerous for most producers —mimicked the actor's faults and mannerisms—he did it so gaily and amusingly, without the slightest suggestion of irritation or malice, that nobody was ever offended.

While at first he allowed his cast plenty of freedom to create their own characters and invent their own business, during the later stages of rehearsal he tightened the reins. As soon as he was satisfied that an actor was on the right lines he proceeded to fix and sharpen the performance. His own technique as an actor was brilliant and he gave his company the benefit of it. By the first night the production was taut, exact, and precise, yet it had an air of spontaneity, ease, and nonchalance. Lines might seem to be "thrown away" but actually they were so exactly pointed, spoken with such immaculate diction that they were sharply effective to even the most distant rows. He had many imitators, but because they lacked his technical skill their productions achieved naturalness only at the expense of underplaying and inaudibility.

Another producer who detested the old method of dictating inflexions and gestures to the cast was Komisarjevsky. He considered that those who did so were not producers in the sense in which he understood the word but merely experts in stage business. Like du Maurier, he would wait to see what the actor was going to do with his part and then help him in the search for the right rendering of the lines and expressive moves and business. When he had to give an actor an inflexion, a gesture, or a movement, he always tried at the same time to arouse the actor's own imagination so that he felt, not just understood, the reason for it. He handled his actors with delicacy and understanding. In *Myself and the Theatre* he wrote: "The 'inside' of an actor—call it 'self', 'consciousness', or whatever you like—with which the producer has to deal, is a very complicated and delicate instrument. That instrument is what matters most on the stage and only an extremely sensitive and careful producer can play on it without hurting the freshness of the actor's conception of the part and his own creation of it."

Komisarjevsky guided his actors through rehearsals so unobtrusively that some of them considered that he "just didn't produce". They used to say, "He just sat there. We had to do it all for ourselves." Only the more intelligent realised how intently he was watching them and listening to them, moulding their performances by an occasional remark which seemed almost casual, sometimes by a single word which exactly summed up what was needed. Gielgud tells how during the rehearsals of *The Cherry Orchard,* after Komisarjevsky had watched Martita Hunt (who was playing Charlotta) rehearsing a scene, he patted her on the shoulder and murmured the one word "Irony". Like Reinhardt, he used the fewest possible words at rehearsal, and chose them with immense care. I have seen Reinhardt stop a rehearsal, go on the stage, walk up and down for a moment or two in silence, thinking, and then address to the actor a single sentence so exact and so illuminating that it was far more telling than the spate of words, vague and ill-chosen, with which some producers try to convey their meaning.

In the series of Chekhov plays Komisarjevsky produced in the middle 'twenties at a tiny little cinema in Barnes, the acting had a sensitiveness and an inner realism, which was something quite new on the London stage. In these productions there were no obvious showy effects but a wonderful sense of atmosphere which was due to Komisarjevsky's ability to make his actors absorb not only the characteristics of their own part but also the mood and the background of the play. Gielgud, who was one of Komisarjevsky's company at Barnes, says that it was from him that he learned how to study a part from the inside, "and then to build it outward so that it came to life naturally, developing in proper relation to the other actors, under the control of the producer".

Like so many great producers, Komisarjevsky was a musician. He made elaborate and subtle use of variations of tempo, modulation of tone, and delicately timed pauses. Before I went on the stage I was working as a journalist and was sent to do an interview with Komisarjevsky. He had come to England after being director of the Imperial and State Theatres in Moscow in the years immediately after the revolution. I had been told to get his views on production in the English theatre, but at first it was difficult to make him talk. He seemed bored and rather grumpy. Then something I said suddenly aroused his interest and he sat down at the grand piano in his room and started to improvise a tune. "It is an English theatre," he said. "The curtain rises. I hear a tune—something like this. The act goes on—and so does the tune, always at the same damn dull pace. Now it is the second act. Still the same tune, still the same tempo. I cannot stand it. I compose myself for sleep. That is very easy—the tune lulls me to sleep. On and on goes that damned tune. But in the theatre it should not be so, it should be like this." Then he played his improvised little tune again with innumerable variations of tone and tempo. It was exactly what Komisarjevsky did in his own productions, giving them intricate patterns of rhythm.

In Gielgud's autobiography *Early Stages* he says that when he produced his first modern play, Rodney Ackland's *Strange Orchestra*, his method of production was a direct imitation of Komisarjevsky's. As a result of working with him, Gielgud has always been reluctant to give his actors detailed instruction during the early rehearsals. Lecturing at Oxford in 1952 he said: "An actor demands some responsibility in his creation of character, and although he expects the producer to have done some homework to help him, he also wishes him to pay him the compliment of observing his potentialities and sensing what he can do best. If everything is prepared beforehand, if the actor is only to mould himself into the shell of the director's autocratic imagination, he feels himself a puppet, unappreciated, and is apt to become rebellious and lazy."

That there are today a number of producers who encourage their actors to use their own initiative is due, not only to the influence of du Maurier and to Komisarjevsky, but also to the arrival in the theatre during the later years of the 'twenties of an entirely new type of producer. Up to then it had been believed that nobody could become a producer unless he had been practically born and bred in the theatre and served a long apprenticeship in it. The new producers were university men. Some of them had no experience as professional actors, others had acted for no more than a year or so in repertory theatres. Tyrone Guthrie, for instance, after a couple of years as a member of the company at the Oxford Playhouse was appointed producer of the Scottish National Players, then two years later became producer at the Cambridge Festival Theatre, and shortly afterwards staged his first production in London. Hugh Hunt went straight from Oxford, where he had gained some experience as a producer for the O.U.D.S., to become the producer at the Maddermarket Theatre during the absence of Nugent Monck. The following year he became the producer at the Croydon Repertory Theatre: only a few months later he was producing in the West End and was then appointed producer at the Abbey Theatre, Dublin. John Burrell directed *Heartbreak House* in the West End at a time when his experience of stage production was limited to working with Michel St. Denis at the London Theatre Studio and producing at the Barn Theatre, Shere. The following year he was appointed producer for the Old Vic. Peter Brook, who began by producing an Ensa show immediately after leaving Oxford, then did a couple of productions at the Birmingham Repertory Theatre and was hardly out of his teens by the time he was producing at Stratford. Peter Hall was appointed producer at the Oxford Playhouse only a few months after leaving Cambridge and very soon afterwards became Director of Productions at the Arts Theatre, London.

Producers such as these had not got the knowledge and experience to drill their cast in the technique of acting so they relied to a very large extent upon creating performances out of what the actors were able to give them. Their task was made easier by the fact that actors were much more highly trained in the technique of their profession than in the old days. There were no dramatic schools in England until 1905, when the R.A.D.A. was founded. (Robert Atkins was one of the first pupils.) It was Tree who started the Academy He was not one of the dictator-producers. "Actors will find their own salvation," he used to say, "if you will only make them believe in what they are doing." But it irritated him that he had to spend so much time showing them *how* to do it. "Why should I pay actors big salaries and then teach them their business," he grumbled. It was because he felt that far too much time was spent at rehearsals teaching actors the technique of their parts that he founded the R.A.D.A. and sent the younger members of his own company to study there. But for many years it trained only an insignificant percentage of those who went on the stage. It was only after the 1914–18 war, when the R.A.D.A. increased in size and other dramatic schools were founded, that the fully-trained actor became the rule rather than the exception. Another fact which made it easier for the new type of producer to direct evocatively was that the profession was now attracting a far larger number of intelligent and educated people than ever before.

One of the healthiest features of the London theatre is its readiness to give opportunities to very young producers and the willingness of even the most experienced actors and actresses to accept their direction. It is now generally realised that producers are born, not made. The actual technique of production is really very simple. It is largely a matter of common sense and that indefinable quality called a sense of the theatre which nobody can acquire if he is not born with it. The ideal producer has an unostentatious, but immediately recognisable air of authority; he has a musician's ear for tone, tempo, and cadence; the painter's eye for the composition of grouping; the tact of a diplomat and the patience of a saint; and the comforting qualities of an old-fashioned nannie. He needs pertinacity and courage so that he does not show the slightest sign of despair to his cast however badly rehearsals may be going. He must be something of a psychologist, not only to analyse the characters in a play but in order to know instinctively how best to handle each member of his cast. Some need to be coaxed and cajoled, some need to be flattered, some need to be deflated, others continually encouraged and a few are all the better for an occasional bullying. He must be able to use words to convey his ideas to his cast precisely and vividly. Yet a producer may have all these qualities and still achieve no more than a smooth and efficient performance if he lacks the ability to stimulate the imagination of his cast.

Bridges Adams has described how Granville-Barker's powers of suggestion were enough to fill a rehearsal-room with magic on the greyest morning. "An actor who did not find a Granville-Barker rehearsal stimulating could count himself dead from the waist upwards. He was not given to wit, but his rather dry humour was everywhere; he had a nimble fancy; his imagination was like flame. He had an extraordinary ear for tone and stress and rhythm. His authority came from himself, and was absolute; he was not at all a pompous, quarter-deck kind of producer. I do not remember any ugly scenes at rehearsals; although you might—and I certainly did—experience the more salutary anguish of being out of key. If things were not going as he liked, he might pace to and fro, groaning a little. If you stopped, he might rather disconcertingly say: 'Go on! Go on!' If there was nothing for it but to turn and rend you, his rebuke was not sardonic, like Irving's, or heavily impish, like Tree's. It was more like the cut of a surgeon's knife, and was often administered with a winning smile."

Reinhardt was a producer who was able to inspire his cast by communicating to them his own zest and enthusiasm. The outstanding characteristic of the acting in all the Reinhardt productions I saw was its gusto. It was said of him that he approached each new production as if it were the most exciting play he had ever undertaken, as if he were convinced that it would be the best production he had ever done.

Producers vary a good deal in their treatment of the initial stages of rehearsal. In the London theatre the first rehearsal almost invariably begins with a reading of the play by the cast. It is a custom which dates from the days when the actors were not given the full script of the play but only their own parts and their cues, so until they had read the play through together few of them had any idea of what it was about. Today, when every member of the cast has the complete script of the play, I sometimes wonder whether it is not a waste of time to spend the first morning of rehearsal on a reading of the play. It is a depressing experience for the producer and the author, because the better the actor the worse he usually reads. I have dismal memories of sitting on draughty stages lit by a single pilot light listening to a company ranged round in a semi-circle, nervously fumbling their way through their parts, the leading players becoming more and more dejected till their voices dropped almost to a whisper. Nevertheless, actors cling to this custom of starting with a reading because in the West End, where every cast is a newly assembled collection of actors and actresses, some of whom have never met one another before, they at least feel that they have become a company once they have endured the communal agony of that first reading. I think Bert Brecht is right when he says that actors should use the minimum of expression and characterisation at the first reading; they are merely making acquaintance.

Some producers keep their cast sitting round reading the play for several more rehearsals while the actors begin to outline their characterisation and experiment with ways of saying their lines. Personally I never hold more than a single reading unless the play is in verse or a period play in which the rhythm and phrasing of the dialogue does not come easily and naturally to the actor. I believe that acting depends so much upon suiting the action to the word, the word to the action, that the two should not be separated even at the earliest rehearsals.

When it comes to moving actors about the stage here again producers differ in their methods. Some producers arrive at the first rehearsal with every move carefully worked out and noted down in their scripts. Others confine their preparation to the basic moves and positions—the exits and entrances, certain groupings and movements which are dictated by the action of the play and about which there can be no two opinions. Guthrie thinks that a producer should not be at all afraid of saying to actors in a quite dogmatic way: "Play this scene sitting on the sofa, and if you are not comfortable let me know later on, but don't decide until we have done it once or twice. Later on, maybe, you may feel like getting up halfway through and going to the window." He is of the opinion that if the actor is allowed to grope it out too much for himself there is a waste of time, "and the dominant personalities start bullying the milder, more unselfish and co-operative ones, which is what we have to be on the look out for". Brecht, during his early rehearsals, deliberately makes the positions rough and provisional "so that the actors have a chance to venture what comes into their heads". Jean Louis Barrault says: "I begin by writing a mise-en-scène. No need to tell you that this cannot be definitive, but the writing of it serves to reassure the company —it is a monster with which we can struggle." He begins rehearsals by reading the play several times for the purposes of casting. Because he is working with his own permanent company he can try out his actors in different parts and often the final casting is very different from what it was at the first reading. "Then," says Barrault, "throwing aside my preliminary-written mise-en-scène, I place the play, without discussion, as rapidly as possible, since actors dislike a vacillating producer. That takes about two or three days for each act."

Myself, I am one of those producers who is unable to work out any but the basic moves in advance. Naturally, after years of experience, I am capable of preparing a script in which every move is planned in detail, so that all the mechanics of the production work efficiently. But the detailed blueprint of a production, made before rehearsals have begun, seems to me to stultify the imagination of both the actor and the producer. During the early rehearsals I want to see what moves the actor makes instinctively or has thought out for himself in studying his part. I use these tentative moves as much as possible when constructing the mechanics of the production. By no means all actors like this method. Some prefer to be told exactly where to go and how to get there. The producer quickly senses which are the actors in his cast who like to use their own initiative and which are those who prefer to have their thinking done for them, and he adapts his own methods accordingly.

Although during early rehearsals the producer may have an open mind about how he is going to move his actors about the stage, what he must never be uncertain about is the exact meaning and significance of every word, line, and scene in the play. Nothing is more certain to shake the confidence of the cast in their producer than that moment when an actor says: "I'm not quite sure of the meaning of this," and the producer's answer after a thoughtful pause, is: "Yes, I'm not sure about that myself." I sometimes suspect that the producer who uses the first rehearsals for a discussion of the play with the cast is merely using the actors to help him disentangle his own ideas about the play.

The producer must come to the first rehearsal with an absolutely clear conception of every character in the play—but not necessarily how they must be played. It is one of the mysteries of acting that a part can be played in several rather different ways and still remain fundamentally the part which the author created—provided, of course, that the actor possesses the essential quality the part requires. If he lacks it, he is miscast and there is very little that the producer can do about it—except blame himself for having engaged the wrong actor for the part. Sometimes a manager who wants to use an actor for a part for which he is not altogether suited, perhaps because he is under contract, will say soothingly to the producer, "You will be able to get it out of him all right." But no producer can get out of an actor what isn't there. He cannot make a charmless actor seem charming, a weak character seem authoritative, an unsympathetic personality seem warm and friendly.

In the West End theatre much of the casting is decided by auditions. These auditions are hateful and embarrassing occasions both for the actor and the producer. Inevitably the actor who has been rejected for a part goes away from the theatre feeling that he has failed to do himself justice because of nerves, or because he was not told enough about the part he was asked to read, or because the audition was too brief. Nevertheless an experienced producer can tell a great deal more from even a brief audition than an actor realises. But I do not think it is wise for a producer to make the acquaintance of an actor for the first time at an audition. He should have had a chance of talking with him beforehand under more relaxed conditions while he listens to his voice, studies his appearance, and gets some idea of his personality. If the producer decides he is a likely actor for the part, he can then tell him something about its main characteristics. In an ideal world the actor would be given the script to study before coming to the audition, but as it is by no means unusual for at least a hundred actors to be auditioned for a play, there are obviously never enough scripts available. But it is essential that when an actor arrives for an audition he should be given a few minutes to study the scene he is going to read. If he has not already met the producer, then the producer should tell him something about the scene and the part and do his best to put the actor at his ease. Nothing is more nerve-racking for an actor than to have his name read out by the stage manager and then walk on to the stage to read a part to a little group of unknown people—the producer, the author and the manager—who are invisible in the black void of the theatre beyond the glare of the footlights.

No sensible producer expects an actor to give more than a rough indication of how he is likely to play the part. But if he seems right in appearance, voice, and personality the producer should discuss his reading with him and ask him to do it again. If he seems to be a possible for the part he should then be rehearsed in a speech which the producer has chosen beforehand as one of the key speeches to the part.

Once rehearsals have begun a producer must always be on his guard against talking too much. Some producers not only talk too much themselves but encourage the cast to do the same. The method of rehearsal which starts with several days of round-the-table discussion seems to me not only time-wasting, but dangerous. The fact that an actor spends much of his life expressing other people's thoughts in other people's words often makes it difficult for him to express his own thoughts clearly and concisely. Besides, a good actor has no clear and concise idea of his part before he begins to rehearse it. Good acting, I believe (though not everyone will agree with me), is a matter of instinct and feeling rather than conscious thought. That is why I think that a producer should not begin rehearsals by lecturing the cast on the play and telling them in detail how he proposes to produce it. "Une oeuvre de théâtre," Jouvet used to say, "ne s'explique pas, elle se joue." During rehearsals the actor who wants to stop and explain in detail an idea he has had about his part is a time-waster and a bore to the producer and the rest of the cast. The actor should explain what he means by doing it on the stage during rehearsal. A producer, too, should show, rather than explain what he means when directing his actors. "Never discuss a passage with a player," was one of Shaw's pieces of advice to the producer. Show how the passage should be done as a suggestion, not an order; and exaggerate your demonstration sufficiently to prevent the player from giving a mere imitation of it."

There are producers with an inadequate and ill-informed knowledge of Stanislavsky who believe that they are following his methods when they interrupt rehearsals for long, woolly discussions about the psychology of the characters and the lives they lead outside the play. Stanıslavsky never did this. If an actor attempted to start a discussion he would stop him by saying: "We are not here to talk, we are here to rehearse." Generally he rehearsed for only three hours a day, from eleven until two. After the rehearsal the company had their midday meal in the theatre. Stanislavsky himself would eat later, so that while the company were at lunch he could move about from table to table, commenting upon the work done during the hours of rehearsal, sometimes sitting down beside an actor and discussing some point at length. Often in the evening, after the performance, he would invite one or two actors back to his house and work with them on a scene. He believed that during rehearsals in the theatre it is unwise to concentrate for any length of time on the difficulties of a single member of a cast as the rest of the people on the stage are apt to become bored and listless, impatient to continue with the play. When Stanislavsky interrupted a rehearsal he did so as briefly as possible while the rest of the cast remained in their exact positions, absolutely silent. Nothing is more destructive to the atmosphere of a rehearsal than a producer who comes on the stage and embarks upon a long discussion with a single member of the cast, so that the rest become bored and begin to chatter and gossip among themselves until the producer finds it difficult to make himself heard above the babble and has to shout for silence.

Tyrone Guthrie contends that the first requisite of a producer is to be a good chairman of the proceedings at rehearsal. But the producer who encourages his company to have their own ideas must have a quick, selective mind otherwise time is wasted in trying out too many ideas. He must be authoritative enough for his rulings to be unquestioningly obeyed. When he has accepted an idea from an actor he must then tend its growth. An actress talking to me about her experience of working with Guthrie said: "You give him a crumb, and he hands you back a loaf." But there are always some members of a cast who have not even a crumb to offer the producer. So the invention must come from him. And even with the most creative members of his cast the producer must always be able to find something to help the actor when he becomes hesitant and unsure of himself. "The actor," says Pierre Fresnay, "tapping his way like a blind man, needs a guide. The producer is the man who guides him from outside, informs him of his position, encourages him along the right path, cries warning when he strays."

To combine the rôles of producer and leading actor successfully is extremely difficult. Many actors feel that it is unfair to themselves and the rest of the cast. They argue that the actor-producer, however sincere and unselfish he may be, cannot help seeing the production primarily from the angle of his own performance. They dislike having nobody 'out front' at rehearsals during the scenes when the actor-producer has to be on the stage. One of the most important functions of the producer is that he provides an audience during rehearsals, someone at whom the actors can, if only subconsciously, aim their performance. If the producer is on the stage, playing a part, actors will tend mentally to play to their producer (who may be standing only a few feet away from them) instead of projecting their performances out into the auditorium.

A few months ago I had a letter from an actor friend of mine who at that time was rehearsing a play directed by an actor-producer. "I find —— charming to work with," he wrote, "and he has some very good ideas about the play, but how I wish he were either producing *or* playing the lead, not both. I have two long scenes with him and I am finding them very difficult to rehearse. It makes me horribly nervous and self-conscious to have to be continually looking straight at the producer while one is struggling with a long and difficult scene instead of having him tucked out of sight in the stalls. Just when I feel I am really getting going, I see, or perhaps I just imagine that I see a look of doubt or disapproval in his face. I lose confidence, wonder what it is that I am doing wrong, and get all jumbled up.

Another difficulty is that in these scenes I can somehow never think of —— as the character he is playing (although he plays it jolly well). I am always conscious that I am speaking my lines to the producer. It's partly his fault. During my speeches he is no longer 'in' the character. Mentally he has changed over from being an actor to become the producer. I notice that after a speech of mine it usually takes him a line or two to get back into character again. On the first night I am afraid neither of us is going to be at our best in these scenes. It's damned worrying."

Bernard Shaw said that Granville-Barker was never at his best as an actor when he was his own producer. "Producing kills acting; an actor's part dies if he is watching others critically. You cannot conduct an orchestra and play the drum at the same concert." William Archer, discussing why Tree rarely did himself justice on a first night, protested that "had he the qualifications of John Kemble and Edmund Kean rolled into one it would be absolutely impossible for him to do himself justice with the whole weight of a huge production on his shoulders. How could he possibly think out his part while he is inventing, arranging, adjusting and regulating this vast machine? How can he throw his whole soul into the imaginative effort of impersonation while his mind is distracted by a thousand anxieties and cares of detail?" When John Gielgud doubles the rôles of actor and producer he often, on the first night, gives the impression of not concentrating entirely on his own performance. Even if the production has had a prior-to-London tour he occasionally seems uncertain of his words, perhaps because he is anxiously watching the other performances, or wondering whether a dimming of a light, carefully rehearsed with the electrician after the dress-rehearsal, has not perhaps been taken too fast, or thinking that maybe he had been unwise to make that last-minute alteration to a piece of grouping. When Gielgud has been at his best on a first night of one of his own productions it has usually been in a part which he has previously played with someone else producing. He had already acted in *Love for Love* and *The Importance of Being*

Earnest by the time he played in them in productions of his own, and the only Shakespearian part which Gielgud has played for the first time with himself as producer is Shylock.

Even if the practical problems of combining the rôles of actor and producer can be solved, a fundamental difficulty remains. The qualities needed to make a good actor are entirely different from those needed to make a good producer. The actor-producer, if he is to be a success in his double rôle, must have a dual personality. For instance, it is essential that the actor should be an exhibitionist; it is equally essential that the producer should not. An actor must take an honest delight in showing off. Unless he has a strong streak of exhibitionism in his character I doubt if he will ever be a good actor. Certainly he will not be able to go on faithfully repeating the same words and gestures night after night, for month after month, unless he thoroughly enjoys exhibiting his performance to an audience. But a producer who is an exhibitionist is a menace to the actor and the playwright. He cannot remain quietly in the background, as producers should. He deliberately makes the production as obtrusive as possible. He thrusts himself in front of the actors and distracts the audience's attention from them by calling attention to himself. "See how clever I am!" he seems to be saying. "Now isn't that an effective piece of business I thought up? And don't you admire that pretty bit of grouping? And I want you to take *particular* notice of the lighting in this scene!"

A good producer must efface himself completely. If after he has finished his production he leaves any positive evidence of his work behind him he inevitably destroys for the audience some of their sense of illusion. If they are conscious that certain bits of business and movement and grouping have been cleverly contrived by the producer, the impression of spontaneity, which is an essential part of illusion, is shattered. The moves which the producer works out must seem to the audience to be the spontaneous movements of the actors themselves, not an ingenious pattern thought up by the producer. Grouping, however pictorially and dramatically effective, must seem to have

277

developed perfectly naturally because of the situation created by the playwright; there must be no sign of the clever producer having been at work composing pretty pictures for their own sake. Good bits of stage business must always seem to have been the invention of the actors themselves; never must the audience suspect that the producer may have had the idea first. Staging and lighting, however beautiful and effective, must never compete with the actors for the interest of the audience. Always the focus must be on the actors. And in the end it is to the actors that the producer must hand all the credit for a successful production.

II

THE END OF AN ERA

The era of the producer is over. Twenty years ago Stanislavsky, Reinhardt, Jouvet, Baty, Copeau, Pitoëff, Dullin, Meierhold, Taïrov and several other producers of genius were still experimenting, developing not only the art of production but the whole art of the theatre. Today there are some brilliant producers in the European theatre but nobody who is contributing anything new to it. Vilar derives most of his ideas from the German theatre of the 'thirties; Brecht harks back to the Russian theatre of the 'twenties; Jean-Louis Barrault is as eclectic as Reinhardt. The theatre is always the mirror of its time, so perhaps the reason why there is so little, if any, genuine experiment nowadays in the European theatre is because this is a period of eclecticism—which, as René Hainaux of the Belgian National Theatre remarked to an interviewer, "is a sign of both civilized standards and creative incapacity".

A year or two ago the Society of West End Managers firmly put the English producer in his place (or at least in the place which they think he ought to occupy in the English theatre) by taking his title away from him and assuming it themselves. Henceforth, according to the official announcement, the title of producer was to belong to "the actual responsible management which provides the money and exercises complete control". The duties of those who used to be called producers were defined as acting as liaison officers between the workers and the management" and being "physically responsible for the correct and appropriate interpretation of the playwright's

279

intentions. It can then," graciously allowed the Society of West End Managers, "be stated that 'The production is directed by Mr. ——'."

There is nothing unreasonable in the West End Managers' claim to call themselves producers if the function of production entails "providing the money and exercising complete control" —as indeed it does. The reason why there have been so few producers of real importance in England since the passing of the actor-managers and the capture of the theatre by the commercial combines is because it is only rarely that a producer has been able to go into management on his own and exercise the complete control so essential if a producer is to direct plays adventurously. The producers who have influenced the development of the art of the theatre are those who have worked under their own management, owning their own theatres with their own permanent companies. Antoine, Stanislavsky, Copeau, Jouvet, Dullin, Baty, Pitoëff, Reinhardt—it applies to them all. And so it used to be in England from the days of Madame Vestris onwards. Granville-Barker was in complete control at the Court and the Savoy, not merely a liaison officer between office and stage; Playfair owned his own theatre; Basil Dean was a partner in the Reandean management. Since then the only genuine experimental productions in the English theatre have been done by producers working for the Old Vic or the Memorial Theatre at Stratford on Avon, two theatres where the producer is given an amount of freedom unusual in the English theatre of today and where the companies, though by no means permanent, are at least not newly assembled for each play. But neither of these theatres has been able to give a producer the opportunity to pick and train a company on a long-term basis, and it is because of this that the many experiments in Shakespearian production have evolved no recognisable style of Shakespearian acting, only a variety of methods of producing and staging Shakespeare.

"Dramatists utilize acting styles, and playhouses preserve them; but directors create them," wrote Kenneth Tynan in one of his *Observer* articles. He went on to argue that if our theatres are filled with a kind of hollow semi-realism for which our authors write, much of the blame must rest with our producers. "Many of them are affable, intelligent men; but none measures up to the continental definition—a dynamic compound of confessor, inquisitor and sage . . . Apart from Granville-Barker and, intermittently, Guthrie, no English director has had much perceptible influence on English acting."

How can he have when he has no company to influence? For three or, at the most, four weeks he rehearses a cast hastily assembled from among actors who happen to be free at that moment, some of whom may never have met one another before. Only in the provincial repertory theatres does the producer have a permanent company to work with—but seldom does he have the time to do any real production except in the very few repertories which run their plays for more than a week and are thus able to allow sufficient time for rehearsal. The advantages of a permanent company working under a single producer are strikingly displayed when the Birmingham and Bristol companies come to the Old Vic and play with a confidence and unity of style which make the resident Old Vic company's style of acting seem tentative and haphazard by comparison.

The only company in London which has stayed together for more than a single year is Theatre Workshop at Stratford. One of the reasons for this company's resounding success at the Paris Festival in 1955 was because the audiences recognized that here at last was a genuine company of players from England, not just a cast. The previous year the English contribution to the festival had been a performance of *The Confidential Clerk*, not by the original company but by a collection of actors got together for the occasion, playing in several different styles. Their loose and maladjusted performance made a very poor showing in comparison with the permanent companies from all over Europe which were appearing at the festival. The mere fact that anyone should have thought it sufficient to send to the Paris Festival a hurriedly got-together collection of actors without any distinctive style is indicative of the fact that the English theatre has lost all understanding of what constitutes a company of players. Both the Old Vic and Stratford on Avon are perfectly content to send abroad under their own name newly assembled groups of players, some of whom have never even stepped upon the stages of those theatres, far less been trained in any particular style of acting. Audiences on the Continent, in America and in the Commonwealth not unnaturally assume that these companies are representative of the style of acting and production to be seen in the theatres to which these companies claim to belong. But anybody who saw all these companies would get a bewildering impression of a jumble of different styles; and if eventually he were to go to the Old Vic or Stratford on Avon to seek to discover what really was the distinctive style of these theatres he would find there was none.

Only a producer-director working in his own theatre with his own permanent company can develop a distinctive style of acting and production. One of the main reasons why there are no producers-in-control in England today has been the Government's refusal to allow any theatre-building for many years after the war. There were young men who came out of the Services with exciting plans to start theatres of their own in however humble a way, but they were thwarted in their ambitions by controls which made it impossible even to convert an existing building, no matter how small, into a theatre.

The English theatre owed much of its vitality in the years following the 1914–18 war to the pioneer producers who were able to have a theatre of their own by converting a drill hall or a warehouse or a derelict chapel or a grubby little cinema, or by refurbishing and reopening some out-of-the-way forgotten theatre such as the Lyric, Hammersmith, which for years had been used as a furniture store until Nigel Playfair took it over and made it one of London's most distinguished theatres. But from 1939 to 1953 it was not legally possible to rebuild a bombed theatre or to convert an existing building into a makeshift theatre. Even if a young producer could raise sufficient capital to go into management in a West End theatre he soon found that he was unable to rent one unless he was prepared to become a satellite of one of the omnipotent theatre combines and sacrifice that independence without which it is almost impossible for any producer to evolve his own individualistic style of production.

During all these years my own small theatre, the Gate, which was damaged in an air raid, remained derelict, although the manpower and material needed to resuscitate it would have been very small. Yet when I took a company on a tour of Germany in 1949 three of the theatres in which we played had been newly built and others were buildings temporarily converted into well-equipped theatres while the foundations were being laid for the rebuilding of the municipal Schauspielhaus.

There will be few laments for the passing of the producer's theatre. In England the public has always been so little interested in who produces the play that the producer's name is billed in front of the theatre in letters far smaller than those which proudly proclaim the presence in the cast of little Miss Somebody-or-Other fresh from her dramatic school who has a tiny part of less than a dozen lines. There are many comparatively knowledgeable theatregoers who still regard the producer as an interloper who considers himself more important than the author of the play. Yet the producer's theatre has always been a playwright's theatre. Admittedly there have been producers who have been more interested in a play because of the opportunities it gave for showy production than because of its intrinsic merits. Admittedly there have been producers who have arrogantly distorted plays, including the greatest of the classics, to make them fit their own conception of life. These producers have been authors' manqué or playwrights' manqué, who have fiddled and meddled with scripts and the actors' interpretation of them because it gave them a sense of creation. But most producers are primarily interested in the play. They see it as a whole, not as a "vehicle". If this book has proved anything it is that the great producers have done far more than the actors for the art of playwriting by inducing men of letters to become men of the theatre.

The weakness of the English producers is that they have failed to do this. Since Granville-Barker very few English producers have done anything to develop the art of playwriting. In fact most of them have confined themselves to the classics. Tyrone Guthrie, Hugh Hunt, Michael Benthall, Glen Byam Shaw, Anthony Quayle, John Gielgud, Laurence Olivier, Peter Brook—these are the producers whose names are known to the public, but their work has been confined almost entirely to the classics. What is the reason for this? Most of them would reply that there are so few good plays in the English theatre that they are driven to work on classics, revivals, and importations from America. But surely it is the producers themselves who are to blame for the shortage of plays. They have done nothing to encourage and develop new authors in the way that Stanislavsky, Granville-Barker, Reinhardt, Antoine, Pitoëff, Copeau, Jouvet and Dullin did. But here we come back again to the great difference between the English producers during the past thirty years or so and their European contemporaries. All the producers who have just been mentioned were in management; they directed their own theatres and their own permanent companies. The English producer is not a manager but a hireling of the commercial combines. He has little say over the choice of play. If he finds a play by an unknown author in which he believes passionately he has little hope of getting it on to the stage unless he can find a big star willing to play in it. Then most managements will accept the play without even troubling to read it.

During recent years only two names of any real importance have been added to the list of English dramatists—T. S. Eliot and Christopher Fry. It is extremely unlikely that either of them would ever have written for the theatre had it not been for two men who were in their small way producer-managers. In 1930, when T. S. Eliot was contemplating turning to the theatre and had already written the fragmentary *Sweeney Agonistes* in an attempt to discover for himself whether he had any aptitude for writing for the actor, he was commissioned by Martin Browne to write a pageant play to be performed at Sadler's Wells in aid of the Forty-five Churches Fund. That play was *The Rock*. The next step in the development of Eliot as a dramatist was a commission from Browne to write a play for Canterbury Cathedral. A few months later he sent Browne the first draft of *Murder in the Cathedral*. It was little more than a scenario submitted for criticism and advice. The play in its final form is an example of how an author of great talent who is unused to the theatre can, during the writing of a play, benefit from the practical knowledge and experience of an intelligent and sympathetic producer. When writing his next three plays, *Family Reunion, The Cocktail Party,* and *The Confidential Clerk,* Eliot followed much the same procedure, beginning by sending his producer the first rough outline and afterwards constantly seeking his advice during the writing of the play.

It was Martin Browne, too, who coaxed Christopher Fry into the theatre by commissioning his first three plays. *The Boy with a Cart* was written for the company of players which Browne directed for the Diocese of Chichester; *The Tower* was commissioned for a performance at Tewkesbury Abbey; *The Child* for a pageant performance in the Albert Hall. When Martin Browne took over the Mercury and made it a theatre for poets he commissioned Fry to write *A Phoenix Too Frequent*. After its run at the Mercury it was transferred to the Arts which was then under the management of Alec Clunes. It was as a result of this that Clunes commissioned Fry to write *The Lady's Not for Burning* which was given its first production at the Arts.

London managements have only themselves to blame for the present shortage of playwrights. They have neither the time nor the inclination to read widely, to recognize a flickering spark of dramatic talent in the work of a novelist or a poet or a biographer and encourage him to write for the theatre, helping and guiding him on his way. It would be grossly unfair to describe the West End managers as mere men of business; they have a genuine enthusiasm for the theatre; but they also have a fatal desire to become all-powerful in the world of the theatre. Continually they seek to enlarge their little empires, running not a single London theatre but several. In addition to their

West End theatres they have companies on tour; they are end-lessly involved in discussions about film rights, radio rights, television rights, repertory rights and the American productions of their London successes; they have no time to ruminate over a script of quality which is not yet stageworthy and to discuss it with the author and keep his enthusiasm alive during months of slow, painful alteration and rewriting. They merely wait for the ready-made article to arrive and lament that it doesn't. Of course it doesn't—except very rarely.

While the work of the producers who concentrate upon the classics is much discussed by the critics because there has been little or nothing new to say about the play, the producers of new plays have often been ignored in the discussion of the merits or demerits of the play itself. The vitality of the theatre ultimately depends upon the supply of new plays, and the English theatre owes much to the small band of producers who have laboured, with little glory to themselves, to do what they could to help and encourage new authors. But without theatres of their own, without the freedom to choose their own scripts or the powers to commission them, they have been able to do little to prevent the art of playwriting in England declining into a dull mediocrity which has at last driven them from the theatre in despair. Had these producers been able to direct there own theatres, with their own companies, I believe the present state of the English theatre would be very different from what it is.

I began this book by vowing that I would be cautious not to overrate the importance of the producer in the theatre, but in writing it, and in studying, as I wrote, the achievements of the great producers, I am more than ever convinced that the healthiest, most enterprising, and most exciting kind of theatre for playwright, actor, and audience is The Producer's Theatre.

A POSTSCRIPT

During the five years which have elapsed since this book was written it has been hardly possible to read anything on production or to listen to a discussion about it without encountering the word 'Brechtian'. Often it is vaguely used merely to describe gimmicks of production and staging, some of which existed years before Brecht adopted them. Properly used the word stands for far more than just a technique of playwrighting and production; more than just the objective style of acting in place of Stanislavsky's doctrine of complete identification with the part; it stands for a definite ideological attitude to the theatre as a whole. While Stanislavsky believed that "the slightest utilitarian tendency kills art instantly", Brecht regarded the theatre as a weapon: "a weapon to be used for the fulfilment of a social revolution which will better the life of Man". Because the Brechtian theatre is the fully developed Marxist theatre of social protest is one of the main reasons why it has had so much influence upon the younger producers all over Europe, most of whom belong to the extreme Left. (Kenneth Tynan has pointed out that the same applies "to nearly every theatre company in Europe of any importance".) Many of these producers follow the Brechtian dogma with so faithful a subservience that they are inhibited from developing styles and ideas of their own. The result on the theatre of the Left has been to create a style of production which, in spite of its enthusiasm, drive, and vitality, too seldom surprises because its doctrinaire approach to every play is almost always predictable.

Perhaps the simplest way of outlining the young Leftist producers' approach to the theatre is to follow the career of Roger Planchon, the most brilliant of the young directors in the French Theatre. A Marxist and a follower of Brecht, he declares himself "a didactic producer". Like so many pioneer producers he began by forming a company of amateur actors.

He was a young bank clerk in Lyons just out of his 'teens when in 1950 he opened the tiny 'Théâtre de la Comédie de Lyons' in the basement of a locksmith's shop. It had only 98 seats. Seven years later he was able to move to a theatre seating fourteen hundred, the 'Théâtre de la Cité Villeurbanne'. In 1959 he was appointed director of the 'Théâtre Populaire de Provence', one of the five provincial theatre centres set up by the Government with lavish financial backing. The aim is to appeal to a genuinely popular audience of all classes. The permanent companies attached to these centres play not only in their own theatre but also in many places in surrounding districts where there is no proper theatre, so their productions have to be simple and ingenious, adaptable to all sorts of stages—a limitation which has stimulated Planchon to develop a style of production which, although simple, is never austere, because of the inventive use he makes of his limited resources.

At the outset of his career Planchon declared that his intention was "to take the best from Vilar's discoveries and from Artaud: the polish and clarity from Vilar, without losing that measure of violence which Artaud urged; not to mention Brecht, of course." When he became the director of the Théâtre Populaire de Provence he said: "We do not popularise; we want to be popular. We don't work for the public: we work with it." His version of the two parts of *Henry IV*, heavily cut and re-arranged, gives a fair idea of his method of production. He chose the play as his first Shakespearian production because it seemed to him that of all the plays this was the one most likely to appeal to an audience more accustomed to the cinema than the theatre. Planchon believes that any producer trying to win an audience from the cinema to the theatre must face up to the fact that the most unfailingly popular films are "Westerns". The turbulent action of *Henry IV*, the fights, the violence, the rowdy tavern scenes, made the play very suitable to Planchon's purpose. In his production he employed cinematic techniques familiar to his film-going audience. He divided the play into a large number of short scenes, playing sequences of them in unbroken continuity, in the manner of the cinema. To achieve this he constantly blacked out the stage and played one scene in a pool of light while the actors in the next scene assembled in the darkness and were instantly picked out by the lighting as the previous scene ended. Sometimes a spotlight would pin-point the face of a single actor, producing the effect of a camera close-up. In spite of the economy of means he was forced to employ, there was nothing bleak about the production. The small, mobile pieces of scenery by his young designer René Allio were brilliantly colourful, the battles were magnificently composed, the tavern scenes were full of lively, swirling movement. The permanent backcloth was a huge map of Mediaeval England. Slides were used to project captions guiding the audience through the intricacies of the plot, and as a further aid to understanding, the rival factions were clearly differentiated by the colours of their costumes which were of ingeniously simplified design.

There was nothing particularly Brechtian in all this. So far the production derived more from Artaud and Vilar. Yet it was essentially a Brechtian production, not just because of the uses of Brecht's alienation effects and many of his methods of stagecraft, but because Planchon's attitude towards the play was faithfully Brechtian. It was used to give a Marxist history lesson and point a moral. Captions and slogans projected on to the set told the audience plainly how they ought to be reacting to the play. Subtleties of characterisation were sacrificed (Planchon dismisses them as "psychological dead-wood") in order to stress what for him had become the primary theme of the play—the jockeying for power, the conflict between Church and State. The heroic elements of the play were expunged. Prince Hal, played by Planchon, became a cunning killer; not a villain on a grand scale but more like an angry teddy-boy. Kenneth Tynan described the play as "boiled down to the bare social bones . . . individual characterisations were subjected to the larger image of declining feudalism. The result was not Shakespeare; it was abundance reduced to relevance, riches cut down to a living wage, a jungle into a cartographical survey. The audience was held not so much by what was happening to the characters as what was happening to the whole society. I admired what I saw, and understood why Arthur Adamov, the leading socialist in the theatrical avant-garde, thinks M. Planchon the best director in France".

It was probably Planchon's anti-heroic, anti-romantic attitude, which led him to produce with such immense relish the long, excessively repetitious, and only intermittently funny burlesque of *Les Trois Mousquetaires* which gave him occasional opportunities to mock kings and queens, cardinals and dukes. Although it was full of comic invention, played with the utmost élan and always enchanting to the eye, the total effect seemed to me trivial, though there were others who professed to find in it a great deal of social and political significance. Probably one of the explanations of why Planchon lavished his considerable talents on this lampoon of *Les Trois Mousquetaires* is that he seems to have great difficulty in finding plays suited to his purpose. There are plenty of young French playwrights who are politically as far out on the Left as he is, but their plays are not sufficiently didactic for Planchon. Other producers of the Left have experienced the same problem. The "Centre Dramatique de L'Ouest", after a meeting with trade union officials, published in its bulletin an article which described the impasse at which they had arrived. "We in the theatre world are torn between productions which become more and more refined (subtlety is the old-age infirmity of civilisation) and fail more and more to reach the people for whom no-one any longer writes plays. Either we perform the usual repertory of the bourgeoise theatre and the few works of art worthy of that name before a limited public or we dream of a vastly wider audience, but know not what to play before it. The seed is not right for the soil, nor the soil for the seed. In the process both are in danger of extinction."

In England Joan Littlewood had the same problem, which is why the repertoire of the Theatre Workshop consisted for many years largely of the classics and "standard works", sometimes slanted to make a sociological comment, but often produced with deliberate over-simplification and immense vitality in the

hope of making them palatable to the working-class audience
which she tried for so many years to capture. Planchon's
production of Marivaux's *La Seconde Surprise de L'Amour*
combined both these methods. It was a curious choice for
Planchon as the play depends largely on the sophisticated style
of the dialogue, the subtlety with which the sentiment is
handled, the "passionate reserve" with which Marivaux's
characters make love. It never becomes physical. Nevertheless
Planchon, presumably with the intention of making the play
more to the taste of his audience, deliberately coarsens it.
Herbert Blau describes him as producing Marivaux like an ill-
read Marxist. "He suffers from a passion for exposé. Thus he
does not permit the lovers to conceal their lust as coquetry
behind the screen of language Marivaux made for such an
evasion. He actually has them in bed; and while the rich make
love the poor are shown freezing over a brazier. Is this
Brechtian? Yes, in an elementary way, blowing the nose of
History with a dirty-linen didactic." When Planchon produced
George Dandin he made it into what one critic described as
"a neo-realist criticism of bourgeoise society." He did this without tampering with the text. One of his devices was to transfer
the locale of the play to the country so that he could introduce
a series of mime scenes (rather in the manner of a film montage)
depicting the under-privileged peasants scraping a miserable
living toiling in the barns and the fields. Other sequences
showed the drudgery of the household servants continually laying tables and clearing them away. As these mime scenes were
brilliantly directed they were good value in exchange for the
conventional ballets which were dispensed with. Although
extraneous to the play, they did no harm to it.

A play which has always fascinated Planchon is *Edward the
Second*. The theme of the play as he sees it is that a king, however civilised he may be, must inevitably come to terms with
injustice. In an adaptation by Adamov it was one of his earliest
productions. In 1960 he returned to it, this time frankly using
it with the liberty with which a film producer treats the script
of a play. An entry in his diary dated May 1960 describes the

beginning of the rehearsal. "Hours of discussion on such and such an intention, on such and such a movement. The actors are only given a theme and a page of notes. Everyone improvises. Allio sketches in a corner. A third of the time spent on improvisation: two thirds on discussion. Exhausted." The production was first seen in the open-air theatre at Orange in July of that year. In December Planchon announced that he was going to begin all over again: "new text, new décor, a new production". The revised production was shown at Villeurbanne the following February. "Can we," he wrote in his diary, "afford to repeat this disconcerting and exhilarating experiment? Yes, the contact between an author and his interpreters in such a total confrontation cannot but enrich a work." But up to now Planchon has failed to find a living author to confront with his interpreters. He himself is well aware of the need to find an author who will join the company and write not just for them but with them, as Obey did for Michel St-Denis' Compagnie des Quinze. Only when Planchon directs new scripts will one be able to see the full extent of his talents.

Although he has been hailed as "France's champion of the didactic theatre", his work has qualities which rarely go with didacticism—such as charm and gaiety. He can hilariously direct a scene of knockabout farce, but he has also a depth of feeling which enables him to make a moment of tragedy or pathos profoundly moving. Although he began as a follower of Brecht, he is too inventive and lively minded a producer to have remained an altogether faithful disciple. Lately he has been sharply criticised by the Leftist critics as a deviationist. Louis Marcorelles, for instance, sternly reproved him for the way in which, trying to find his own individual style of production, "he has unfortunately gone further and further away from the fundamental Brechtian lesson: care for the concrete". Planchon's production of Gogol's *Dead Souls* ended, according to Marcorelles, in the worst sort of formalism. "He merely managed to create something in the picturesque Barrault-Vilar tradition. Brecht was forgotten."

Eric Bentley, one of Brecht's translators, has protested that in Brechtian circles "Brecht is the only artist who authentically exists, the others are of interest, when they are, only as influences on him". The history of the theatre in the twentieth century has frequently shown how debilitating can be the effects of attempting faithfully to preserve and imitate the methods of a great producer after his death. What was a fresh and living inspiration while his work could be seen at first hand is apt to become a stultifying formula in after years. Towards the end of his life Brecht himself was uneasy about the way in which many of his theories were being misinterpreted. For instance, he protested that his alienation of the action "was not intended to drum emotion out of the theatre, as some have interpreted it, but to bring about a combination of reason and emotion". In an interview in *The Times* Lotte Lenya, who acted in many of Brecht's productions, warned that it is extremely difficult to interpret Brecht's written theories correctly without first-hand knowledge of his personality and the circumstances in which his ideas were expressed. "For one thing, in his later days every single utterance was taken with the greatest seriousness. I watched a number of rehearsals of the Berliner Ensemble when I last visited him in 1955, and he seemed to me then the same as ever—he coaxed the actors along, made jokes, contradicted himself, used one approach with one actor, another with another, just as any good director does, but always there were three disciples with notebooks taking down every word he uttered; to add, presumably, to their own holy scripture made up of the master's pronouncements.

"In the picture the public receives of Brecht at work with actors the one thing which never emerges is the *fun* we all had, the free-and-easy atmosphere in which we would always be free to make our suggestions, laugh and joke, and generally work together as a happy company should. No-one was ever less rigid in his interpretations of his works than Brecht, and the works we produced together were always in a sense collaborative efforts. If he liked an idea, wherever it came from—Weill, me, his secretary, Hauptmann, anyone—he would happily accept it, and no producer could interfere less with his actors. Their truth was what counted; the way they felt things. But he hated argument about interpretation, or even intense discussion. 'Don't tell me, show me', was his constant cry."

Of all the Brechtian devices, the much-imitated "alienation effect" was the device about which he himself eventually came to have misgivings. In his last years he lamented that in spite of all his efforts to prevent his actors "creating empathy", his audiences still insisted on becoming emotionally involved in the play. They admired Mother Courage instead of despising her as "a capitalist exploiter, a hyena on the battlefield of the Thirty Years' War". They warmed to Galileo and forgave him his ultimate lack of courage in the defence of his discoveries, instead of condemning him as a coward. Charles Marowitz, in his recent book, *The Method as Means,* maintains that the whole Brechtian concept of the anti-illusionist theatre has failed in its intention because the audience's desire to be deluded is so strong that it blots out everything which conspires to dispel their illusion. "Audiences continue to feel empathy and become involved no matter how vigorously Brecht tries to disillusion them. Breaking the Fourth Wall, eliminating scenic authenticity, dispensing with coloured lights, disrupting the chain of events, ignoring tempi—all of these things have not overcome the spectator's desire to feed on make-believe. And this is because it still *is* make-believe . . . illusion is not the exclusive property of the stage; it is a built-in predisposition of the spectator. If one wanted to remove it really, one would have to lascerate the viscera of a man's imagination."

The true influence of a producer is not in his theories but in his example. Brecht was one of the great masters of the art of production, and it is hard to believe that any producer could have watched one of his productions without becoming in some way stimulated and influenced; but nobody is going to learn to produce like Brecht by studying his involved and often confusing writings. While so much has been written about his political-theatrical theories, there is very little precise information about the way he worked with his actors. There are countless eye-witness reports of Brecht at rehearsal, but most of them are too fulsome and adulatory to be of much practical value, and are usually the result of watching only a very few rehearsals. The few would-be factual accounts of Brecht at work are fogged and distorted by the writers' determination to relate everything which Brecht said and did at rehearsal with something he had written—often many years before. One longs for more cool, technical appraisements of Brecht at rehearsal, preferably by other producers, uncommitted to any particular political doctrine. One wants to know more, in precise detail, of how Brecht trained and directed his actors to create the finest ensemble of players since Stanislavsky's Art Theatre Company.

Brecht's method of working with a designer was unusual and interesting. During the month of discussion round a table, which was how Brecht's rehearsals invariably began, the designer sat with the company. The set had not yet been designed. It was only when the company moved on to the stage and various positions were being tried out that the designer started planning the sets. Various ground plans were marked out on the stage to suit the tentative groupings. Sometimes the designer might propose an entirely new plan which would stimulate Brecht to try out a fresh pattern of movement. But it was only after the grouping and movement had been agreed upon that the setting was finally designed. Needless to say, it is not a method practicable in the English theatre, where the time between the first rehearsal and the first night is so short that if the set is to be ready in time it has to be on its way to being built before the actors have assembled for the first rehearsal.

English productions of Brecht's plays, including Theatre Workshop's *Mother Courage* and the Royal Court Theatre's *The Good Woman of Setzuan,* have demonstrated that the producer needs more than an understanding of Brecht's methods: he needs actors trained in the Brechtian style. Because it was a style which often seemed easy, relaxed, informal, too little credit has been given to the Berliner Ensemble for the sheer technical brilliance of their acting under Brecht's direction. They made their effects with absolute precision, but it was a precision seemingly so effortless that the technical skill with which it was achieved was unnoticeable. The diction and phrasing of the company was impeccable, and when called upon to do so they could attack a scene with flashing swiftness without any sacrifice of clarity. Their movement and gesture had a lightness and grace hitherto unknown in the German theatre. An English company lacking the rigorous training of Brecht's actors and without their elaborately integrated teamwork simply cannot achieve the detached style of acting which Brecht demanded. In attempting it they merely seem offhand, casual and vague. A further handicap for an English producer attempting a Brecht play is that it costs a great deal of money to stage the plays in the Brechtian manner. He was a lavish producer with a lavish subsidy to support him. When the Berliner Ensemble went to the Paris Festival with *The Good Woman of Setzuan*, Brecht equipped the Théâtre Sarah Bernhardt with a revolving stage, built his own proscenium, and installed a new curtain. He took with him seventy-five actors, an orchestra, an army of technicians, load after load of scenery and hundreds of costumes. Yet when in the English theatre any play is staged with stark economy, someone is sure to praise the production for its "Brechtian simplicity". Admittedly some of his productions seemed simple and economical: *Galileo*, for example, in which the harbour of Venice was enchantingly suggested by a fleet of model ships suspended from the flies, and a fountain or a balcony or a tapestry sufficed to indicate a change of locale. But the ships and the set-pieces were, as was everything on Brecht's stage, beautifully and expensively constructed; and the permanent set with its great walls of burnished copper and its tiled floor served to emphasise another feature of Brecht's productions—the beauty of the costumes and groupings.

Another essential for a Brecht play done in the Brecht manner, which no English producer of the plays has yet been granted, is a really large stage. Brechtian stagecraft demands it because of his use of "space-staging"—isolating solidly built impressionistic sets in the centre of the stage, a method which has been popular with German producers since the early 'twenties. The size of the stages certainly contributed to the success of two of the most effective productions of Brecht's plays directed by other producers—Planchon's production of *Schweich in the Second World War* on the huge stage of the Théâtre Champs Elysées, and Vilar's productions of *Mother Courage* and *The Resistable Rise of Arturo Ui* on the even larger stage of the Palais de Chaillot. But the Brechtians criticised Vilar's productions for being deviationist. Michael Kustow, for instance, protested that Vilar had failed to point the Brechtian moral that "wars will continue only so long as you have the Capitalist system of barter and market": instead, he left the audience with the feeling that "war is terrible, but it must go on for ever, like Mother Courage's song, so shrug and persist".

Vilar, who used to be regarded as the leading Leftist producer in France, is now being accused by the critics of the Left of "dislocating drama from its social context". He is lectured for having become too introspective in his productions, failing to direct his plays so as to stress a social attitude, becoming more concerned with the individual than with society. All this is simply the old Meierhold dictum that detailed portrayal of individual emotions is "worthless soul junk". Vilar is an austere, ascetic producer. His scenery is reduced to the barest elements, severely practical, giving little pleasure to the eye. His lighting is sharp and cold. Like Brecht, he lights his night scenes as brightly as his daytime scenes, suggesting darkness to the audience by the miming of his actors. He makes no attempt to fill out the vast width of the stage of the Palais de Chaillot, playing most of his scenes in pools of light. In spite of the austerity of his methods, his Théâtre National Populaire draws a huge audience, many of them new theatregoers. There are many reasons for his success with this audience—the firm outlines of his productions, the exactness with which he makes his points, the dramatic tension he creates, and the excitement of his grouping and movement which compensates for the lack of other pleasures to the eye in his mainly black and white productions. His company combines vigour and attack with the utmost clarity of diction and phrasing, especially when speak-

ing the hexameters of Corneille and Molière. At first the delivery
of the verse was plain to the point of being prosaic, but in recent
years the style of the company has become, when necessary,
more lyrical, more romantic. Vilar never fantasticates the
classics, yet his approach to them is essentially modern; instinctively he sees what is contemporary in the plays and stresses
these elements in his productions, but without resorting to
gimmicks and ingenious inventions.

Michel St-Denis, talking to the seminar for professional
producers organised by the British Drama League, said that the
main thing he had learned from Vilar was about the use of space.
"In the open-air theatre at Avignon he has been used to enormous
space—his stage is nearly one hundred yards wide. In *Ruy Blas*
there is a moment, a very precise moment, when the Queen,
who is in love with Ruy Blas, obliges him to go and shut the
door, just to annoy him—and the door was fifty yards away.
Usually these things are calculated between producer and
designer so that they are at a seemly distance—otherwise there
will be such a silence! So when I saw that moment coming I
said to myself, 'How will he do it?' But it was perfectly all
right. The whole scale of the movement is much bigger than
we are used to—that is all there is to it. It shows that we allow
ourselves to be imprisoned by ideas of the kind that if we
lengthen a pause through the use of space it will be dead—and
that is not true.

"Vilar, I think, is a very difficult character. He is a very
solitary man. His actors often complain they are not enough in
touch with him, but they are full of confidence in him, because
through the way he works with them he brings them regularly
to success. There is a little book (*De la Tradition Theatre*) which
Vilar wrote some years ago in which he says that we rehearse too
much. He says we have not got enough confidence in the actors.
An actor who is really an actor—one should put a lot of confidence in him. One of the ways Vilar works is to put notes on
the notice-board. Suddenly he has an idea about the meaning of
this or that and he scribbles a note about it for the board, or he
sits for a long time round the table discussing. He says we

never sit for long enough. The actors want to rush to action because they want to be drunk with emotion before they understand why. 'We should,' he says, 'sit for a while with cool heads and our backsides on a chair.'

"In England the only professional theatre with a definite 'social attitude' is Theatre Workshop, which was founded in 1945 and spent its first eight years touring the industrial towns of the North, with an occasional appearance at the Edinburgh Festival, before settling down at the Theatre Royal, Stratford-atte-Bow, in London's East End. One of its manifestos stated that it 'seeks to put on plays that have either a directly working-class appeal, or an appeal that goes beyond the middle-classes . . . we aim to produce plays that lack the modern introspective attitude and choose those which take a positive line. As the modern middle class is nihilist, this criterion provides a fairly safe gauge'."

Among the authors which Theatre Workshop found to suit its purpose were Molière, Ibsen, Chekhov, O'Casey, Aristotle, O'Neill, Pirandello, Synge, Shaw, Lope de Vega, Gogol, Shakespeare and several other Elizabethan and Jacobean dramatists. In Joan Littlewood's productions of the classics her aim was to relate these to the modern world, and particularly to contemporary social conditions. Some of the plays yielded readily to her purpose; as, for instance, *Volpone*, produced in modern dress, with immense relish and comic invention, as a satire on the greed, acquisitiveness, and graft of modern society. On the other hand, *Macbeth* was one of her least successful productions. Her determinedly anti-poetic treatment of the play reduced Macbeth himself to no more than a craven killer. The attempt to portray him as a ruthlessly ambitious dictator was altogether too much at variance with the lines. The play was produced as if it were happening during a civil war in Scotland, but instead of making the play more contemporary, it made it seem fantastically unreal because, as *The Times* critic protested, it substituted for a coherent society a never-never land. The most successful of her Shakespearian productions was *Richard II*. Bolingbroke became the leading part, the typical Marxist hero, the revolutionary who overthrows a régime. Needless to say,

Miss Littlewood was not the first to see Bolingbroke as the hero of the play. The day before Essex's rebellion against Queen Elizabeth I, the conspirators bribed Phillips, the manager of the Globe, to put on *Richard II* as an example of how a weak and vacillating ruler can be deposed by the determined leader of an insurrection. Walter Raleigh in one of his Oxford lectures remarked that it is difficult to take sides against Richard without taking sides against Poetry. As Joan Littlewood has always been determinedly anti-poetic, she had no compunction about depriving Richard of his poetry and his pathos, stripping him down until he was displayed as no more than a weak, treacherous, decadent pervert. But because she also refused him the arrogant authority with which Shakespeare endows him at the beginning of the play, much of the drama of his decline was lost. The drama of this production was in the relish with which the rebel faction hunted down their whimpering prey. For those who like blood sports it must have been an exhilarating evening. It was a production of immense vitality because of the conviction with which it was directed and acted. There have been plenty of "must-do-something-different" Shakespearian productions which have done as much damage to the poetry and balance of a play for reasons less sincere than those which inspired this production. Joan Littlewood has produced other classics with immense zest without attempting to slant them in any way. For instance *Arden of Faversham* and *The Duchess of Malfi*, because she has a relish for melodrama and violent action and believed that her audience (or rather, the working-class audience which she hoped would eventually fill her theatre) also relished them.

Her success with the public far beyond Stratford East dates from the time she started producing a succession of good new plays. They were plays with a working-class milieu, but with little of the "social significance" which Joan Littlewood had injected into the revivals she had produced at Stratford East. What appealed to the public was not just the plays, but the way they were done. *The Quare Fellow* was an exact, straightforward, realistic production, but the others were produced in a manner reminiscent of the "workers' theatres" in Germany and

Russia immediately after the revolution. The producers in those days seemingly had no illusions about the intelligence of the workers, as everything—characters, ideas, emotions—were reduced to the simplest possible terms, every point was heavily underlined, the humour was made as broad as possible, every opportunity for bawdry was seized upon, the actors took their audience into their confidence with leers, winks and asides, and the whole performance was bashed out with the maximum of noise and vitality. It was ironical that a style of production originally aimed at "the workers" proved, when brought to London's West End, to be just the thing for business men entertaining their clients on their expense accounts. But it is understandable enough. The deliberate lack of subtlety in these productions, their vigour and gusto, the flavour of vaudeville, the introduction of songs, the mateyness between actor and audience, the cheerful ribaldry, the engaging suggestion of impromptu—all this is very much to the taste of the more jovial kind of West End audience which likes to "do a show" without being asked to exert itself overmuch. The style of production achieved popularity for plays which, produced more conventionally, would probably have been enjoyed by only a minority audience. But of course it achieved more than this. It refreshed and revitalised the London theatre with a great blast of rowdy, zestful gusto just when it needed it most. But it did not make Joan Littlewood happy. She decided, for a time at least, to give up the direction of Theatre Workshop and go abroad. "The West End," she complained, "has plundered our talent and diluted our ideas . . . it is not unusual for someone to leave a situation in which they cannot do the work for which they are qualified. That is my case."

Shortly after Joan Littlewood left, a production arrived in the West End from Stratford East which was startlingly different from anything which had been seen there under her régime. The play was Thomas Murphy's *A Whistle in the Dark*, written with immense power, tensely directed by Edward Burnham and magnificently acted. It was about a brutish family of Irish labourers working in Coventry. Here was working-class

realism of a kind one never saw at Stratford in any of Joan
Littlewood's productions, a play of relentless, ferocious realism,
unrelieved by humour. Its impact was profoundly shocking.
Compared with this, Joan Littlewood's productions of plays of
working-class life were jolly, boisterous high jinks. They were
peopled with pimps, prostitutes, petty-thieves, confidence-
tricksters, drunks, layabouts, spivs, the lot; but they were presented primarily as entertaining characters, rather endearing
in spite of their failings. Presented realistically they would have
given a picture of working-class life which would have been
ugly, distorted and lop-sided. But Joan Littlewood was out to
entertain her audience in these plays, and she succeeded—sometimes for hundreds of performances—though the audience was
not the sort she had intended to entertain. Bamber Gascoigne
in an article in the *Spectator* maintains that her influence "has
usually been a boon to her actors and a disaster for her writers.
She gives actors a comic style which enables them to turn almost
any drivel into an entertaining evening, but at the same time
she reduces her authors to turning out stuff which needs precisely this salvaging quality from the actors". He cites *The
Hostage* and *The Lion in Love* as plays in which "everything
was sacrificed for entertainment, no joke was too extraneous, no
gag too old to be included".

In her direction of her actors Joan Littlewood's method of
rehearsal is based on the fact that in her early days as a producer her company was largely amateur so that she had to train
them as she rehearsed them. Talking to actors who have worked
with her in recent years one finds on the whole (though admittedly this is a generalisation) the more experienced and
better trained an actor is, the less responsive he is apt to be to
some of Miss Littlewood's methods. For instance, before rehearsals began on Brendan Behan's *The Quare Fellow*, the actors
trudged for hours in a circle round and round the grimy roof of
the Theatre Royal imagining that they were prisoners at exercise. One actor told me that he found this a sheer waste of
rehearsal time as far as he was concerned; he claimed he was
perfectly capable of imagining what it was like to trudge round

a prison yard, because at his dramatic school he had done exercises of this sort designed to stimulate and develop his imagination. But another actor, less experienced, assured me that the boredom, and dreariness, and chilliness of tramping the roof made him realise something of the drabness of prison life. When *A Taste of Honey* was being produced the two actresses in the opening scene spent an hour or so dragging heavily weighted suitcases round the stage, miming scenes in which they were unable to get on crowded buses and improvising arguments with landladies. By the time they started work on the opening scene in which they arrive at the lodgings they had caught the bored, tired, querulous mood in which it has to be played. To me this seems to be the negation of the art of the actor who must create from his own imagination, not merely from what he has physically experienced. When I was in New York in the late 'thirties, at the time when the Group Theatre's methods were being followed by several companies, I was shown a couple of truckloads of earth which had been dumped in the yard behind the theatre and told how each day the actors started rehearsals by digging in this earth for half an hour to help them to get the feeling of being farm-labourers coming back from work—which was how the opening scene of the play began. In another production which began in the basement kitchen of a sleazy café, the set included a sink with running water, and each night for an hour before the curtain went up, the actress who was playing the part of a little drudge in this kitchen washed a pile of dirty plates and glasses sent in from a neighbouring restaurant. It may be useful for an actress in a part like this to work for a little in a restaurant kitchen so that all her business is real and efficient, but if each evening she cannot think herself in the right mood without requiring such elaborate stimulus, then surely she is deficient in the ability to recreate each night what should have been imaginatively experienced during rehearsals.

So much has been written about Joan Littlewood's method of encouraging her actors to improvise dialogue that many people have the idea that much of the text of the play is created by the actors rather than the author. All that actually used to happen was that often while the actors were improvising a scene, an idea for a speech would emerge which the author would incorporate in the script. It is not a particularly new or revolutionary idea. During any production in which an author is on good terms with his producer and the cast he will sometimes ask for the collaboration of the actors in a scene which is not altogether satisfactory and say to an actor, "Tell me the sort of thing you feel the character would say here." But in the four weeks' rehearsal, which is the maximum allowed for a West End production, there is no time to spend hours on improvising around a scene or indulging in elaborate make-believe about how the characters would behave in scenes outside the play. Much of the difference between Joan Littlewood's methods and those of other English producers depends on the fact that she has generally been able to spend at least six weeks rehearsing a play.

For a time Joan Littlewood encouraged her actors to improvise, not only at rehearsal but also during the performances, because she believes that as soon as a performance is regarded as finalised it wilts and dies. But there is a law which decrees that not a word must be spoken on a public stage until it has been approved by the Lord Chamberlain's office. So a court case and a fine put an end to this form of improvisation. In August 1960, *Encore* published an article called 'Working with Joan' which was a symposium of accounts of her methods of production by actors who had worked with her. One wondered if some of these actors had ever worked with any other good producer, as some of the ways of rehearsals described seemed to be regarded as unique to her, although they are the normal practice of many other producers. For instance, it is explained how she never says, "On this line you move downstage; then you will not be masking and you will be ready for your next cue." That may be the method of some producers in weekly repertory desperately pressed for time, but to describe it as the method "used by the great majority of directors" displays a very limited knowledge of English production. Nearly all producers I know do exactly as Joan Littlewood is described as doing in this symposium; they give the actor an objective and a motive for moving from one point of a stage to another, and to a considerable extent collaborate with an actor in working out the moves, often asking him when and where he feels he would like to make a move. What I find exasperating about so many devotees of Joan Littlewood is that their idea of what goes on in the West End Theatre is about thirty years out of date. For instance, I simply cannot recognise among any of the producers I know the type who is described as "coming into the theatre with a preconceived idea of what he wants and bashing at the actor until he gets it".

The fact that not all of Joan Littlewood's methods of production are unique in no way detracts from her stature as a producer. By all accounts her genius lies not just in her exceptional ability to win the complete confidence of her actors, but also in the way she can inspire her actors with confidence in themselves. English actors during rehearsal are usually far too cautious, shy and inhibited. It is extraordinarily difficult to induce them to rehearse adventurously. But Joan Littlewood has the gift of persuading them to be courageous enough to take risks, even if it may end in their doing something silly which may make them look ridiculous. There is an illuminating account by an actor of what happened when he went to an audition. "She gave me a script and she said, 'Read all the parts—play all the characters.' I said, 'I can't do this,' and she said, 'Go ahead and do it, you are either an actor or you can't!' Well, I did it. Women, children, old men, young men. I was terrible—you know—I felt such an idiot. She said, 'Well, at least you don't mind making a fool of yourself—and any man who has courage on the stage and is willing to make a fool of himself can, in fact, become a good actor." But although this often results in the actor discovering that he can do much more than he believed he could, she does not make the mistake of trying to drive an actor beyond his capabilities. To quote another of her actors, "Her greatest capacity is to know the limitations of each individual actor—to know what he can do—and even more important, to know what he can't do." There is a general idea among the acting profession that she despises technique. She does demand that her actors must not fall back on a safe, well-tried, technically skilful method of solving a difficulty without trying different means first; but at times her direction of an actor is purely technical, especially in the matters of timing and getting a laugh.

When this book was finished five years ago there was a dearth of talented young English producers. In the London Theatre the only one discernible was Peter Hall. Since then nearly a dozen new producers have made names for themselves. They include Lindsey Anderson (*The Lily White Boys*), Peter Coe (*Oliver*), John Dexter (*The Kitchen*), Michael Elliott (*Brand*), William Gaskill (*One Way Pendulum*), Val May (*Mourning Becomes Electra*), Tony Richardson (*Luther*), Minos Volanakis (*The Oresteia*) and Peter Wood (*The Iceman Cometh*). Several of these have come into the theatre from television, one or two from the films. On the other hand, some who started in the theatre now work from time to time as free-lance television directors. From radio the theatre has acquired Donald Mc-Whinnie, whose production of *The Caretaker* owed so much to his meticulous attention to exact phrasing, variation of tone and tempo, and delicate use of pause that one came away from it feeling that most directors would benefit from occasional spells of radio production to compel them to concentrate for a while exclusively on the sound of their productions.

The to-and-fro of producers between the theatre and other mediums has been much to the advantage of the theatre. Otherwise some of the best young producers in the London theatre would have been compelled to earn their living by grinding their talents away in weekly repertory. As the number of theatres in London decreases, and the length of the runs increases, the number of new productions grow fewer each year; so it becomes increasingly difficult for a producer to exist in the London theatre unless he can earn money from other sources. Occasionally he may hit the jackpot with a play which runs for two or three years, providing him with a steady weekly royalty on his production, but more often he will work on a play for many months, first with the author on the script, next on the casting and auditions, then on the rehearsals, followed by the out-of-town opening and weeks spent tracking the production round the provinces, polishing and tightening it, until it eventually arrives in London where, after more rehearsals, it opens perhaps to tepid notices, runs for a very few weeks to poor business, and earns the producer no more than five hundred pounds. There are only two theatres in London with a policy of short runs which give opportunities to several producers in the course of the year. They are the Old Vic and the Royal Court. But the fact that the number of performances of each play is limited inevitably means that the sum which can be paid to the producers is also very limited. Nevertheless, one of the many ways in which the English theatre is indebted to the Royal Court is for giving chances to new producers, not only in their monthly productions, but also in their Sunday night productions without scenery.

The pattern of Shakespearian production in the English theatre remains much the same as it was a few years ago. If one picks out at random a few dramatic criticisms of Shakespearian productions staged during the past five or six years most of them might equally apply to the productions of the previous decade. There are the same complaints about over-strained originality, inaudibility due to the mangling of Shakespearian rhythms, and the determined refusal to allow the great rhetorical passages to be spoken as poetry. At the Old Vic, Michael Benthall has continued firmly with what he has described as "our rather colloquial method of speaking the lines. We try very hard to speak them as if they are realistic, and at the same time to keep the rhythm of the verse". This is surely attempting the impossible. Colloquial speech has its own characteristic rhythms, which have little in common with the rhythms of the iambic pentameter. One of the characteristics of Benthall's productions, which is a result of his realistic treatment of the verse, is the immense care he takes to ensure that his actors speak the lines as spontaneously as possible, as if they had just thought of them, not as set speeches. This is as it should be, but he seems to fear that lines and speeches already familiar to the audience will no longer sound like spontaneous utterances of the characters, so either he directs his actors to speak famous speeches slowly and hesitantly, with many pauses, as if they were having difficulty in putting their thoughts into words, or he dashes them through familiar passages at high speed so that they have flashed past before the audience has had time to recognise them. A *Times* notice of one of Benthall's recent productions pointed out that this attempt at realism defeats its own purpose. "A man coining a fine phrase as he talks will roll it lovingly on his tongue. To rush through it as most of these actors did and manacle the image with over-charged emotion is not only unpoetical, it is unreal."

It is puzzling that so many directors besides Michael Benthall should want to transmute Shakespeare's verse into something which bears an unconvincing resemblance to everyday speech. Perhaps it is because so many producers today are under the misapprehension that if Shakespeare is spoken musically it will be intoned and sound, to quote Michael Benthall again, "lovely but meaningless". Shakespeare never intended his plays to be spoken "musically" all the way. There are long stretches which simply demand to be spoken swiftly, rhythmically and sensibly; but there are the speeches which are written as music and demand to be spoken musically. We still have a few leading players who prove again and again that there is no reason why these speeches should not be spoken in a way that combines sound and sense as Shakespeare intended. If the audience is given the sense without the sound, they are being unfairly deprived of one of the greatest pleasures of the Shakespearian theatre.

When Peter Hall became director at Stratford-upon-Avon, he announced that he was engaging a company on long contracts and bringing John Barton from Cambridge to train the company to speak verse in the best traditions of the Marlowe Society. As a result there has been a noticeable improvement in the general standard of speech; the most vicious massacres of Shakespeare's sound and sense are now mostly perpetrated by imported actors who are not members of the permanent company. Peter Hall protests, fairly enough, that the director of a Shakespeare play is often in the position of a choreographer asked to stage a ballet with people who haven't had a lesson. But he himself must take the blame for casting actors and actresses in leading parts, seemingly for no other reason than that they have just had a fashionable success in the West End in a realistic play. More care in discovering beforehand whether they had some aptitude for speaking verse, at least with a sense of its rhythms, would have saved several players from gravely damaging their reputations at Stratford. Sometimes casting seems to have been deliberately eccentric in order to excite surprise and speculation, as for example in the 1961 season, when an admirable character actor was piteously miscast as Hamlet, presumably on the principle that it would make an interesting change if the part were played by an actor physically, temperamentally, and vocally almost the exact antithesis of Hamlet. Lately Peter Hall seems to have lost his belief that actors can be taught to speak verse and has fallen back on the theory that "by and large training consists in doing it. The verse imposes itself on them at last, and after struggling to turn Shakespeare into modern prose, and suffering agonies, the actor sooner or later finds it plays itself". But meantime the critics and the audience might fairly protest that they too are suffering agonies.

The charge that producers continually strain for originality at all costs is largely due to the fact that new productions of the same plays are far too frequent—and this in spite of our having only two Shakespearian theatres. A producer starting on a play which he (as well as the critics and the public) has seen several times in recent years not unnaturally feels that somehow he must think up a fresh approach to the play. He fears that, if he simply directs it straightforwardly, his production will be thought dull and uninventive. But as he thinks back over the productions of the play he has seen, as well as those he has read about, he finds it increasingly difficult to think up business which has not already been done or unorthodox characterisations which have not already been tried; so in his striving after originality he is apt to be driven into eccentricity. In most continental repertory theatres a production of a Shakespeare play, if it is judged to be a good one, is kept in the repertoire for several years, while in England the Old Vic and Stratford may, between them, produce the same play half a dozen times in the course of five years, with half a dozen producers exercising the utmost ingenuity in trying to make their production different from the others. But at last there are signs that the rate of the output of new productions is slowing down. Now that Stratford has a permanent company, it is able to continue a production for longer than a single season, and this has already been done with *Twelfth Night* and *The Taming of the Shrew*. The Old Vic too is reducing the number of new Shakespearian productions by bringing other authors besides Shakespeare into its repertoire.

The most straightforward performances of Shakespeare seen in London in recent years have been Michael Croft's productions for the National Youth Theatre. W. A. Darlington, while approving Croft's method of trying to do each play as if it had never been done before, declares, somewhat despairingly, that to do this with a professional cast "would mean putting most of them through a process of brain-washing to which they would put up an unconscious but tough resistance. With a cast of schoolboys no preconceived ideas exist and no brain-washing is needed". Fortunately during the last five years there has been a sufficient number of straightforward and finely effective productions to prove that actors are not quite as indoctrinated as Mr. Darlington believes, and they are ready to respond to a producer who can convince them that even the most familiar of the plays can still be lively, fresh and exciting without being rigged out in fancy dress and given a shot in the arm.

Such a producer is Michael Elliott, whose *As You Like It* at Stratford in 1960 I count among the best Shakespearian productions I have ever seen. It enchanted the audience, because it conveyed to them the producer's own delight in the play. Plainly he found so much pleasure in it, had so much faith in it, that he felt there was no need to do anything but produce it as faithfully as possible. The romance, the gaiety, and the melancholy were beautifully mingled. The balance of the production was delicate and exact, especially in the contrast between the realism of the rustics and the artificiality of the Court. The setting was simple and pleasurable. Many of the parts were played better than I have ever seen before, without attempting any unusual interpretations. The verse was impeccably phrased, spoken with a seeming simplicity yet with subtle variety of tone and tempo. It is difficult to believe one will ever see a better production of this play. Another very satisfying production at Stratford that season was William Gaskill's clear, vigorous, dramatic, honest-to-goodness production of *Richard III*.

Peter Wood's *The Winter's Tale* during the 1959 season was a fine production which told the story of the play firmly and dramatically. The grouping, movement and scenic effects were brilliantly contrived; they gave immense pleasure to the eye, but were never fussy, and never distracted one's attention from what was being said. In the same season a superbly effective production of a different kind was Tony Richardson's *Pericles*. Here is a play which deserves no reverence, so the producer is fully justified in exerting all his ingenuity to make it enjoyable for a modern audience, who are apt to find the story just plain silly. What Richardson did was to have the narrative passages sung by Edric Connor, in the manner of a calypso, to a group of sailors who became an audience within the play, which was produced as a dream fantasy; a splendidly colourful barbaric fantasy, with naïve and exaggerated costumes such as the sailors might have imagined as they listened to the story. Many producers, having hit on this idea, would have been content to go no further and do a production which was just "rather fun". Richardson never condescended towards the play. He managed to make the story seem vigorous and dramatic and often very touching by giving full value to the scenes of genuine pathos towards the end of the play. Incidentally, it is odd that Peter Wood and Tony Richardson, after brilliantly producing exceptionally difficult plays, should have had comparative failures with much easier plays, Wood with *Hamlet* and Richardson with *Othello*. The ingenuity and inventiveness which Richardson brought to *Pericles* was embarrassingly misapplied to *Othello*, a play which is well able to look after itself.

Among other outstandingly good productions of the past five years were Tyrone Guthrie's *All's Well That Ends Well* transported to Ruritania; Zeffirelli's *Romeo and Juliet* (although it collapsed in the last act); Peter Hall's *Coriolanus* and *Twelfth Night;* Michael Benthall's *A Midsummer Night's Dream* giving full scope to his talent for gay and beautiful movement and grouping; and John Barton's *The Taming of the Shrew,* which transformed what I had always seen as a cruel and loutish farce into a lighthearted, charming comedy. Perhaps I ought to add to the list *Troilus and Cressida* produced by Hall and Barton in front of an unchanging backcloth on a bleak stage bare of everything except what looked like a circus ring filled with real sand. Because of the lack of décor and different acting levels, I found the production visually monotonous and tiring to the eye. I dislike being asked to provide my own scenery when I go to a Shakespeare play, and I certainly can't do it as well as a good scene designer who nowadays can give pleasurable variety to the eye without distracting from the play or impeding the swift flow from scene to scene with pauses while the stage hands get to work—as happened in Zeffirelli's magnificent but ponderous Stratford production of *Othello,* which he designed himself.

Recently in Moscow I saw Okhlopkov's *Hamlet,* which must be the most lavish Shakespearian production of all time. As soon as the curtain rises one realises that the setting has been suggested by Hamlet's words, "Denmark is a prison". Instead of a front cloth there are vast, solid, prison-like doors which open to reveal the palace. Astonishingly effective use is made of these doors in the play scene, when they are swung back to serve as the sides of the setting with all twelve of the great panels opened to form three galleries crowded with spectators. The producer and his designer do not confine themselves just to the interior of the palace, the ramparts, and the graveyard. There are scenes by the seashore, in the garden, on the top of a cliff, in the courtyard of the palace and at the quayside, where a ship waits for the journey to England. When Hamlet comes upon the King at prayer, it is in a chapel dominated by a huge statue of the Madonna. Scene follows scene without pause because of the skill and ingenuity with which the elaborate equipment of the theatre is used. The settings are sombre and beautiful, not excessively realistic. On the immense stage one never feels they are swamping the actors or encroaching upon their playing space. Like so many Russian theatres, the Mayakovsky combines an enormous stage with a smallish auditorium about the size of the New Theatre in London, so in spite of the scale of the production, there is a feeling of intimacy between actor and audience. The production employs the theatre's full company, nearly a hundred and fifty actors. When Laertes bursts into the palace, he is at the head of a huge revolutionary mob which swarms up the great iron grille protecting the King, furiously attempting to burst through the bars. Ophelia's mad scene is played in the palace square, watched by a horrified crowd. All through the play the crowds are used to emphasise that this was not just a family tragedy, but also the story of a State in turmoil. Apart from stressing the revolutionary element, the production is not slanted in any way. The only interpolation is a brief scene in which Ophelia is seen in the garden playing a game with some of her friends and singing a song which is afterwards echoed in the mad scene. At the performance I saw the Hamlet, contrary to all we hear about the casting of this part in the Soviet Theatre, was played by a boy of twenty.

Peter Hall, after his visit to Russia with the Stratford Company, described the Soviet Theatre as "a beautifully kept and well presented museum of dramatic art". This is true of only a part of the theatre. For instance, at the Moscow Art Theatre I saw a production of *Anna Karenina* which had been in the repertoire for twenty-seven years, yet it looked as if it had been running for only a month or two. It is a pity that this production could not be seen in England, for we think of the Moscow Art Theatre too exclusively in connection with Chekhov and overlook the fact that many of its productions are on a very grand scale.

There are twenty-seven scenes in *Anna Karenina* and more than a hundred actors. It is a production of the utmost elegance which re-creates the aristocratic life of Tsarist Russia, not only in meticulous detail, but also with charm and glamour. The enormous revolving stage of the Art Theatre is used for a series of wonderfully spectacular scenes including the whole of the dress-circle of a theatre, the staircase at the Opera, a race course with stands packed with spectators, the stables, and the final scene in which Anna throws herself in front of a train steaming towards the audience. But what is even more impressive than the luxuriousness of the production is the extraordinary detail of the acting in the ensemble scenes when the stage is thronged with actors.

At other theatres I saw productions which have been many years in the repertoire without showing any sign of ageing, and if I had confined my theatregoing to productions of the classics I would probably have agreed with Peter Hall's description of the Soviet Theatre. But in Leningrad, Moscow, and Kiev I saw a number of new productions which gave one a very different impression. They were not in any way unorthodox or experimental, but they were certainly not old-fashioned. The settings were realistic, but not in the heavy, unimaginative old-fashioned style of the ballets and operas I saw. What all the productions had in common was a large number of scenes, a great many actors, and usually some stunningly sensational piece of stage-craft, such as the dynamiting of a coal mine by saboteurs in a play I saw at Kiev. This is the sort of theatre which the Russian audiences like; and producers have to give the public what they want, not because the theatres have to pay their way, but because the Government considers that any theatre which is not attracting big audiences is not properly fulfilling its function. The end of the great era of experiment in the Soviet theatre of the 'twenties was brought about, not just by Stalinism, but because audiences drifted away from the experimental theatres, plainly showing their preference for more lavish and realistic productions.

But there is one theatre where productions in the style of

the experimental theatre of the 'twenties can still be seen. It is the Satire Theatre, which was closed down for many years, but was allowed to re-open in 1954. It is the smallest theatre in Moscow, simply a large room in the first floor of what used to be the home of a wealthy family. The stage is almost as cramped as in those little makeshift minority theatres which used to exist in London before the war, though in some scenes an astonishing number of actors are crammed on to it. The three plays which are the mainstay of the Satire Theatre's repertoire were originally produced by Meierhold, and the present productions are very much in the same style. Make-ups and costumes are wildly and amusingly exaggerated, the settings consist of very funny satirical backcloths resembling blown-up cartoons, the actors jump around on little platforms, ramps, and ladders, as they used to do in the days of the "constructionist" settings, the acting is all clowning and buffoonery done with tremendous zest and humour. The actors continually take the audience into their confidence, and at one point during *The Bedbug* they swarm into the auditorium distributing a newspaper. The audience is as lively as the actors, laughing uproariously, shouting their approval of satirical lines and again and again breaking into bursts of applause. An evening at the Satire Theatre is noisy, bustling, exhilarating and immensely entertaining, even if one cannot understand what is being said.

All the new theatres I saw in Russia were of conventional design, but I was shown a model of the Theatre of the Young Spectator, a children's theatre which was to be built in Leningrad, which is an open stage theatre. Like Bernard Miles's "Mermaid Theatre", the stage is not raised, it is simply the floor of the building which has a very steeply raked auditorium so that the audience look down on the stage. Most of the new theatres I saw have excessively large auditoriums. The theatre of the Palace of Culture in Leningrad, for instance, where the Stratford and Old Vic companies performed, has a cinema-like auditorium which stretches away and away from the stage. A much more likable auditorium is that of the Soviet Army Theatre, in which the seats curve towards the abnormally wide stage. So far as I could discover there are no longer any theatres-in-the-round. Okhlopkov, the pioneer of this kind of theatre (one of his productions is described in Chapter 8), is now working happily in a proscenium-type theatre. When I asked why these theatres had disappeared, I was told that at first audiences enjoyed the novelty of playing a game of make-believe with the actors, but when the novelty wore off they preferred to go back to the proscenium theatre. One hears no talk in Russia about the anti-illusionist theatre which nowadays has so many advocates in England. "We have outgrown that sort of theatre," said a Russian producer with whom I was talking. "Our audiences are now so much better educated and more sophisticated than they were in the early days of the Soviet theatre. In those days we used deliberately to expose the mechanics of the theatre, show the scene-shifters at work, reveal the lights above the stage, make the actors talk direct to the audience instead of pretending that they did not exist, use any device we could think of to remind the audience they were in a theatre and prevent them from believing that what they were seeing was real life." He went on to tell me how, in an Ostrovsky play when a poor peasant girl was about to submit to become the mistress of a rich old man to provide money for her starving family, the audience threw money on to the stage so that she would not need to sell herself. Which is how the equally unsophisticated audiences of the Victorian fit-up companies behaved when they shouted warnings to the hero as the villain was stealing upon him. But the present-day audience in England is perfectly well aware that what they are watching is a theatrical performance and not real life, so I can see no good, logical reason why some producers should be so intent upon reminding the audience of the fact.

The anti-illusionists detest the proscenium theatre, the "magic box" as they call it, a box of tricks for bamboozling the audience into believing that they are watching something real. Personally I detest most of the proscenium theatres in England for a different reason, because of the effort the actor has to make to "get across" to his audience, but this does not apply to the older proscenium theatres such as the Haymarket, the New Theatre, and the Criterion. In nearly all the London theatres built from the 'twenties onwards, the relation between the stage and the cinema-like auditoriums could hardly be worse. When at last, many years after the war, a new theatre, the Royalty, was built in the West End, it repeated all the faults of the worst type of proscenium theatre and with indecent haste became a cinema—the purpose for which one suspected it had really been designed, though planning permission for pulling down the Stoll Theatre to build an office block had only been given on condition that the building incorporated a theatre. The new Belgrade Theatre at Coventry combines a splendidly designed front-of-house with a wretchedly inadequate stage with, for the actors, the added handicap of a large permanent forestage, which in a realistic play becomes a blank no-man's-land across which they have to project their performances.

In England the interminable arguments about the merits and demerits of the proscenium stage. the open stage, and the theatre-in-the-round are all based upon theory, not upon experience, because we have no properly designed modern proscenium theatre, no theatres-in-the-round which are not temporary makeshifts, no open-stage theatres except the one which is annually rigged up in the Assembly Hall at Edinburgh for the Festival. But the Chichester theatre, which is now being built, will give us at last an open-stage theatre on the lines of the Festival Theatre at Stratford, Ontario, which seems to me the ideal stage for Shakespearian productions. It is lamentable that the Government refused to implement its promise to build the National Theatre, as there would have been two theatres under the one roof, an open-stage theatre and a proscenium theatre. Then it would have been possible to discover by trial and error which were the kinds of plays suited to each theatre. I am convinced that there is no one type of theatre in which all plays can be best performed.

Today any theatre built for profit will inevitably be unsatisfactory. Because of the price of land and the high cost of building, the stage has to be shrunk to make room for as many seats as possible. Fortunately a number of local authorities are either building theatres or planning to do so, among them Manchester, Croydon, Guildford, Plymouth, Leicester, Nottingham, Edinburgh and Crawley New Town. But from what one hears some of these theatres will be unhappy buildings, because they have been designed without full consultation with all the branches of the theatrical profession who will work in these theatres, and without examining the new types of theatres recently built on the Continent.

Although new theatres are desperately needed, what the English theatre also badly needs is something of which there is at present no sign—a young producer who has the faith and determination to gather together a few actors into a permanent company and set to work in even the most appallingly inconvenient premises. Planchon, starting in the basement of that shop in Lyons, within ten years has made his company one of the most famous in Europe. Before him Antoine and Copeau and Pitoëff followed the same path. Only a permanent company working under a single producer of great talent can bring into the English theatre anything really new in the way of production and acting. If he cannot find the actors to share his faith, and the hardships it will entail, he must do what Antoine and Copeau and Pitoëff did—begin by recruiting his company from amateurs. It is what Stanislavsky and Barry Jackson and Joan Littlewood did, too. In the old days it used to be said that every actor began his career determined to become an actor-manager. Unless the young producer of today starts with the determination to become a producer-manager, he must resign himself either to wearing away his talents in a succession of repertory theatres, or to producing for television while he waits for an occasional production in the West End or at Stratford. It is not an exhilarating prospect for anyone who cares a great deal about the theatre.

POSTSCRIPT 1975

During the twelve years which have passed since the last chapter was written the deaths of Okhlopkov, Piscator, Vilar and Tyrone Guthrie have deprived the European theatre of four great directors. Peter Brook, after his production of *The Dream* in 1970 withdrew to France to found the International Centre for Theatrical Research. Behind the closed doors of a Paris warehouse he conducted an arduous series of experiments with a group of actors from several different countries. At the Shiraz-Persepolis Festival they performed *Orghast*, most of it in an invented language consisting of phonetic sounds rather than words, in an attempt to find a common international idiom. After wandering with his actors through Asia and Africa seeking the possibility of a new relationship between actor and audience, he is back in Paris where he has established himself at Les Bouffes-du-Nord, a near-derelict old nineteenth-century theatre in a suburb of Paris. Planchon still believes as strongly as ever in the didactic theatre but he no longer re-writes or contorts a classic to fit in with his own political beliefs. His production of *Troilus and Cressida*, for instance, was entirely faithful to the text and he has become a superb director of Molière. Speaking of *Georges Dandin* he says: "I and my company love this play because it seems to have been written last month; that's our definition of a classic." He has constantly sought, without much success, to find new playwrights to express his own convictions. Now he has decided to write the plays himself. In order to concentrate on writing he has declared that henceforth he will seldom direct, so he has chosen a young man in his middle twenties, Patrice Chéreau, to direct in his place and be the co-director of the company. Barrault, in contrast to Planchon, remains "basically anti-politique". He sees "no reason at all for over-statement and over-emphasis of politics in the theatre."

So it is somewhat ironical that in 1968, when rioting students invaded the Odéon and jeered him off the stage when he tried to reason with them, the result was that he was evicted by the Government from the theatre because of a mistaken idea that he had allowed it to be used for student demonstrations. Deprived of his subsidy, he moved to a hall in Montmartre which had been used for all-in wrestling. Here, for his production of *Rabelais*, he installed bare platforms running the length and breadth of the hall, intersecting one another at right angles, with the audience seated in every corner. In 1972 he moved to the near-abandoned Gare d'Orsay on the Left Bank, where he erected a gigantic circus tent housing another arrangement of bare platforms.

The number of highly talented directors in the European theatre is probably greater than it has ever been but nobody has emerged with the stature sufficient to fill the gaps left by the losses of recent years. Nevertheless the status and influence of the director has been steadily increasing until he has now achieved what many theatre people believe to be a grossly inflated importance. Some leading directors have been so much publicised, written about, interviewed and talked about that their names are as familiar to the public as those of many leading players. Too frequently this has resulted in an arrogance towards the play and the players which is increasingly resented within the theatre itself. Michael Elliott, himself a distinguished director, thinks that "the proper function of the director has become almost lost under the ambition and megalomania of its members." He goes on to say that "usually the object of their malevolent advances is a great but difficult play. By giving it a 'new interpretation', which in fact corrupts the play but serves excellently the director's intention of showing off his talent, he will appear to give new life to dead material." John Russel Brown, the literary director of the National Theatre, describes such directors as manufacturers and salesmen. "To function in this way they need to coin images, to find a new conception of each production of each play."

Postscript 1975

There are, of course, many directors for whom the play and the players are more important than their own ego, but there are far too many of the arrogant, exhibitionist directors, some of them not particularly intelligent judging by their complete misunderstanding of the play they are directing. For instance *Le Malade Imaginaire*, brought by the Comédie Française to the World Theatre Season in 1973, began with a long scene in dumb show invented by the director, Jean-Laurent Cochet, to make it plain that Argon is not ill, does not even imagine that he is ill, but is engaged in an elaborate confidence trick. The result was to make near nonsense of the rest of the play and its title. A mimed prologue to a classic is becoming a favourite gimmick. For instance, there is the scene Ingmar Bergman invented for *Hedda* before he began Ibsen's play. At Chichester in Pilikian's production of *Oedipus Tyrannus* we were given, as a bonus, a prologue depicting the murder of Laius.

Until recently the exhibitionist directors confined themselves mainly to Shakespeare, but now other great playwrights including Chekhov, Ibsen and Strindberg are being mauled by them. Chekhov is the one who has suffered most. When the Moscow Art Theatre came to the World Theatre Season in 1970 they performed *The Seagull* in a version which can only be described as having been "messed about with" by Livenov, the director, who had clumsily edited the play, written new speeches, and sometimes re-arranged the text, as for example when the long duologue in the third act between Konstantin and Nina was sliced in half and the two halves performed in different scenes. At Bremen, Noelte in his productions of Chekhov has been making what he considers to be some much needed improvements on the text. At Warsaw's National Theatre Hanusz-kewicz's production of *The Three Sisters* is performed in an abstract setting, a pruned version lasting two hours without an interval. Lately it has become fashionable to deprive Chekhov of the realistic settings his plays demand. In all of them the relation of the characters to their surroundings is an integral part of the play. At the Finnish National Theatre I saw a production of

The Three Sisters by Georgi Tovstonagov from Leningrad's Gorki Theatre performed against a vast mud-coloured backcloth, the stage bare except for the furniture which from time to time during each act was moved round into different positions by the revolve. Our own National Theatre's production of *The Three Sisters* also had an oddity—Svobada's setting consisting of innumerable lengths of stretched string (or was it wire?) completely at odds with a production meticulously realistic in the choice of furniture and props. Even more difficult to fathom was the reason for Robin Philips' production of the play in a setting of glistening black with glittering metal decorations. In the National's production of *The Cherry Orchard* there was a curiously pointless innovation. At the end of the play as the sound of the carriages driving the family away faded into the distance and as one waited for the entrance of old Firs, forgotten and left behind in the locked-up house, the stage suddenly revolved to reveal him improbably locked in his bedroom. The director, Michael Blakemore, does not normally indulge in tricks to draw attention to himself, so one suspects that having done a production faithful to Chekhov's intentions he was at the end assailed by that fear which seems to haunt so many directors of the classics nowadays, the fear that unless they think up something unexpected the production will be dismissed as "ordinary" and they themselves regarded as dull and uninventive. Perhaps the same fear drove Bergman, in his superbly directed and acted production of *The Wild Duck*, to spoil the ending by turning Ibsen's stage directions upside down so that the great closing scene between Gregers and Hjalmar was dissipated by the sight of Hedwig crouched on the forestage (which we were supposed to imagine to be the attic). In Ibsen's stage directions the entrance to the attic is in the back wall of the set, and throughout the scene Hedwig is out of sight behind its closed door.

Directors who tinker with masterpieces might heed Michael Elliot's reminder that "if the play is a classic its merit is not in doubt, and the director can be reasonably certain that the genius which created it was superior to his own." Georgio Strehler, the founder of the Piccolo Theatre in Milan, is fond of quoting similar advice given to him, when he was a very young director, by Jouvet. "You are not Mozart," he said "nor Molière. But without you, without a theatre, a director, without interpreters, Mozart and Molière are but pieces of paper; valuable, interesting, but still only paper. It is you who bring them to life. But *never* permit yourself to think you are they."

Nowadays a director working on a play written two or three centuries ago usually seeks by various means to stress whatever is particularly relevant to the present. One of the most usual methods is to up-date it and it was this device which recently rescued Molière from centuries of misunderstanding and neglect in the English theatre. First there was Frank Dunlop's romping production of *Scapino* set in present-day Italy, a production full of comic invention not imposed upon the play but the legitimate comic developments of situations and characters— characters no longer hidden beneath the costumes of Molière's day, so unfamiliar and unreal to English actors and audiences. Then at the Nottingham Playhouse there was David Williams' production of *The Misanthrope* up-dated to the Twenties but scrupulous in its avoidance of the easy laughs which would have been raised by the slightest over-emphasis on the clothes and mannerisms of the period. Next came John Dexter's dazzling production of the same play at the National, set in the last days of the de Gaullist regime. In neither production were the settings modernised: only the clothes and manner of behaviour. Both were played in seventeenth-century salons of the utmost elegance but obviously rooms which were lived in, with here and there pieces of modern furniture such as comfortable armchairs, and, of course, a telephone, and in the National's present-day production, hi-fi equipment. All very restrained compared with Oslo's Scene 7 Theatre's production of *Les Femmes Savantes*, described in *The Times* as "up-dated to the befringed 1920's with a couple of beefy males in the bluestocking roles". An unexpectedly successful example of up-dating was David Giles' production of *'Tis Pity She's A Whore* for the Actors' Theatre, transferred to Sicily in the early years of the century. The plot gained in realism because the schemers and killers in their black pin-striped suits and wide trilby hats reminded one of the criminals of the Mafia. The colonnaded setting and the suggestion of oppressive heat evoked exactly the right atmosphere for the violent passions of the play. So far as I know, this masterpiece of the Elizabethan theatre had never, since its own time, been staged for more than an occasional single performance, but in this production it was so successful that it became a part of The Actors' Theatre repertoire.

Shakespeare in modern dress has long ceased to be a novelty. One can think of few of the plays apart from the English histories which have not been thrust into modern clothes during the past dozen years. One of the most successful of these experiments was the way Robin Philips enlivened the tedious unattractiveness of *Two Gentlemen of Verona* for the Royal Shakespeare Theatre by setting it round a swimming pool with the characters in up-to-date beach clothes. A good example of how modern dress can bring minor characters much more alive for to-day's audience was the playing of Antonio as a bloated, cigar-smoking tycoon. There was a nice moment when he handed to his servant Parthino his sun glasses, his ostentatiously monogrammed beach wrap and his still glowing cigar to hold while he took a dip in the pool. Much less successful was the National's *Merchant of Venice* presented as happening at the end of the last century. Jonathan Miller's idea was that the sight of business men in frock coats and top hats carrying brief cases would emphasise to the audience that the theme of the play is Money. But money is *not* the subject of the play. It is only one of its several themes. This picking out one theme in a Shakespearean play and heavily stressing it at the expense of the rest of the play is becoming increasingly common. *The Merchant* is essentially a fairy tale which could hardly have been more effectively stifled by the stuffy, ugly costumes of the period of this production. Besides, up-dating the story reduced the plot to nonsense. As I overheard one of the audience remark in the interval, "in these days Antonio would have had his fleet insured at Lloyds, so he would have had no difficulty in repaying his debt to Shylock".

The outstanding event of the Shakespearean theatre of the past twelve years was Peter Hall's bold and splendid idea of joining together the English histories, making them, with John Barton as his collaborator, into three plays under the title of *The Wars of the Roses*. They were united by John Bury's permanent setting of iron and steel, emphasising the harshness of the story and dramatically contrasting with the splendour of the costumes. Barton's snipping and stitching was done with the utmost skill and discretion, but years later his production of *King John* contained so many passages written by himself and so many borrowings from other sources that one critic described it "as an inchoate amalgam of disparate elements presented under a misleading title in the name of an author who did not write it". Much the same criticisms were brought against Strehler's audacious adaptation of Shakespeare's Henry trilogy performed at the 1973 Salzburg Festival under the title of *The Game of the Mighty*. There are 144 in the cast, 39 scenes, and it lasts for eight hours spread over two evenings. In spite of the fury with which it was attacked by many of the critics it was retained in the Salzburg repertoire for the following year. The R.S.C. attempted to defend itself against the angry criticisms of its *King John* by describing it as "an experiment to see whether a play which has been virtually dead in the past 50 years can be made to live for an audience of to-day." But it is worth remembering that the youthful Peter Brook at the Birmingham Repertory Theatre breathed life into this "virtually dead" play with such success that he went straight on to direct at Stratford-upon-Avon.

Barton quickly regained the esteem in which he had been held with his production of *Cymbeline*, perhaps the most difficult of all Shakespeare's plays for the director—and for the audience too. Dr. Johnson's opinion was: "To remark the folly of the fiction, the absurdity of the conduct, the confusion of the names and manners of different times, and the impossibility of the events in any system of life, were to waste criticism upon unresisting imbecility, upon faults too evident for detection, and too gross for aggravation". Barton brilliantly edited the play, cutting some 800 lines, and introducing a narrator who—sometimes with a nice touch of humour—guided the audience through the intricacies of the plot. So for once the story became understandable and the play enjoyable, because as Johnson admitted, "it has many just sentiments, some natural dialogues, and some pleasing scenes".

It was Peter Brook's *A Midsummer Night's Dream* which was, needless to say, the other outstanding Shakespearean production of the period. Brook has explained his approach to the play as based on the fact that he could think of no symbols which would conjure up fairyland for a modern audience. "So I turned to the arts of the circus, the tumblers, the acrobats, the jugglers and the slapstick comedy of the clowns. I wanted to make it a joyful production and I felt a display of sheer physical virtuosity would achieve this." So for many weeks the cast went through a strenuous course in acrobatics. Explaining the setting of bare, lofty white flats, Brook said he designed it because he felt "this removed the sense of being earthbound and made it seem natural for the characters to fly". Juggling as well as acrobatics were among the skills which the cast had to acquire. There was an enchanting scene between Oberon and Puck, each swinging on a trapeze, in which the magic flower, love in idleness, was represented by a silver disk magically spinning as they passed it to and fro on conjurers' wands. The fairies, nearly all of them played by male actors, were in costumes resembling track suits of grey. silk Puck, who in one scene appeared walking on stilts with the mortals scurrying around in alarm below him, wore a yellow clown's suit with a blue skull cap. The "rude mechanicals" were dressed as present-day workmen in cloth caps and overalls. In the almost unanimous praise heaped on this production perhaps too little of it was given to the speaking of the verse. Brook had obviously taken infinite care that it should be spoken with full appreciation of its changing rhythms, tone and tempi together with an exact understanding of even the most delicate nuances in the text. Never before can this play have given so much pleasure to the ear. It was the ultimate magic of the production.

A rewarding experiment in Shakespearean production was the National's all-male *As You Like It*. Clifford Williams, the director, described himself as "searching for an atmosphere of spiritual purity which transcends sensuality". Most of the critics agreed he had achieved what one of them described as an atmosphere of "luminous purity". J. W. Lambert suggested that why the absence of actresses had produced this effect was because in the 300 years during which women players have been accepted on the English stage "they have acquired what might be called an excess of femininity: not content with being women, they have fallen into the way of behaving 'womanishly' to a quite unnecessary degree". The women's parts in this production were not played by boys. They were played by permanent members of the company, young men in their twenties. The result effectively demolished the myth that Shakespeare's women were played by young boys. It is inconceivable that Burbage played Macbeth opposite a boy of fourteen, or that Volumina or Gertrude were played by children. There is evidence that Robin Goff, the first Juliet, almost certainly played Cleopatra seven years later.

The list of Shakespearean productions during recent years in which the directors have felt impelled to "do something" with the plays is too long to enumerate here. The most frequent have been those where the director has been intent upon expressing what he usually describes as his "personal view" of the play, which doesn't bother overmuch about what Shakespeare's view may have been and often entails cutting lines, characters, and even whole scenes not in accord with his own highly individual conception of the play. Then there have been the directors who even before they have begun rehearsals explain to the press and radio the particular "angle" from which they view the play, but the results have usually proved that the angle from which they have approached it has given them only a partial view of the play. Slanting a production in an attempt to make political propaganda is, in the English theatre, usually confined to occasional manipulations of the text, the heavy over-emphasising of a few lines and speeches and the caricaturing of one or two characters. But the National gave us an example of what can happen to Shakespeare when he is given the full propaganda treatment. It was the production of *Coriolanus* by two ex-members of the Berliner Ensemble, Manfred Weckworth and Joachim Tenschert. The text was mercilessly hacked and twisted as the directors attempted to make it fit their theories. As a production it failed utterly for the simple reason that the propaganda point the directors were trying to make was precisely the opposite of the point Shakespeare made when he wrote the play.

Perhaps we have seen an end to the era of gimmicky productions of Shakespeare as a result of the wrath of the critics over *Measure for Measure* at Stratford in 1974. Keith Hack's direction went just about as far as possible in deliberate misinterpretation of the text, misconceived characterisation, and irrelevant invention. "Why, o why, can't they trust Shakespeare?" was the theme of most of the notices. Kenneth Hurren wondered if the reason Keith Hack had been invited to join the R.S.C. was that he had "doubtless previously displayed somewhere that hostility to Shakespeare which is so valued at Stratford these days". Hurren thought the production "an insufferable affront to any audience who may attend in innocent expectation of seeing a play of Shakespeare's". To B. A. Young the evening's proceedings seemed "no better than an insult thrown in the face of the audience".

Fortunately there have been a number of straightforward productions in which the imagination and skill of the director have been used simply to enhance what Shakespeare wrote. A surprise success was Terry Hands' production for the R.S.C.

of *The Merry Wives of Windsor* which had come to be regarded as coarse-grained and boring. The critics were frankly astonished to find that this production was full of gaiety and genuine merriment, that the last scene had an entrancing sense of magic, and that the characters, usually considered to be so sketchily drawn, had come vividly to life. How was this achieved? Simply, I think, because Hands liked the play, enjoyed it, developed an affection for it, and directed it with a lightness of touch which made one forget the galumphing antics with which the comic scenes had been played in the past. As to the characters, Shakespeare is said to have been given only a fortnight to write the play, so had no time to do more than sketch the characters in outline. One felt that Hands had done what Shakespeare would have done with them given time—filled in the outlines, and coloured and developed the characters. If there is any doubt about whether Shakespeare wrote *The Merry Wives* in a fortnight it is an undeniable fact that Clifford Williams directed his now famous production of *The Comedy of Errors* in a fortnight. Owing to illness, a production of the R.S.C. had to be postponed and *The Comedy of Errors* was hastily staged to fill the gap. One wonders to what extent the exhilarating zest and comic invention of this production and the actors' obvious faith and delight in the play would have survived all the many weeks of preparation now considered necessary for a Shakespeare production.

Two other productions not belonging to the theatre of bright ideas were John Barton's *Twelfth Night* and Laurence Olivier's *Love's Labour's Lost* at the National. *Twelfth Night* is the most difficult of all Shakespeare's comedies because of its complex mingling of often conflicting moods and emotions. In Barton's low-keyed, almost grave production this was beautifully achieved. The fun was there but it never became farce, and the underlying melancholy of the play was subtly suggested. As to Olivier's *Love's Labour's Lost*, what one admired about the production was the way he accepted the fact that this has always been one of the least popular of the plays and made no attempt to introduce gimmicks in an attempt to popularise it. Shakespeare never intended it to be a popular play. At a time when the theatres were closed by the plague it was commissioned by one of the great Elizabethan noblemen to be performed at his country seat; so Shakespeare was writing for an elitist audience and it was for just such an audience that Olivier directed it, relying upon them to enjoy sophisticated verbal wit, to take pleasure in graceful verse spoken with full appreciation of its musical cadences, and to enjoy the visual delights of the settings, based on mediaeval missals, and the glowing colours of the sweeping satin gowns.

Olivier is curiously underrated as a director in spite of the variety of plays he has directed with the utmost skill and understanding. Probably the reason is that in his productions he never calls attention to his own handiwork, never gives interviews about how he is going to direct a play, has never written about his theories of production. He does not regard himself as an intellectual, in fact he believes himself to be, if not exactly uneducated, at least ill-educated, quite unfitted to begin rehearsals in the fashionable way with a dissertation to the cast. In an interview he said: "I'd rather run a scene eight times than have wasted that time in chattering about abstractions. An actor gets the right thing by doing it over and over, not by arguing about motivations. There are directors who encourage that sort of thing too much. Instead of doing a scene over again that's giving trouble, they want to discuss... discuss... discuss".

Overmuch attention is concentrated upon directors of the classics. It is natural enough, because a critic has little new to say about a famous play, so he has space to discuss the performance at length. Until a few years ago this would have meant the performances of the leading players, nowadays it generally means assessing the various degrees of success with which the players have fitted themselves into the director's conception of the play. If a director badly misconceives and misdirects a classic the play has suffered only temporary damage. Eventually another director will come along to repair the damage in a more intelligent production. The continuing health of the theatre in any country depends upon its new playwrights, so a director accepts a far heavier responsibility when he undertakes a new script, especially if it is the work of an unknown author. If he miscasts it and misdirects it he may consign that play to oblivion and so dishearten the author that he decides the theatre is not for him and returns to churning out a stream of radio and television scripts.

Fortunately to-day in the English theatre there are many good directors to choose from. In the late thirties James Agate in *The Sunday Times* calculated that we had no more than a dozen good, intelligent, fully experienced directors. To-day the number is at least five times as large. The explanation is that a director who did not succeed in getting established as a West End director had to grind down his talents, week after week, in "weekly rep". Now weekly rep is confined to a few summer seasons at the seaside. There are nearly sixty repertory theatres in the regions with State and Civic subsidies enabling them to give reasonable time for rehearsal and longer runs for their productions. Consequently the directors have opportunity to develop their talents, and as an increasing number of these theatres also have small studio theatres it is possible, without incurring much risk, to give opportunities to aspiring young directors who otherwise would find it difficult to get a start. In London the Royal Court with its two theatres and its unvarying policy of giving a large number of plays for short runs (despatching its biggest successes to other theatres) has been the richest source of new directors, although there have been times when the teaming together of an inexperienced director and an inexperienced playwright has been disastrous to both.

If a playwright is unlucky he may find his play in the hands of a director who is determined to stamp upon the play every possible indication of what he believes to be his own particular individual style and personality—the exact opposite of John Dexter who has said of himself: "I'm a bit chameleon-like I suppose. I'm the kind of director the play seems to suggest I should be". He directed the first five of Arnold Wesker's plays, but it was ten years before he directed another of his. Asked in an interview with Ronald Haymer why he had not liked the three plays Wesker had written in the interim he explained why and then added: "I could see things to do with them but to *do* things with a play, to turn it into something else, is not the object of directing".

In recent years there have been several successful long-term partnerships between authors and directors. For instance David Storey and Lindsey Anderson; Tom Stoppard and Peter Wood; Peter Nichols and Michael Blakemore; Alan Ayckbourn and Eric Thompson. The methods and extent of their collaboration vary considerably. Peter Wood provides an editorial (as well as directorial) talent which is just what Stoppard's plays need. Peter Nichols writes several drafts of his script before showing it to Michael Blakemore; then, he says, "we work quite a lot on the script before we get to the draft we want to rehearse. During rehearsal often you feel like changing it, but it is best not to, I think". On the other hand the script which Alan Ayckbourn's director reads for the first time is the finalised version. This well suits Eric Thompson who has modest ideas about the contribution of the director. An actor for 20 years, he made an immediate reputation as a director when his first production, *Journey's End* for the 69 Company in Manchester, was brought to Town. He thinks a great deal of rubbish is talked about the actor's processes and too much valuable rehearsal time wasted in discussion. "I believe", he says, "that about 70 or 80 per cent of actors know exactly how they should play a part the first time they read the script". He sees the job of the director as mainly a question of channelling. "What as an actor you can't judge is the question of tempos and noise-levels and climaxes. All that is different from the playing of the part. For the director it's a question of making sure things don't get out of frame. If you get really good actors you don't often have to show them what to do. You say 'You must go less far there and further there.' Directing is a lesser business than acting". To that one might add that directing is a lesser business than playwriting.

The longest of the author-director partnerships has been between David Storey and Lindsey Anderson. It began when Anderson was directing the film of one of Storey's novels. Here again the author, unlike Stoppard and Nichols, does not involve his director in the preparation of the text. "Lindsey accepts the script and that's it basically." Storey says the outstanding quality Anderson brings to the plays is "clarity, directness—allowing them to live their own life and not imposing an interpretation on them. His tendency with actors is to let them have their head, and if what happens is real he accepts it, and if it's not he'll say so, rather than determine beforehand what's required". Probably Anderson's years as a film director contributed to the brilliant visual sense which he brings to his theatre productions. In *The Changing Room* there were often seventeen or eighteen people crowded into the room with a constant to-and-fro as the players got ready for the match and afterwards showered, cleaned up, got dressed and drifted off to their homes or the pub. Anderson was scrupulously careful never to call attention to an effective piece of grouping, the flow of elaboratedly integrated movement, or an inventive and revealing piece of business; so the effect was that the players were milling about the stage on their own. Yet so skilfully was the production composed that amid all the bustle the eye was always directed to wherever the director wanted to focus attention, however momentarily. But Anderson's visual talent is only one of his many talents—such as his ability to evoke from an actor a performance just that little bit better than he has ever given before. His direction of Storey's *Home*, a play with a small cast and few opportunities for movement, demonstrated the subtle use he can make of delicate variety of tone and tempo in static scenes which could have dragged a little in the hands of a less skilful director.

It is unlikely that the elaborate realism of Anderson's direction of *The Changing Room* and *The Contractor* would have won so much admiration a few years ago when the anti-realists were in strength among so many directors and theatrical theorists. What finally made realism respectable again in England outside the commercial theatre was the success of Peter Gill's productions at the Royal Court of the D. H. Lawrence trilogy, beginning with *The Daughter-in-Law* in 1968. Here was the sort of detail which the anti-realists all over Europe believed they had swept off the stage—the solidly built realistic set, the sink with running water, the kitchen range on which pots were cooking, the fire to be stoked, the miners washing themselves down with soap and water when they came home from work. But of course the realism of these productions was not merely visual. It was matched by the detailed naturalism of the acting, together with the warmth and understanding of Peter Gill's direction of the plays.

The decline of the campaign against realistic theatre has simply been due to the fact that playwrights, particularly in England, have continued increasingly to write plays demanding realistic settings. Because of the number of English plays produced in the European theatres the propaganda against realism has diminished there too. But some directors persist in imposing irrealism upon essentially realistic plays. For instance, Ingmar Bergman's production of *Hedda Gabler* at the Royal Dramatic Theatre in Stockholm was played in a blood-red abstract setting (described by one critic as representing back-to-the-womb-with-loathing) so heavily over-stressing one aspect of the play that at times it nearly overwhelmed the acting of a superb cast directed with a subtlety and realism completely at variance with the crude setting. To take just one other example, in the production of *Spring Awakening* at the National all the interior scenes were played against a vast sheet of aluminium stretching the full length and height of the stage, with the minimum of furniture, sometimes only a single chair. What these scenes need is the atmosphere of claustrophobic stuffiness in the over-furnished rooms of a small German household at the end of the last century. As a flamboyant declaration of the director's hatred of realism that vast sheet of shining metal curtaining made the point—but mercilessly, at the expense of the play. One wonders why the Royal Court insists on proclaiming its allegiance to the anti-illusionist cause by invariably exposing all the lighting equipment hanging above the stage even when great pains have been taken to make the set as realistic as possible. In *The Changing Room* when the caretaker switched on the solitary light hanging in the middle of the room at least forty visible spotlights came to life suspended in a huge circle above the stage. It is fifty years since Meierhold exposed the mechanism of the theatre as a means to "destroy the illusion of actuality." Need his example still be followed so slavishly?

There is no need nowadays to take sides over realism or anti-realism. There are plays, old and new, for directors who resolutely oppose realism, but most first-rate directors are uncommitted and can adapt their methods to the style of the play. Typically, on two consecutive nights, one could see John Dexter's scrupulously realistic production of *Pygmalion*, and next night his entirely different handling of *Equus*, a play which demands an irrealistic production. Both, in their different ways, were equally fine and it is interesting to recall that Peter Gill, who because of his production of the Lawrence plays was regarded as excelling as a realistic director, later proved his versatility when he directed a graceful, imaginative *Twelfth Night* for the R.S.C.

It is unfortunate that so many new theatres in England were planned at a time when such a diversity of theories, mostly insufficiently tested, were being vociferously advocated. The proscenium theatre must be abolished, the actors must come out of their frame and act among the audience, illusion was no longer to be the business of the theatre. A theatre with a balcony (what used to be called the dress circle) was declared to be "socially divisive", not only in England but in some European countries, particularly Germany. The whole audience must be contained in a single tier of seats. The older theatres with their separate entrances and bars for the stalls and circle, the upper circle and the gallery, are certainly divisive, but if there is only a single circle sharing the same entrances, foyers and bars it is difficult to understand why this should be considered "socially divisive". Ideally a seating capacity of around 450 is the maximum for a single tier theatre. After that row after row of the audience are increasingly too distant from the stage unless there is a balcony projecting over part of the lower tier so that all the audience in both parts of the house are reasonably near the stage. Double that figure of 450 to 900, put them in a single tier, and you have one of the most disastrous new theatres in the country, the Birmingham Repertory. Seated in one of the back rows one experiences to the full The Loneliness of the Long Distance Viewer. Not only does one feel remote from the stage but also remote from most of the rest of the audience stretching row after row into the distance in front of one. Some planners, realising the drawbacks of too many rows far distant from the stage, saw the solution as a simple one. Just extend the length of the rows of seats so that more rows are nearer the stage. But that means extending the width of the stage too. The result has been some appalling jumbo-sized stages the width of the acting area greater than at the Royal Opera House and Drury Lane. Both of these are 42 feet; Billingham is 44 feet; Birmingham and Leeds 49 feet; Exeter 51 feet. Bolton, an adaptable theatre, has a platform 54 feet wide when used as an open stage, and at the Gardner Centre at Sussex University, another adaptable theatre, the open platform stage stretches to nearly 60 feet. The difficulties and expense of producing on these stages the kinds of plays performed by repertory companies are so obvious that there is no need to enumerate them. What is less obvious is why the planners were seemingly oblivious of the artistic and financial handicaps they were imposing upon those who were to work in these theatres.

There were many who believed that the opening of the Chichester Festival Theatre would initiate a new era in playwriting, acting and direction. The theatre was modelled on Tyrone Guthrie's Shakespeare Festival Theatre at Stratford,

Ontario—a stage thrusting far out into the auditorium and surrounded by the audience on three sides. What the Chichester planners did not sufficiently take into consideration was that Guthrie had designed what he called "the non-scenic theatre", intended primarily for Shakespearean productions, a bare stage with a permanent unchanging neutral background and a balcony with flights of stairs leading up to it on either side. The advantages and disadvantages of such a stage for Shakespeare have already been discussed in an earlier chapter, "The Producer and the Playhouse", but Chichester was never intended to be a Shakespeare Festival Theatre and it was soon obvious that among the variety of plays produced there few could be staged in the permanent set. So massive amounts of scenery were lugged on to a stage never intended for it, because so many of the plays just *had* to have scenery and furniture and props if they were to be performed at all. The same has been happening in other open stages. Eric Shorter of the *Daily Telegraph*, a critic who spends much of his time at the regional theatres, and has seen several productions in each of the open stage theatres, has come to the conclusion that "none of these theatres seem capable of satisfactorily containing anything but epics, chronicles and pageants". The fundamental weakness of stages such as Chichester and the like is that except in crowded scenes of swirling movement it is impossible for the director and an actor to make a simultaneous effect on the entire audience unless the actor flattens himself against the back wall of the stage. It is curious that those who consider a two-tier theatre to be divisive are usually enthusiasts for the thrust stage, the most divisive and undemocratic of all forms of theatre. If one can pay for the best seats, in the centre of the theatre facing the stage, one is comfortably positioned to enjoy the whole play. But the less fortunate members of the audience in seats flanking the stage can only hope to enjoy parts of the play, because no directors, however ingenious, can solve the problem of how to avoid the actors turning their backs to a part of the audience part of the time. There is also the problem of audibility. It is

337

not just that there is a fall in volume when the actor turns his back to a section of the audience. Audibility is connected with visibility. Every actor knows that if he is underlit he is in danger of being inaudible because audiences find him more difficult to listen to if they cannot see his face clearly and the emotions it expresses. Which is why in an open stage production sometimes a section of the audience sits rather glumly wondering why the rest of the audience is so amused.

Most of the drawbacks of the three-side open stage theatre vanish or diminish in the little studio theatres, such as the Stables Theatre in Manchester, where there is only room for a tiny audience. Audibility is no problem, the actors can use subtle variations of volume, tone and inflexion impossible in a large open stage theatre; and the sense of intimacy between the players and the small band of spectators goes a long way to compensate for the disadvantages of the thrust stage on a larger scale.

The National Theatre, not yet in operation at the time of writing, has an open stage in one of its three theatres, but the relation between actors and audience is different from that on any other form of the open stage. "The point of command"—the position on the stage where the actor can command the whole audience with no more than the slightest turn of the head—will be near the front of the stage. In fact it is an open stage in the literal sense of the word because it is not enclosed on two sides by the audience. By the time this book is published that stage will have been so much discussed that there is no need to deal with it here.

The National also has a proscenium theatre, which infuriates those who proclaim that "a new revolution is needed to destroy, finally and completely, the proscenium theatre and the social habits which go with it". Unfortunately the word proscenium is still associated in many people's minds with the heavy, ornate white and gold picture-frame prosceniums of the older theatres, most of which no longer exist. The modern proscenium theatre has no picture frame. It is the side walls of the theatre which

338

are the limits of the acting area so that the boundary between auditorium and stage is smoothed away. The edge of the stage is no longer a straight line but curves outwards towards the audience, breaking down another rigid division.

Among the enormous number of theatres built in England during recent years the number of appallingly bad ones is depressingly high. Many have elementary faults because of insufficient consultation with experts. Too late, architects are beginning to realise that a theatre is probably the most difficult of all buildings to design. Few theatres have been put out to competition, too often they are regarded as part of the work of the civic architect, an extremely busy man who simply has not got the time for the preliminary study necessary before starting to design a theatre. It is not enough to study plans of other theatres, and visit some of them. It is not enough to call in experts to advise on the technical requirements and to discuss with actors the placing and design of the dressing rooms, and so on. The architect must sit in the auditoriums of many theatres watching the play, and watching it from seats in different parts of the house, because a good theatre is one in which there is a happy relationship not only between actor and audience but among the audience themselves. Bridges Adams once defined what is essential above all else for a good theatre architect. "A teetotaller might design a bar, but a theatre designer, whatever his technical efficiency, is only asking for trouble if he is not possessed of a theatre sense. Mere audience sense is not enough. He should feel an urge to strut and spout upon his own stage and become someone else and weave spells and be admired."

Nowadays there are directors who are happy to escape from buildings which in any way resemble a theatre. Luca Rosconi, for instance. His production of *Orlando Furioso* was first given in a disused Italian church. There were no seats. The whole area was shared by audience and actors except for a stage at each end of the building on which some of the scenes were played. Sometimes both stages were used simultaneously. The audience could choose which one they wanted to watch, pushing their way towards it through the crowd of spectators, sometimes having to dodge out of the way of a knight mounted on a wheeled horse, politely murmuring "permesso, permesso" as he rode by. But on another occasion the knights charged through the crowd, scattering it in all directions, and there were times when soldiers pushed it back to clear the way for a procession. It was a production designed to be played indoors or out-of-doors, given the space. On its Italian tour the town's piazza was generally used for the performance. At the Edinburgh Festival it was given in a huge, gaunt building originally built as a roller-skating rink.

Another away-from-the-theatre company is Le Théâtre du Soleil. Its director is a young woman, Ariame Manchkine. The company had been working for seven years by the time they arrived in Paris in 1970 with *1789*. It was a production they had been rehearsing for a tour of the French provinces, but during rehearsals they heard of a huge disused shed in Vincennes on the outskirts of Paris which had once been a cartridge factory and an army rifle range. It would suit them nicely, they thought. This seemingly crazy idea resulted in one of the biggest successes in Paris. For the audience, except those with a car, it meant a journey to the last station on the Métro and then a bus ride to Vincennes, a desolate, dilapidated place which had once been a prosperous garrison town. If one arrived early enough one might get a seat on what looked like an improvised grandstand of planks on a village football field. Otherwise one had to stand on the floor, or perch, until the performance started, on one of the five stages linked by an intricate system of cat-walks. Waiting for the performance to begin one could pass the time by watching the actors making-up at long trestle tables and getting into their costumes as they chatted with the nearby audience while you ate the supper you had brought with you, if you had been sensible enough to do so. Soon the floor was thronged by the audience who, like those at *Orlando Furioso*, had to look out for themselves. Respectfully they squeezed back as the Royal Guards pushed their way through them shouting

"Make way for the King", and later they were scurrying to avoid the onrush of an excited band of revolutionaries. As the play gathered momentum the audience on the floor ceased to be just spectators, as they were at *Orlando Furioso*, and became, if only subconsciously, part of the Paris mob. Gradually the actors drew the audience surrounding them into the play. After the fall of the Bastille many of the actors gathered little groups of spectators around them, each telling their own story of the storming of the Bastille and their own share in it. Then, suddenly, the jubilation. Every light blazed. Loud speakers blared raucous fairground music. On each of the five stages there were sideshows, wrestlers, tumblers, a coconut shy, all the fun of the fair. In the cheering crowd actors and audience mingled together. Eventually, seemingly spontaneously, they formed a crocodile which grew longer and longer as again and again it wended its way round the stages and across the catwalks, shouting, singing, cheering. There was no sign of the actors cajoling or bullying the audience into taking part— as so often happens in avant garde companies which declare "audience participation" to be one of their missions.

1798 is no ordinary documentary. It uses mime, life-sized puppets, tableaux vivants, music, the devices of the Commedia dell'Arte, all done with tremendous zest. The script is the collectivist result of the invention and imagination of the company under the guidance of Ariame Manchkine, but the production has the firm, highly professional direction so often lacking in those "we-did-it-all-ourselves" productions. Also unusual is that in spite of the opportunities offered by the theme of the play, there is no Marxist or extreme Left Wing propaganda.

Jérôme Savary, who founded what used to be called Le Grand Théâtre Panique, now Le Grand Magic Circus, is another director who does not believe in political theatre. "We speak to the senses", he declares. On his first visit to London with an exhilaratingly crazy entertainment based on Arrabal's *Le Labyranthe* the senses he appealed to most were a sense of fun and a sense of the ridiculous. But when he brought his company to the Round House in 1973 in *Robinson Crusoe* the sense to which he was speaking seemed to be almost exclusively the sense of shock. At first it was all very jolly. One was greeted by clowns with a welcoming handshake, and a welcoming wave from stilt-walkers, to a background of brass band circus music and the excited babble of the audience, many of them children. What followed included episodes in which a savage ripped open a corpse and devoured the entrails; a doctor copulated with the corpse of a girl killed in a scene in which she was raped and strangled by a sexual maniac; a couple of pantomime zebras copulated with one another; Christ on the way to Calvary twirled the cross like a drum-majorette, and later, nailed to the cross, vomited from it. Throughout the evening the audience were continually harassed and molested. Actors, mostly near-naked, stumbled about among them, fireworks were let off from time to time in different parts of the auditorium, odd objects fell into one's lap, and there was a moment when, without warning, a car was driven through the audience. Savary justi-fied all this on the grounds that the effect of shock and disgust is to stimulate and reinvigorate the mind—a fashionable theory at that time. But there was also much to amuse and even charm. A great deal of the charm came from Savary himself who acted as master of ceremonies in the manner of a ringmaster. The humour had some of the inspired dottiness and knockabout craziness of their previous shows. Some of the critics were enthusiastic, even ecstatic. One who wasn't, thought some of his colleagues' notices told us more about them than about the show.

The hope is sometimes expressed that a new director of genius may emerge from among what are usually described as the Experimental Groups. An unlikely hope, because most of these groups do not feel any need for a director. In their manifestos there is much about "collectivist creation", impro-visation, a "refusal to rely upon anecdotal narrative or descrip-tive pretext". Some claim to express themselves in "the language of the body", which generally results in the unco-ordinated squirmings and writhings of insufficiently trained bodies. That the language of the body has a considerable vocabulary when used by a highly professional director and cast was proved by Lindsay Kemp's *Flowers*, a wordless interpretation of Genet's *Our Lady of the Flowers*. Other groups proclaim their aim is "the development of non-verbal language", presumably inspired by what they have heard of Peter Brook's experiment, but without realising that the non-verbal language was initially the work of a poet, Ted Hughes, and developed during many months of experiment and rehearsal based on the study of the speech sounds of the actors from several different countries who comprised the company. The result had nothing whatsoever in common with the largely self-inspired strangulated cries, grunts, moans, screams and chantings of Brook's imitators. In addition to these groups, who spend much of their time on tour, there is the fringe theatre in London and Paris, performing wherever they can find room for themselves and an audience, however small—the upstairs room of a pub or a café, a basement or an attic, a warehouse due for demolition, sometimes a place dignified by the name of "studio theatre", and, in one case, a disused synagogue. Reluctantly one has to agree with J. W. Lambert, in his *Drama in Britain, 1964-1973*, that "Neither category has yet produced a dramatist of anything like the stature of those in the mainstream theatres; neither category has yet produced experimental stagings which rival in stimulus the more adventurous full-scale theatre; and neither category has shown much sign of attracting the degree of talent to be found in young actors and directors in the mainstream. In short, fringe and experimental theatre in Britain proliferates, but cannot be said to flourish".

The one sturdy survivor among them all is Charles Marowitz's cellar theatre, the Open Space. Here his own productions have included his collage versions of *Hamlet* and *Macbeth* and his re-written version of *Othello*. Seemingly genuinely bothered, as many others have been, by the apparent lack of motive for Iago's hatred of Othello, he makes them both black. Iago despises Othello as a traitor to his people because he believes he can only have reached the rank of general by toadying to the whites. Marowitz argues, with some justification, "that by making Othello the establishment Negro and Iago the Black Power militant I have made the conflict between the two much more credible".

Nowadays the Director's Theatre does not mean quite what it did. In fact many actors interpret Director's Theatre as meaning a theatre in which the director hogs far more than his fair share of rehearsal time by talking too much, with the result that the actor goes on the stage under-rehearsed, sometimes not even firm on his lines through lack of practice in his part. Actors are also apt to associate Director's Theatre with rehearsals beginning with a long dissertation explaining in detail how each part is to be played. Most good actors in the early stages of rehearsal want to be allowed to show (*not* to explain in words) their own conception of the part. Then the actor can turn to the director and say: "Is that the sort of way *you* see the part: if I play on these lines will it fit with the rest of the production?" What an actor particularly dreads when rehearsing a classic is being talked into playing a part in a way completely at variance with the author's intentions because the director sees the part in a "new" way. The result is that the actor, however hard he tries to follow the director's conception, usually seems rather less good than he really is.

Seventeen years ago I finished this book by declaring my belief in the Director's Theatre as the healthiest form of theatre. Now I have doubts. It is all too possible, as John Barbour warned in an article in the *Daily Telegraph*, that we may be approaching the days when directors are richer, cleverer, more famous and more in demand than authors – or indeed actors. "I find it", says Barbour, "a disturbing thought". So do I.

BOOK LIST

The following are the authors to whom I have been particularly
indebted during the writing of this book.

Adams, Bridges, *The Lost Leader.*
Appia, Adolphe, *Die Musik und die Inscenierung.*
Brassilach, Robert, *Les Animateurs de Théâtre.*
Coward, Noel, *Present Indicative.*
Craig, Gordon, *The Art of the Theatre; Towards a New Theatre.*
Dalcroze, Jacques, *L'Oeuvre d'Art Vivant.*
Davies, Robertson, *Renown at Stratford.*
du Maurier, Daphne, *Gerald, a Portrait.*
Duncan, Isadora, *My Life.*
Farjeon, Herbert, *The Shakespeare Scene.*
Fuchs, George, *Die Schaubuhne der Zukunft.*
Fuerst and Hume, *Twentieth Century Stage Decoration.*
Gielgud, John, *Early Stages.*
Granville-Barker, Harley, *On Dramatic Method.*
Hunt, Hugh, *The Director in the Theatre; Old Vic Prefaces.*
Jelagin, *The Taming of the Arts.*
Kitchin, Laurence, *Mid-Century Drama.*
Komisarjevsky, Feodor, *Myself and the Theatre.*
MacGowan, Kenneth, and Jones, Robert Edmond, *Continental
    Stagecraft.*
Magarshack, David, *Stanislavsky, A Life.*
Pearson, Hesketh, *Bernard Shaw; Gilbert and Sullivan.*
Playfair, Nigel, *The Story of the Lyric Theatre, Hammersmith.*
Poel, William, *Shakespeare and the Theatre.*
Rose, Enid, *Gordon Craig and the Theatre.*
Shore, Bernard, *The Orchestra Speaks.*
Short, Ernest, *Theatrical Cavalcade.*
Simonson, Lee, *The Stage is Set.*

Southern, Richard, *The Open Stage.*

Stanislavsky, Constantin, *My Life in Art; An Actor Prepares; Building a Character.*

Stern, Ernst, *My Life, My Stage.*

Symons, Arthur, *Studies in Seven Arts.*

Tynan, Kenneth, *Curtains.*

van Gyseghem, André, *Theatre in Soviet Russia.*

INDEX

Index

Index

Index

Index

Index

Index